Classic Cars

Classic Cars

BY
PIERO CASUCCI

RAND McNALLY & COMPANY
**CHICAGO
NEW YORK
SAN FRANCISCO**

Contents

Introduction

During the 34 years between 1905 and 1939, there was considerable development in every element of both interior and exterior car design. Engines were initially slow-revving, having single or twin-cylinders. These only developed a limited horse-power, which is why the more prestigious cars came to have a very high cylinder capacity. The 1915 Packard introduced the fashion for very powerful cars. The 'Twin Six' had twelve cylinders, and was the first American model to have aluminium pistons. At that time there was a great variety of types, especially among the vehicles with smaller cylinder capacities. There were air or water-cooled engines mounted either in the middle (even under the floor), in front, or at the back; single or twin-cylinder, laid out in line, 'V' or opposed, operating on the 2 or 4 stroke cycle. Then during the 1930s, 8 cylinders in line became a common arrangement until this was replaced by 8 cylinders in 'V' formation.

Hot bulb ignition was replaced by the coil, or ignition by means of high or low tension magnetos. Side valves became overhead valves, sometimes operated by a double camshaft. In time the 'L' head developed into the 'T' (with side valves operated by two separate camshafts, originally adopted because they were easier to maintain). In the 'L' the valves were situated on the same side, and the spark plug was mounted beside the inlet valve, so as to be cooled by the incoming mixture. Cars which initially only had two-speed gearing acquired three or four gears. The system of gearing was soon to be considerably changed, however. The early movable gear-wheels gave way to a proper gearbox, the invention of Emile Levassor. This consisted of a sliding gear-train providing two or three gear ratios plus reverse.

The electric gearshift made its first appearance on the Cadillac in 1912. The introduction of removable wheels represented another important advance. The Isotta-Fraschini was

the first car to mount brakes on the front wheels in 1910. For a long time, however, front-mounted brakes were considered to be dangerous and did not come into widespread use until the mid 1920s. In 1921 a Duesenberg was developed with revolutionary hydraulic brakes which were adapted three years later on the Chrysler. At the same time, during this period, car bodywork saw a progressive development in structure. Open cars gradually were altered to have enclosed bodies for greater passenger comfort.

Proportions changed, partly due to style and partly due to the need for streamlining to accommodate greater speeds. Pneumatic tires replaced the solid rubber and provided a smoother, safer ride. There were subtle improvements such as windshield wipers, dipping headlights and interior heating and cooling.

Early car suspension was either semi-elliptical, fully elliptical or cantilever leaf-springing. The steel coil spring was introduced and eventually refined into the modern suspension system of springs and shock absorbers.

The history and development of the car industry in Britain, America, Italy and France was, and indeed still is, closely linked with motor racing. Most motor manufacturers either participated directly in motor races, or, like Citroen, organised great rallies to display the robustness and reliability of the vehicles they were offering for sale to the general public.

Motor racing had a decisive influence on car engines, encouraging the development of light and resistent metal alloys, particularly during the period from 1934 to 1937, when the most important competitions imposed maximum and minimum weight restrictions. The object of the regulations was to force the makers of racing cars to use engines of relatively low cylinder capacity so that they were not too powerful. Even then, people were shocked and concerned at the high speeds which were reached by the single-

seater racing cars. Serious accidents were invariably attributed to the extremely high speed averages achieved on certain tracks. The availability of new light-weight metal alloys and special fuels, however, meant that all the motor manufacturers were able to overcome the obstacle of the maximum weight restriction. They produced cars with extraordinarily powerful engines with the only restraint being that they needed to limit the weight to 1,650 lb (750 kg). As the restriction of weight did not regulate the speed as it was intended, later rules almost always imposed a maximum cylinder capacity and a minimum weight for each vehicle. By contrast, especially at the beginning of the century, racing had provided a constant incentive to reduce the weight of cars; and this trimming-down (if only of sports cars) occasionally produced sensational results.

While Bentley, Isotta-Fraschini, Fiat, Alfa Romeo and Renault relied on racing as a highly-effective form of advertising, manufacturers in the U.S.A., except for small specialist firms, soon lost interest. They were concentrating on mass production which was much more attractive and advantageous to them. Henry Ford led this trend with the Model T, introduced in 1908. Other manufacturers were quick to follow his example. American car-buyers were mainly interested in being able to buy a car cheaply. They were not concerned with speed or winning races. Mass production resulted in the construction of a network of suitable roads, and in 1916, President Woodrow Wilson signed the Federal Aid Road Act, making possible the creation of an impressive national roadway system through a fifty per cent direct grant, the other fifty per cent to be provided by the individual States.

The first motorway to be built in Italy was the Milan-Lakes section, begun on September 21, 1924. Ten years later the Germans were to plan a comprehensive road system (mainly with

military purposes in mind). In the meantime, Italy had opened various other motorways: the Milan-Bergamo (1927), Naples-Pompeii (1928), Bergamo-Brescia (1931), Turin-Milan (1932), Venice-Padua (1933) and a road suitable for trucks between Genoa and Serravalle in 1935. The first Canadian motorway, from Toronto to Niagara Falls, was opened in 1939, whilst in every other country, including France, motorways were planned only after the Second World War. Italy also embarked on an ambitious national program after the War that has made it, after Federal Germany, a country with one of the best road systems in Europe, with motorways totalling about 3,700 miles (6,000 km).

The spread of the motor car has created numerous problems, first and foremost that of accidents. In six years (from 1969-1974) in the nine countries of the Common Market, 360,535 people died in road accidents, and some 10 million were injured. In the U.S.A. more than 50,000 people are killed every year. In Germany there are more than 18,000 road deaths, while in France more than 16,000 people die each year. Governments began to be concerned about these accident figures after the War and the U.S. government launched a safety campaign in the late 1960s.

They insisted on improvements in motor car construction and maintained that the worst faults lay in the design. Every company that exported cars to the U.S.A. was involved in the American ESV program (Experimental Safety Vehicle). Plans were studied for new, better-constructed cars and it was hoped that safety measures could be devised that would rectify even the drivers' mistakes. The ESV program was a failure which cost all the motor manufacturers concerned a great deal of money.

Techniques and the demands of safety clashed; meanwhile American experts were investigating another problem, that of pollution.

The energy crisis, which rapidly developed in 1973, has created another enormous problem, which is literally revolutionising car design. Most countries are concerned about the steady rise in the price of oil and the fact that sources of energy are not inexhaustible. The countries most conscious of this, politically, are those that have to rely on other oil-producing countries for their raw materials. Ironically, however, the traditionally oil-rich U.S.A. has been the hardest hit. For years they produced very heavy, powerful cars (4,000-4,400 pounds/1,800-2,000 kg on average) which are massive fuel-consumers. They are now scaling down their production models, and making them much lighter. This operation requires immense design changes and an investment of billions of dollars (General Motors has allocated 13 billion simply to the first stage of the reconversion operation from large to medium-sized cars and from medium-sized to small cars). The need to reduce energy consumption has accentuated the movement towards the restructuring of cars, even if the idea of driving smaller vehicles has little appeal for car-buyers in the U.S.A. The V-8 engine, so widespread today will gradually be phased out and the 6-cylinder, which had almost vanished in America, and above all the 4-cylinder will be re-introduced.

Faced with uncertain fuel supplies and the reality of having to pay ever more for crude oil, most countries have no alternative but to scale down their motor industry.

After the excitement of the pioneering and expansion earlier in this century, car manufacturers are now having to work hard to guarantee the survival of their current models.

Motor design seems to have come full circle. As we admire and appreciate the powerful classic cars of bygone eras, we still look forward to new design concepts for ever safer and more efficient motoring.

—body by Pierce-Arrow

PIERCE-ARROW

United States of America

As in France, England and Italy, steam-driven vehicles were enthusiastically developed in the U.S.A. between 1800 and 1900. Such pioneers were Frank Curtis who produced a steam-driven buggy and White and Stanley who worked on designs for steam cars.

The first car, in the modern sense, made in America goes back to 1893, when Charles E. Duryea, a cycle maker from Illinois, and his brother Frank built a vehicle with electric ignition. In 1895 Charles and Frank Duryea started the Duryea Motor Wagon Company at Springfield, Massachusetts.

In the same year George Baldwin Selden was granted a patent (presented as long before as 1879) concerning a 'car fuelled by liquid hydrocarbons with internal combustion engine, the transmission shaft moving faster than the wheels of the vehicle, and equipped with clutch or device to separate the engine from the drive-wheels'. This apparently elementary patent forced motor manufacturers to pay a royalty on their cars, except for Henry Ford who refused to acknowledge it. Ford was sued and lost but successfully appealed in 1911. The Selden patent was broken by a technicality—it was based on the Brayton design whereas

cars were being built with engines based on that designed by Otto.

1895 saw the first race between 4-wheeled mechanical vehicles, the first specialised journal (*The Horseless Age*), and the first recognised club, the American Motor League, in Chicago. In 1896 the Duryeas completed their third vehicle.

The following year, the Pittsburgh Motor Vehicle Company, and the Pope Manufacturing Company began to make motor cars. In 1900 about 48,000 people went to the first automobile exhibition in New York's Madison Square Garden, where 300 different models of cars from 40 manufacturers were on display. Prices ranged from a minimum of $280 to a maximum of $4,000.

In 1899 Ransom Eli Olds' Motor Vehicle Company in Detroit began to achieve success with the Classic Curved Dash Oldsmobile, which had a chain driven single cylinder engine. The early part of the twentieth century saw the creation of hundreds of automobile factories, some of which did not produce even one car. In the 'American Car since 1775' *Automobile Quarterly* gives a detailed list of 5,000 different American firms (from Abborn to Zip), together with the names of another 165 (from Acme to Widmayer) that merely designed motor vehicles without ever managing to build any. It also lists 116 bodywork factories (from American Body to Woonsocket), which operated and expanded alongside the chassis factories. Statistics for production in America date from 1898, when 15 cars were made (13 Duryea, 1 Ford, and 1 Winton): up to 1900 the figures are modest, Columbia emerging clearly at the head of the field, with 500 vehicles in 1899 and 1,500 in 1900. The Locomobile held first place from 1901 to 1902. In 1903 and 1904 Oldsmobile took the lead with an already impressive output for the times (4,000 and 5,508 vehicles respectively).

In 1906 Oldsmobile lost its lead to the Ford Motor Company which produced 8,729 vehicles; Cadillac and Buick were not far behind. Ford gained substantially over the others with the presentation of the Model T on October 1, 1908. In that year Ford made over 10,000 cars, in 1909 production was up to 17,000, and in 1910 it reached 32,000 vehicles. From 1911 on, thanks to the growing success of the Model T, Ford made truly remarkable progress, by 1922 the company was producing over a million motor cars. Inevitably, however, the popularity of the T began to decline, and history was made in 1927 when Ford lost its lead to General Motors. The two companies were hotly competitive for the next two decades before the battle of mass production was decisively won by General Motors' most popular model, the Chevrolet.

By 1939 a total of 75 million vehicles had been manufactured in the U.S.A. On the technical level, the 1930s saw the gradual establishing of certain designs. In 1933 the study of aerodynamics brought streamlined shapes to the car body. The first pointed or V-shaped radiator cowlings appeared, together with the first servo-assisted brakes. The Chrysler Airflow introduced in 1934 encouraged the trend for more daring and functional lines. In 1936 in some cars the handbrake was moved to the left of the driver's seat, to give the driver and front passenger more room. For the same reason, in 1937, in some models, the gearshift was mounted below the steering-wheel. By about 1938 General Motors had introduced a technical innovation to many models: fully synchronised gears.

The need to produce larger and larger numbers of vehicles to feed the gigantic industry centred almost exclusively on Detroit, and resulted in a new philosophy based on an annual revision of each model. The originator of this new philosophy was the head of General Motors, Alfred Sloan. In contrast to Henry Ford's principles and practice (the Model T saw few alterations from 1908 to 1927), General Motors started a system of annual changes. These were limited to one or two aesthetic details, however, and from then on the expression 'face-lift' was used to describe the updating of models.

The motor car therefore began to be regarded as a status symbol, a visible embodiment of the owner's affluence as well as a means of transport.

Auburn was one of the great names among American cars in the 1930s before mass production, when there was still demand for refinement and prestige cars.

The factory took its name from the town in Indiana where it was set up. It was founded in 1874 by Charles Eckhart, a German immigrant, who had gained experience with Studebaker when it was still making its famous Conestoga Wagons. Frank and Morris Eckhart continued their father's work, initially producing twin-cylinder cars, then later vehicles with 4 and 6 cylinders. Business did not prosper, however, and in 1919 the firm was taken over by Ralph Austin Bard and William Wrigley. The turning-point in the factory's history was the arrival, in 1924, of Errett Lobban Cord, creator of the car of

Car: **Auburn 851 SC**
Year: **1935**
Engine: **8 cylinders in line**
Bore and stroke: **77.7 × 120.6 mm**
Cylinder capacity: **4572 cc**
Gears: **3 forward**
Brake horse power: **150 (with supercharger)**
Maximum speed: **100 mph**
Wheelbase: **10 ft 7 ins (3.22 m)**
Suspension: **front and back: semi-elliptic leaf-spring**

that name. There then began a period of thriving activity, and the 851 SC of 1935 reflects this successful era. The Lycoming engine of the 851 SC came either with supercharger (115 bhp) or without (150 bhp). It had a cast-iron cylinder block, aluminium head, side valves, water cooling, coil ignition, shaft transmission, and hydraulic brakes on all four wheels.

The 851 SC could reach 100 mph. Auburn also made a 12-cylinder model. In 1937 the factory ceased production.

Brewster was a make better known for its bodywork than engineering. It began in New Haven in 1810 with coaches. In 1856 production moved to Long Island, New York. When cars began to flood through America, Brewster had agreements with the best European car manufacturers, especially Rolls-Royce to fit out cars exported onto the American market.

For about a decade, starting from 1915, Brewster produced cars under its own name, adopting Knight sleeve-valve engines with removable head, magneto ignition, pressure lubrication, pump cooling, cone clutch, and brakes on all four wheels. Brewster cars were rather high-priced, however, ($8,300 for the Berlina, $8,800 for the Touring Landaulet, and $7,200 for the Runabout). The prices quoted included, so the catalogue stated, windshield removable tires, pump to blow up the tires, engine speedometer, ammeter, voltmeter, and horn. In 1925 Brewster was bought by Rolls-Royce. In 1932 it regained its independence, and operated by fitting out other makes, mostly Fords. In 1938 production ceased. From 1932 to 1938 the company had only produced some 300 cars. Brewster also made bodies for Buick, Cadillac, Lincoln, and Oldsmobile.

Car: **Brewster**
Year: **1915**
Engine: **4 cylinders in line**
Bore and stroke: **101.6 × 139.7 mm**
Cylinder capacity: **5528 cc**
Gears: **3 forward**
Brake horse power: —
Maximum speed: —
Wheelbase: **10 ft 5 ins (3.17 m)**
Suspension: **front: semi elliptic leaf-springs: back: cantilever leaf-springs**

This Company had a vital impact on the history of car manufacture, although it existed only very briefly (from 1907 to 1910).

It pioneered coil spring suspension at a time when the vast majority of companies were using semi-elliptic leaf-springs. Another characteristic of the Brush was its wooden chassis and axles. The engine was water-cooled (10 bhp), with a multi-disc clutch. The wheels were made of wood. The lights were acetylene. Only a single model was produced, the 2-seater Roadster. In England it cost £100 in 1910. Alanson P. Brush founder of the firm, and designer of the car, was keen to make his name known abroad, despite the small size of his business. In 1910, however, Brush was absorbed into the U.S. Motor Company, which specialised in

Car: **Brush**
Year: **1910**
Engine: **single vertical front cylinder**
Bore and stroke: **101.6 × 127 mm**
Cylinder capacity: **1030 cc**
Gears: **2 forward**
Brake horse power: **10**
Maximum speed: **45 mph**
Wheelbase: **6 ft 8 ins (2.05 m)**
Suspension: **front and back: coil springs**

trucks as well as producing a wide range of cars. In its 1912 catalogue it featured a Liberty Brush, with the same mechanical details as the 1910 Brush, at $350, or, with lights, hood, and windshield included, at $400. The Brush Roadster was priced at $485. It still had chain transmission, and could carry only two people. There were also still only two forward gears.

17

Buick 24/30 HP
Buick Six
Buick Series 40

David Dunbar Buick, born in Scotland, was only two when he and his family arrived in the United States and settled in Detroit. As a young man Buick developed an interest in the motor mechanics. He created several models of various cylinder capacities, and arrangements. But, though skilful in the workshop, Buick was no businessman, and in the early days his company had a variety of backers. In 1908 it found success, becoming one of the four big factories in Detroit. Involvement in motor sport, particularly hill racing (winning 166 times in 1909 alone), brought the company to the public's attention.

The Buick 24/30 dates from 1911, and could seat five passengers. The steel chassis was described in the instruction manual as resilient. The wooden wheels were the 'artillery' type, with easily removable rims. The twin-block engine had overhead valves, and was mounted on three bearings. The engine was water-cooled (with pump), and had high-tension magneto ignition, a multi-disc clutch, and brakes on the back wheels. It cost $1,850 from the factory. The extras included hood, windshield, engine speed indicator, and the tools for removing and replacing the wheels.

The Six dates from 1918. It had 6 cylinders, and appeared for the first time in the Buick line in 1914 (the 4-cylinder had meanwhile started to disappear from the firm's list). The Six sold for $895, providing good value for the time. The best indication that production was now significantly

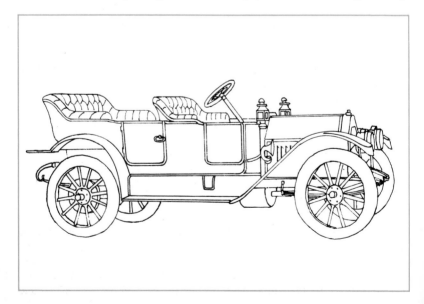

improved is that from now on Buick no longer made 'special cars' to customers' personal specifications. To make up for this, it offered an extensive range of models which included two limousines and a 2 plus 2-seater coupé. The Six remained in production up until 1923 with few modifications (electrical system, shape of the radiator, removable engine head, and brakes on all four wheels). 201,000 cars were made in 1923.

The Series 40 dates from 1936, and was called 'the Doctor's Friend' because of its sturdiness, which allowed it to be used continuously. It was one of the most successful and widespread models to be produced between the wars. The 8-cylinder in-line engine had five main bearings, coil ignition, and twin down-draft

Car: **Buick 6**
Year: **1918**
Engine: **6 cylinders in line**
Bore and stroke: **85.7 × 114.3 mm**
Cylinder capacity: **3954 cc**
Gears: **3 forward**
Brake horse power: —
Maximum speed: —
Wheelbase: **10 ft 4 ins (3.14 m)**
Suspension: **front: semi-elliptic leaf-spring; back: cantilever leaf-spring**

Car: **Buick 24/30 HP**
Year: **1911**
Engine: **4 cylinders in line**
Bore and stroke: **108 × 114 mm**
Cylinder capacity: **4175 cc**
Gears: **2 forward**
Brake horse power: **32**
Maximum speed: **55 mph**
Wheelbase: **9 ft 8 ins (2.94 m)**
Suspension: **front: semi-elliptic leaf-spring; back; elliptic leaf-spring**

carburetor. The two top gears had synchro-mesh. In that year hydraulic brakes were adopted, together with a handbrake acting on the rear wheels alone. There were eight models with two engines (3800 and 5200 cc) and

19

four different wheelbases in the range.

The 40 was the cheapest model and the most popular. It weighed over 3,700 lb (1,700 kg). The engine developed 93 bhp and its maximum speed was about 80 mph. It could accelerate from 0 to 50 mph in 12 seconds. The 1940 version incorporated the special 4-speed transmission made by General Motors, which was semi-automatic. This transmission was initially available only to Buick and Oldsmobile.

Buick was one of the first in the General Motors group to adopt the 8-cylinder engine in all its cars. It introduced independent front suspension, completely overhauled the bodywork and adopted aluminium pistons and hydraulic brakes.

One of the presidents of Buick at one time was Walter Chrysler. In 1919 he left because of disagreement with the directors of General Motors. But he did not leave the industry. He started his own firm, which then later became one of the big Detroit companies. The times were propitious for enterprising men, and the story of the American car industry is full of dramatic developments and of firms growing up and vanishing, all in an extraordinarily short period of time.

Car: **Buick Series 40**
Year: **1936**
Engine: **8 cylinders in line**
Bore and stroke: **78.6 × 98.5 mm**
Cylinder capacity: **3821 cc**
Gears: **3 forward**
Brake horse power: **93**
Maximum speed: **80 mph**
Wheelbase: **9 ft 10 ins (2.99 m)**
Suspension: **front: independent wheels with coil springs; back: semi-elliptic leaf-springs**

Cadillac Series 314-7
Passenger Sedan
Cadillac 452 B
Cadillac Sixty Special

This firm bears the name of the French general Antoine de la Mothe Cadillac, founder of the city of Detroit in 1701. A timber merchant, William H. Murphy, adopted the name in 1902 when he started up a car factory. The company quickly acquired a name for good quality craftsmanship. Murphy was lucky to have a young engineer, Henry Martin Leland, who was particularly skilled in motor mechanics. On August 22, 1902 the Cadillac Car Company was born out of a merger with Leland & Faulconer, and Henry Leland assumed control.

The first Cadillac, given the date, had a single cylinder, but had nothing to distinguish it from its competitors other than its unusual height off the ground, designed for rough roads.

The company received great publicity from a test held in 1908 on the Brooklands circuit in England, when it was demonstrated that all the parts of any car in the Cadillac range were interchangeable. The test, later made official by the Royal Automobile Club, consisted of stripping down three of the eight Cadillacs that were in London at that time, mixing the parts up, and then re-assembling them back into three cars. These three cars were then test-driven for 500 miles at Brooklands without the least hitch. The same year Cadillac joined General Motors, as its prestige mark, a role which it still has today.

Another well-known engineer, Charles Kettering, helped to make Cadillac's name by persuading the head of the company to use 8-cylinder V engines. This innovation was announced in September 1914, and from 1915 onwards all Cadillacs adopted them. In 1925 the firm was joined by Lawrence P. Fisher, one of six brothers reputed for their bodywork. It thus acquired a specialist to introduce another quality element to the trade-mark.

The Series 314-7 Passenger Sedan was powered by an 8-cylinder V engine, with the cylinders at an angle of 90°, developing 85.5 bhp at 3,000 revs, and with compression ratio of 4.7:1. The cylinders were set in two blocks of four; the head was removable. Although the same as previous engines in terms of bore and stroke, it may be considered completely new (the rods were shorter). It weighed almost 130 pounds (60 kg) less. The chassis was also made lighter, and the rear suspension modified. The coachwork, by Fisher, had been improved in certain details, yet despite this it

still cost $500 less than the Standard and Custom models. The windshield opened and the mirror was adjustable; the windshield wipers worked automatically. The Standard models also had front and back bumpers.

The 452 B (1930) incorporated a 16-cylinder engine, in two blocks of 8, over an aluminium crank-case. It had overhead valves, operated by push-rods and rockers, and central camshafts; the crankshaft and camshaft had five bearings.

The 16 cylinders developed 165 bhp at 3,400 revs. For the ignition there

was a Delco-Remy distributor with twin 6-volt distributor heads and twin coils; a two-disc dry clutch, pressed chassis with longitudinal and cross members, and vacuum-assisted, mechanically-operated drum brakes.

The 1938 Sixty Special was greatly admired for its bodywork. Its engine developed 135 bhp, and the three-speed gears were operated by a lever mounted under the steering-wheel (it was the first car to use this arrangement). The unusually low chassis lent itself to striking stylistic innovations, which accounts for the Sixty Special's immediate popularity. It abandoned the running-board; a trend which was followed by all American and European cars.

Car: **Cadillac 452 B**
Year: **1930**
Engine: **16 cylinders V**
Bore and stroke: **76.2 × 101.6 mm**
Cylinder capacity: **7413 cc**
Gears: **3 forward**
Brake horse power: **165**
Maximum speed: **90 mph**
Wheel base: **12 ft 4 ins (3.75 m)**
Suspension: **front and back: semi-elliptic leaf-spring, integrated with hydraulic shock-absorbers**

▲

Car: **Cadillac Series 314-7 Passenger Sedan**
Year: **1925**
Engine: **8 cylinders V**
Bore and stroke: **79.37 × 130.17 mm**
Cylinder capacity: **5173 cc**
Gears: **3 forward**
Brake horse power: **85**
Maximum speed: **80 mph**
Wheelbase: **11 ft 0 ins (3.35 m)** *or* **11 ft 6 ins (3.5 m)**

Car: **Cadillac Sixty Special**
Year: **1938**
Engine: **8 cylinders V**
Bore and stroke: **88.9 × 114.3 mm**
Cylinder capacity: **5676 cc**
Gears: **3 forward**
Brake horse power: **135**
Maximum speed: **90 mph**
Wheelbase: **10 ft 7 ins (3.22 m)**

▼

It is estimated that in about ten years Chadwick built no more than 300 cars, of which only two survive today. Their creator, however, Lee Chadwick, is held in the highest esteem for his application, ability and perfection in all he produced.

Lee Sherman Chadwick, an engineering student at Purdue University, invented a mechanism for a washing-machine manufacturer when he was only 24. He ended his career as director of the Perfection Stove Company, specialising in the production of cooking stoves. As one American historian has put it very aptly, his career began in the washroom and ended in the kitchen. Of the various models he made, the most famous was the Six Model 19, which was produced in 1910, and which, for a supplementary $376, could include a

Car: **Chadwick Six Model 19**
Year: **1910**
Engine: **6 cylinders in line**
Bore and stroke: **127 × 152.4 mm**
Cylinder capacity: **11577 cc**
Gears: **4 forward**
Brake horse power: **75**
Maximum speed: **96 mph**
Wheelbase: —
Suspension: **front and back: semi-elliptic leaf-springs**

supercharger. There was no need for a supercharger, however, as even without one the Chadwick Six could exceed 96 mph, developing 70-75 bhp at 1,100 revs. An essential feature of the engine (three-block, 6 cylinders, with inlet valves in the head, and exhaust valves at the sides), was the cooling system, which consisted of a copper cover around each group of two cylinders, with water circulating inside it.

Chevrolet Model C
Chevrolet Four Ninety
Touring
Chevrolet Superior
Roadster

The largest motor manufacturer in the world came about through the meeting of two exceptionally talented men, one a major industrialist, the other a first-class driver, and a designer open to new ideas. When they met, William C. Durant, creator of General Motors, was pursuing his dream of creating a vast car manufacturing group, whilst Louis Chevrolet was a test driver for Buick. Durant was born in Boston in 1861. Chevrolet was born in La Chaux-de-Fonds, Switzerland in 1878 and emigrated to the U.S.A. with his parents.

Durant gave Chevrolet the job of designing the prototype for a car which was to develop into a massive undertaking. The enterprise eventually grew to a colossal size, making the Chevrolet mark the backbone of General Motors.

Chevrolet was officially founded on November 3, 1911, under the name Chevrolet Motor Company of Michigan, and its first car had a 6-cylinder engine (4850 cc) and was called the Classic Six. Surprisingly, 2,999 of these were made in 1912. The car sold for $2,150. Durant's boldly commercial way of doing business did not coincide with that of Louis Chevrolet, who resigned in 1913, accepting the harsh condition that he would never use his name on any other commercial product. Chevrolet was an engineer with no over-riding ambitions in life. He eventually set up his own small engine-transformation business under the name of Frontenac. This gave him satisfaction from a creative point of view, but was not particularly successful financially. Chevrolet is remembered in history as being a person with

Car: **Chevrolet Model C**
Year: **1911**
Engine: **6 cylinders in line**
Bore and stroke: **90 × 127 mm**
Cylinder capacity: **4845 cc**
Gears: **3 forward**
Brake horse power: —
Maximum speed: —
Wheelbase: **10 ft 0 ins (3.04 m)**
Suspension: **front and back: semi-elliptic leaf-springs**

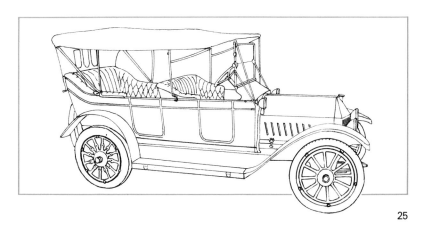

enormous mechanical talent, but lacking in any business sense.

Durant's aim was to make Chevrolet rival Ford. This he achieved stage by stage, though his success rapidly increased when, in 1915, after the 1911 Model C (6-cylinder), he produced the Four Ninety (4-cylinder), the name of which referred to its list price. Whereas it cost $490, the Ford Model T was selling at $680. In 1916 Ford hit back by reducing the price of the Model T to $345.

The Four Ninety, like the Ford T, came in only one colour, black, and could seat five, with the steering-wheel on the left. It had wooden wheels, splash lubrication, water cooling with pump and ventilator, and electrical ignition system. The price included windshield, horn, removable wheels, emergency tools, and in the case of the sedan, curtains. This car enabled Durant to strike a first blow at Ford's supremacy. To be more effective he ensured that the Four Ninety was made in as many different factories as possible. In 1915 he produced 70,701 vehicles, in 1917 125,882, and in 1920 150,226 out of an overall production figure that year, within General Motors, of 393,075 vehicles.

When Durant resigned from

Car: **Chevrolet Four Ninety Touring**
Year: **1921**
Engine: **4 cylinders in line**
Bore and stroke: **93.66 × 101.6 mm**
Cylinder capacity: **2800 cc**
Gears: **3 forward**
Brake horse power: **30**
Maximum speed: **50 mph**
Wheelbase: **8 ft 6 ins (2.59 m)**
Suspension: **front and back: ¾ elliptic leaf-springs**

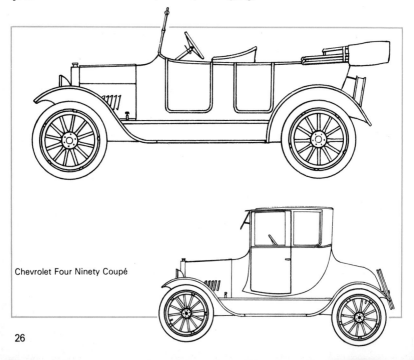

Chevrolet Four Ninety Coupé

General Motors in 1920, to be replaced by Pierre S. du Pont, Chevrolet's future was still not certain. However, du Pont and Alfred Sloan, his right-hand man, decided to make the company the true rival to Ford, and evolved a strategy based on price and quality. If in the future, Chevrolets became more expensive than Fords, they would have the reputation of being better cars.

The first vehicle to be born out of this new strategy was the Superior, a direct descendant of the Four Ninety. Its designer, Ormond E. Hunt, intended it to be indeed 'superior' to the Ford which gave it its name.

The Roadster, which cost $490, like the Four Ninety, was clearly inspired by its sister car but no-one had imagined that by 1923 production figures would be touching the half

Car: **Chevrolet Superior Roadster**
Year: **1924**
Engine: **4 cylinders in line**
Bore and stroke: **93.66 × 101.6 mm**
Cylinder capacity: **2800 cc**
Gears: **3 forward**
Brake horse power: **35**
Maximum speed: **56 mph**
Wheelbase: **8 ft 7 ins (2.61 m)**
Suspension: **front and back: ¾ elliptic leaf-springs**

million mark (480,737). The Superior also came complete with a range of accessories, including a windshield in two sections.

Armed with the Four Ninety and the Superior, General Motors began its aggressive marketing attack on Ford, winning control of the American market eventually, after years of dramatic developments and rivalry. But it is curious that the Chevrolet has never lost its 'prima donna' role, and is still the standard-bearer for General Motors.

Chrysler coupé 50
Chrysler CD

Like many other founders of car manufacturing companies, Walter Chrysler showed outstanding enterprise and spirit of initiative. At 45 he was already an important figure in the industry (head of Buick, and deputy vice-president of General Motors). But then his ideas began to clash with those of Durant. Rather than waiting for things to smooth over, he went his own way, and started again from the beginning, by joining Willys-Overland, which was in trouble at the time. After helping to sort out problems at Willys, he joined Maxwell-Chalmers, which was in the same state as Willys had been before his arrival. The success of this double rescue operation, and his faith in three young engineers, Fred Zeder, Owen Skelton, and Carl Breer, persuaded him to start his own business. A year later, in 1924, he had already produced a vehicle of exceptional quality. It had a 6-cylinder engine with side valves, developing 68 bhp at 3,200 revs, aluminium pistons, and hydraulic expanding brakes on all four wheels (Lockheed)—the first time these had been used on a standard car. It was very successful and 100,000 vehicles were sold in 1925.

The Chrysler coupé 50 appeared in 1927, when Walter Chrysler extended his range. It was a two-seater coupé, with wooden wheels, a crankshaft on 3 bearings, thermo-syphon cooling, choke, and disc clutch. The accessories included windshield wiper, electric horn, anti-theft device, removable wheels, and rear-view mirror. The ideal car, therefore, for Chrysler to put up in competition against Ford and General Motors. To cover all sectors of the market, he pushed forward the Dodge and brought out two new models, the De Soto and the Plymouth. All his cars were characterised by certain important innovations, such as the down-draft carburetor and the swing-valve engine.

The CD dates from 1931. It was inspired by the big 6300 cc Custom Imperial, but had a shorter wheelbase, a less complicated engine (on 5 bearings), a mechanical feed pump, hydraulic brakes, a thermostat for the radiator, and a 4-speed transmission. The CD sold for $1,565. The engine was considered to be under-powered, so the cylinder capacity was increased twice that year, bringing the bhp up from 80 to 100. The four-speed gearbox was abandoned after 1933, in favour of 3 speeds.

In 1934, pursuing his desire for innovation, Chrysler brought out one of his most original, but at the same time most controversial models, the Airflow. The engine was sited between the axles, for increased comfort.

Walter Chrysler died in 1940, leav-

Car: **Chrysler CD**
Year: **1931**
Engine: **8 cylinders in line**
Bore and stroke: **85.7 × 127 mm**
Cylinder capacity: **5857.6 cc**
Gears: **4 forward**
Brake horse power: **100**
Maximum speed: **72 mph**
Wheelbase: **10 ft 4 in (3.14 m)**
Suspension: **front and back: semi-elliptic leaf-springs**

Car: **Chrysler coupé 50**
Year: **1927**
Engine: **4 cylinders in line**
Bore and stroke: **92.07 × 104.7 mm**
Cylinder capacity: **2790 cc**
Gears: **3 forward**
Brake horse power: **38**
Maximum speed: **55 mph**
Wheelbase: **8 ft 6 in (2.59 m)**
Suspension: **front and back: semi-elliptic leaf-springs**

ing behind him the third largest motor manufacturing company in America. Later, together with Ford and General Motors, the company was to become a multi-national, with many factories in Europe.

One of the most outstanding Cord motor cars was the L 29. The engine was an 8-cylinder in-line Lycoming (the same as the engine used in the Auburn, but mounted the other way, with the clutch at the front). The bodywork, front and back, was designed by Leo Goessen. The quarter elliptic leaf-spring suspension and inner brakes and radiator were by Miller. The structure of the bodywork also derived from Auburn.

Produced in 1929, the car sold at $3,095 for the sedan, and $3,295 for the convertible. The front-wheel drive, it was feared, would mean that it had little power going uphill, especially since the engine was behind the front axle, but these fears were not justified.

Cord was in fact a finance company, which combined Cord (named after its founder Errett L. Cord), Auburn, Lycoming, the Kalamazoo Limousine Body, the Stinson Aircraft Factory and Duesenberg. Errett Lobban Cord's own undisciplined vitality lay at the heart of the difficulties encountered by all the firms he had gathered into his empire; but the quality of Auburns, Cords, and Duesenbergs made him one of the most prominent figures in the American automobile industry.

Car: **Cord L 29**
Year: **1929**
Engine: **8 cylinders in line**
Bore and stroke: **82.5 × 114.3 mm**
Cylinder capacity: **4881 cc**
Gears: **3 forward**
Brake horse power: **125**
Maximum speed: **77 mph**
Wheelbase: **11 ft 5½ ins (3.49 m)**
Suspension: **front: ¼ elliptic leaf-springs; back: semi-elliptic leaf-springs**

The date of this model shows that this car has nothing whatsoever to do with the post Second World War Cunningham, which was purely and simply a racing car. James Cunningham, Son and Company started in New York in 1838, as a coach factory, and began making cars in 1908, specialising in a slighly unusual area—ambulances and hearses. The market was right for a de-luxe semi-racing car, and this is precisely what Cunningham produced, with little heed to cost.

The Speedster's engine had aluminium pistons, head, and engine block. Parts of the body were also aluminium. The 8-cylinder V engine developed over 90 bhp at 2,400 revs, then later 110 bhp at 2,500 revs. The 4-speed transmission and detachable wheels were both something of a

Car: **Cunningham Speedster**
Year: **1919**
Engine: **8 cylinders V**
Bore and stroke: **95 × 127 mm**
Cylinder capacity: **7204 cc**
Gears: **4 forward**
Brake horse power: **90**
Maximum speed: **95 mph**
Wheelbase: **11 ft 0 ins (3.35 m)**
Suspension: front: **semi-elliptic leaf-springs;** back: **¾ elliptic leaf-springs**

novelty at the time. It could reach 95 mph.

The commercial success of the Cunningham was due in part to the famous Italo-American driver Ralph De Palma, who set up world records driving a Cunningham at Sheepshead Bay.

Cunningham ceased production in 1936, because the owners decided to turn to making electrical equipment, which was obviously more profitable.

1934—De Soto Airflow SE   USA

De Soto, founded in Detroit in 1928, was part of the Chrysler group until 1960, when, for commercial reasons, it ceased production. The 1934 Airflow model was a fairly typical De Soto model, but it was not a success. It is possible that it arrived on the scene too early. The shape of the body made access to both trunk and engine difficult, and sales soon showed that the Airflow was not particularly popular (about 14,000 vehicles in 1934, 4,600 in 1937). In almost every respect the version brought out by De Soto resembled the Chrysler, and the engine was the only 6-cylinder engine in the Airflow range. Its maximum speed was just over 85 mph. Efforts were made to break records, to bring the car to the public's notice. A De Soto Airflow reached an average of almost 75 mph over a distance of 500

Car: **De Soto Airflow SE**
Year: **1934**
Engine: **6 cylinders in line**
Bore and stroke: **85.7 × 114.3 mm**
Cylinder capacity: **3956 cc**
Gears: **3 forward**
Brake horse power: **100**
Maximum speed: **85 mph**
Wheelbase: **9 ft 7½ ins (293.3 m)**
Suspension: **front and back: semi-elliptic leaf-springs**

miles. Another crossed the United States from New York to San Francisco using, on average, a gallon of gasoline every thirty miles. Demand for the model continued to fall, however, and in 1937 it was decided to sell only the Chrysler version although this move did not help the sales. The Airflow did, however, represent an attempt at innovation, and proved once again that among American car buyers such attempts always receive a cool reception to begin with.

Dodge was the creation of two brothers, John and Horace Dodge, who, with a thorough mechanical knowledge learnt from their father's firm, left their home town of Niles, Michigan for Windsor, Ontario where they made bicycles, and then later spare parts for cars. In 1901 they moved to Detroit and were successful in supplying parts to various firms, especially Ford. Relations with Ford became difficult and the brothers resolved to set up their own company. In November 1914 the first Dodge car came on the market. The reputation they had acquired as suppliers greatly helped them and by 1915 they had produced 45,000 vehicles. By 1920 they were making 625 cars a day.

The car illustrated here is an early model. The engine had side valves and developed 35 bhp. It had a cone

Car: **Dodge Four**
Year: **1915**
Engine: **4 cylinders in line**
Bore and stroke: **98.4 × 114.3 mm**
Cylinder capacity: **3478 cc**
Gears: **3 forward**
Brake horse power: **35**
Maximum speed: **45 mph**
Wheelbase: **9 ft 2 ins (3.25 m)**
Suspension: **front: semi-elliptic leaf-springs;**
　　back: ¾ elliptic leaf-springs

clutch, brakes on the back wheels, and magneto ignition. The poor gear layout with 2nd and 3rd gear on the left was one of the defects of the car.

In 1917 the Dodge brothers brought out what is held to be the first car with an all steel, closed body. In 1925 the company had been bought for $146 million by Dillon, Read, and Company, and Dodge was absorbed into the Chrysler organisation in 1928.

1918—Detroit Electric

It may seem surprising that at a time when there was no energy problem, a market for electric cars grew up and flourished in the U.S.A., with, at one point, some 21 different manufacturers involved. It is also odd that electrically-propelled cars were made in Detroit until 1941.

Detroit Electric, founded in the American car capital in 1907, experienced a period of prosperity for much the same reasons that favour electric propulsion today: manoeuvrability in town traffic, silence, and fuel economy. In 1910, Detroit Electric sold 1500 cars.

The salient feature of the car was the positioning of the 3 bhp motor between the two axles, with back-wheel drive. For many years the car was steered by a tiller (the wheel being adopted only in 1914). Its maximum

Car: **Detroit Electric**
Year: **1918**
Engine: **electric, beneath the floor**
Gears: **5 forward**
Brake horse power: **3**
Maximum speed: **25 mph**
Wheelbase: **8 ft 4 ins (2.54 m)**
Suspension: **front: semi-elliptic leaf-springs; back: elliptic leaf-springs**

speed was only 25 mph but it could run 125 miles before its batteries needed to be recharged. The batteries were situated at the front and back. After 1914 the electric car was only available with a closed body. Its rather high price ($2,500) made people gradually lose interest in this kind of vehicle. No-one could have imagined that 35 years later the car industry would be concentrating on electrical traction and it is ironic that today's electric cars have a similar performance to the 1918 Detroit Electric.

Duesenberg Model A
Duesenberg J
Duesenberg SJ

In a country where more people drove cars than anywhere else, and where hundreds of firms were making brave but often unsuccessful innovations, Duesenberg remains a special case and will always be unique. Super-luxurious, super-fast, gigantic, yet highly manoeuvrable, heavy, yet requiring the minimum of effort to steer, these cars created an aura of perfection that defies the years. The few still in existence today are quoted at high prices, as in the 1930s when no Hollywood star was seen without one.

Even thirty years after the disappearance of Duesenbergs from Indianapolis, there are many who maintain that they were the best cars ever produced in America and that there is nothing even today to compare with them, even considering such luxury cars as Cadillacs and Lincoln Continentals.

Born in Lippe, Germany, Fred and August (Augie) Duesenberg emigrated to the U.S.A. with their parents in 1885. The brothers first became interested in cars at the turn of the century. Fred helped a friend in Wisconsin build the Rambler; then he opened a garage in Des Moines, Iowa, determined to produce a car of his own design as soon as he was financially able to do so. One of his customers, a lawyer named Mason, offered him the means to realise his dreams. The car he built was called 'The Mason Motor Car'. It had a twin-cylinder engine, with horizontal opposed cylinders. Advertised as the toughest and fastest American twin-cylinder car, it sold at $1,250.

The company was later bought by Frederick Maytag, which probably pleased Fred Duesenberg as his thoughts were now elsewhere. The first thing he did was to make a 4-cylinder car, for the production of which the Duesenberg Motor Company was founded in Saint Paul, Minnesota, in 1913.

On the outbreak of war Duesenberg began contributing to the War-effort by working for the American Army and Air Force. He continued to produce 4-cylinder engines, which meanwhile had acquired 4 valves per cylinder and two camshafts (the Air Force used it in training aircraft). At the same time they introduced the 16-cylinder Bugatti, which the Duesenbergs and their chief designer, Charles B. King, had extensively modified, as well as a 16-cylinder of their own design. They designed a 12-cylinder engine, for Air Force use, and a 4-cylinder (160 bhp) engine for the Army. All their output during the war came from a factory at Elizabeth, New Jersey, where the Duesenbergs had moved before the outbreak of hostilities. The sale of this factory to Willys Motors, and that of the manufacturing rights on the 4-cylinder Model G to the Rochester Motor Company enabled the Duesenbergs to move once again. They chose Indianapolis and concentrated initially on a straight-8 engine with overhead camshafts, of which four were made in 1920. Three of these went into cars which came 3rd, 4th,

and 6th at their first showing in the 1920 500 Miles race. They then produced a 16-cylinder engine (two blocks of 8 coupled together) for a record-breaking car in which Tommy Milton reached more than 155 mph at Daytona. Car-racing occupied almost all their energies in these early years in Indianapolis, and made their name. Their cars won first prize in 1924 (Corum and Boyer, at over 98 mph), 1925 (Peter de Paolo at over 100 mph), and 1927 (Souders, averaging over 96 mph).

At this stage they produced a de luxe touring vehicle, that was introduced to the public inside the Commodore Hotel, New York, in October 1920. The engine in the Model A, as this first car was called, derived from the Duesenberg 3000 cc racing engine, but the cylinder

Car: **Duesenberg Model A**
Year: **1922**
Engine: **8 cylinders in line**
Bore and stroke: **73 × 127 mm**
Cylinder capacity: **4261 cc**
Gears: **3 forward**
Brake horse power: **88**
Maximum speed: **95 mph**
Wheelbase: **11 ft 2 ins (3.40 m)**
Suspension: **front and back: semi-elliptic leaf springs**

capacity was raised from 3000 to 4200 cc. There was only one camshaft in the head, and two valves per cylinder as against three in the racing-car (one inlet, two exhaust). It developed 88 bhp at 3,600 revs, and could exceed 95 mph. The Model A was also the first American car with hydraulic brakes on all four wheels, and a tubular front axle; it incorporated the first balloon-type tires.

It was a highly revolutionary car (priced at $8,300), and the Duesen-

berg brothers wanted to demonstrate its qualities by making it run the equivalent of the breadth of the continent: 3,000 miles (4,828 km), on the track at Indianapolis. The car was re-filled with water and fuel and the drivers exchanged without halting. In fact there were two stops for tire-changes, but the engine remained running. It averaged over 68 mph. In 1922, the first effective production year, 92 were made: then in 1923, 140 vehicles were produced. The Model A, of which a total of about 500 were produced, was followed by a mysterious Model X, which differed from the A in having a longer wheel-base and increased power (from 88 to 100 bhp). Only about a dozen of the Model X were produced.

Despite the success of the Model A and the reputation they now had, the

Car: **Duesenberg J**
Year: **1931**
Engine: **8 cylinders in line**
Bore and stroke: **95 × 120.5 mm**
Cylinder capacity: **6882 cc**
Gears: **3 forward**
Brake horse power: **265**
Maximum speed: **115 mph**
Wheelbase: **11 ft 10 ins (3.60 m)**
Suspension: **front and back: semi-elliptic leaf-springs**

Duesenberg brothers started to find themselves in financial difficulties, and would perhaps have closed shop had it not been for Errett Lobban Cord, who was building up a new corporation and had bought Auburn in 1924. Cord took over Duesenberg and the brothers were then able to set to work again with fresh vigour. At the New York show of 1928 they launched the Model J. Underneath an eagle on the radiator stood the words Duesenberg Straight Eight. The

Model J was immediately acclaimed as the best American car ever made. The 8-cylinder in-line engine had two camshafts in the head, 4 valves per cylinder, and rods heat-treated in aluminium alloy. The car developed 265 bhp at 4,250 revs. Despite its weight of two tons it had a maximum speed of around 115 mph and, most important of all, could achieve 0-100 mph in 21 seconds. It could exceed 100 mph in second gear. Although designed entirely by Fred Duesenberg, the J engine was actually made by the Williamsport, Pennsylvania company, Lycoming. It featured among other items: servo-assisted brakes, speedometer (showing up to 150 mph), rev counter, 8-day clock, chronometer (from 1/5 second to 30 minutes), altimeter, oil pressure indicator, fuel indicator, engine temperature indicator, and ammeter.

All the instrument dials were coloured white on black. On either side of the dashboard was a light, the right-hand one indicating every 700 miles (1,126 km) that the engine needed more oil. The light on the left warned that 1,400 miles (2,253 km) had been covered and the distilled water in the battery had to be filled up. To keep the total weight as low as possible, there was extensive use of special alloys. The bodywork was the work of specialists, who were given two chassis, one with a wheelbase of 11 ft 10 ins (3.03 m), the other of 12 ft 8 ins (3.83 m). The cost of a chassis varied from $8,500 to $11,750. The eagle emblem could be added for an extra $25.

In 1932 the Model SJ appeared-differing from the J in having a super-charger. The SJ developed 320 bhp, and had a maximum speed of around 125 mph, with a possible speed of over 100 mph in second gear. It could reach 100 mph from stand-still in 17 seconds. Aesthetically it differed from its sister car in its 4 chromium plated exhaust-pipes mounted on the left-hand side. SJ owners were proud of this distinctive feature, but it became 'vulgarised' when, probably under pressure from J owners, Duesenberg added 4 exhaust-pipes to the J also, for an extra cost of $900. It is estimated that 104 SJs with side exhaust-pipes were made, of which 36 actually had super-chargers. Total production of the J and SJ is thought to have been between 470 and 480.

Obviously both models fired the imagination of many car-body designers (in 1930 Duesenberg offered 18 different styles, and listed seven different bodywork firms). Murphy, from Pasadena, made the largest number. In practice, no two cars were the same, as each buyer who wanted something exclusive came away satisfied: the firm put an engineer at the disposal of customers, to explore all possible variations. Murphy would draw the proposed body on an enormous blackboard, so that the exact dimensions could be reproduced. Duesenbergs were supplied with bodies in Europe by Saoutchik, Letourneur and Marchand, and the Italian, Castagna. The cost of the bodywork was around $2,500, which together with the $8,500 or $9,500 for the chassis came to quite a sizable amount of money. The SJ chassis cost $11,750 in 1932.

Sadly, the end came at last for

Duesenberg. In 1937 Cord ran into difficulties with Auburn, and the Cord Corporation went into liquidation. Among the various attempts to revive this famous name, the efforts of Fritz Duesenberg, August's son, in 1966, should not go unrecorded. He had solid financial backing, and his aim was to provide the American market with a super de luxe car along the lines of the Duesenberg J and SJ. The bodywork design was entrusted to Virgil Exner, and the production of it to Ghia, in Turin, Italy. The engine chosen was a Chrysler V8 developing 425 bhp. Line, instrument panel, and final details were to be based on the original J and SJ. The total price was fixed at $19,500. A prototype was made and exhibited in the States, but the lukewarm reception it received convinced everyone that the Duesen-

Car: **Duesenberg SJ**
Year: **1936**
Engine: **8 cylinders in line with compressor**
Bore and stroke: **95 × 120.5 mm**
Cylinder capacity: **6882 cc**
Gears: **3 forward**
Brake horse power: **320**
Maximum speed: **125 mph**
Wheelbase: **11 ft 10 ins (3.60 m)**
Suspension: **front and back: semi-elliptic leaf-springs**

berg now belonged to the past, and that no substitute, however sophisticated, could replace the cars of the 1930s. This one prototype was nevertheless sold at auction for the enormous sum of $37,500 in 1966. Since then there have been at least two other Duesenberg companies, one making a replica of the 1936 SSJ 2-seater, and another making a modern-styled 4-door sedan selling at about $100,000.

39

1921—Du Pont Touring USA

The American public came to know of Du Pont after the New York car exhibition of 1919. The firm was founded by Paul du Pont, whose family owned an important chemicals factory and had for many years also been involved with marine engines. Paul du Pont wanted to make a car that would rival the most celebrated American cars of the time, including the Duesenbergs, and he planned a series of highly-refined vehicles of which only 537 were ever made.

The 1921 Touring was one of the first, and could seat five people. The 60 bhp engine was pump cooled; it had high tension magneto ignition, and a multi-disc dry clutch.

In 1925 Du Pont went on to make a 6-cylinder car, and at the 1928 New York exhibition launched the Model G, with 8-cylinder in-line Continental

Car: **Du Pont Touring**
Year: **1921**
Engine: **4 cylinders in line**
Bore and stroke: **100.01 × 130.17 mm**
Cylinder capacity: **4090 cc**
Brake horse power: **60**
Maximum speed: **70 mph**
Wheelbase: **10 ft 4 ins (3.14 m)**
Suspension: **front and back: semi-elliptic leaf springs**

engine of 5,275 cc (125 bhp in the standard version, 140 bhp in the Le Mans). Du Pont ceased production in 1932. Paul du Pont's passion for cars had been cooled by the prohibitive expense of his company's limited production, even though the cars that they produced were first-rate. Even following the publicity gained by its participation in the 1929 Le Mans 24 hours, the Model G, perhaps the most highly admired of the Du Pont range, still had no commercial success.

Ford Model K
Ford Model T
Ford V8 Model 18

The car that was to become the most popular make in the world, introducing the concept of mass production, started life officially in 1903. A company was formed by a group of 12 men led by Henry Ford. The 12 included the Dodge brothers, who later themselves became car manufacturers. The firm's premises in Mack Avenue, where production of the Model A began, were modest. Henry Ford was, in fact, already busy designing and making cars in 1896 (a quadri-cycle, a development from this, and two racing-cars). The Model A was driven by a twin-cylinder water-cooled engine with horizontal cylinders under the seat, and had chain transmission and epicyclic gears with two ratios. It was made for two years, and replaced by the Model C, which also had a two-year production span. The first 4-cylinder car was made in 1904; 1906 saw the model K, ostensibly a de luxe model, with a 6-cylinder engine. Ford and his collaborators quickly realised that this car was not going to make much impact on the market that was rapidly expanding and swarming with competitors. The K was manufactured for two years, and the best indication of Ford's lack of interest in it is the fact that it was built in the Dodge factory, and then assembled in his own.

It should, nevertheless, be stressed that the Model K's 6-cylinder engine was an exact 'square', both piston bore and stroke being the same, and that there were two epicyclic forward gears: this gearbox was to become characteristic of all Fords. However, particularly in this model, it appeared unable to absorb and transmit the power of the engine. This was one of the most basic criticisms levelled at the car.

The K's lack of success convinced Ford that, at least in those early years, the future of cars lay in a popular model, simple in design and capable of being produced in large quantities if possible. Step by step, he arrived at a solution with the 4-cylinder Model N. After this, twin-cylinder engines were abandoned.

The Model T, later to become so famous as the means of 'motorising America', was introduced in 1908, and stayed in production up to 1927. Exactly 15,007,033 vehicles were built—a record beaten only by Volkswagen after the Second World War over forty years later.

Many books have been written about the Model T, not all of them correct in every detail. One of Ford's most commonly misquoted remarks about the car concerns the colour of the body. 'You can have a Ford in any colour,' he is reputed to have said, 'as long as it's black.' This does not entirely correspond with the facts, for at first the T came in various colours. By 1914, however, production was so rapid that it was found that only black Japan enamel would dry quickly enough to keep the conveyor belts moving at the required speed. Therefore for a number of years black was the only colour available.

It is also untrue to say that T's remained the same from 1908 to 1927. Structurally indeed they did not change; but they were being continually updated—partly because, unable to satisfy demand, Ford was obliged to have certain components made elsewhere. Only in 1920, 12 years after the model had been launched, was Ford in a position to totally build the car himself.

Apart from the look of the body, which immediately created a sense of solidity, and the many variants available, a fundamental characteristic of the T was its epicyclic gearbox. The company had already used this in other cars. In this system the engine was not engaged by means of movable gears. When the pedal was pressed down, a band-brake operated on the rim of the crown-wheel correspond-

Car: **Ford Model K**
Year: **1906**
Engine: **6 cylinders in line**
Bore and stroke: **114.3 × 114.3 mm**
Cylinder capacity: **7033 cc**
Gears: **2 forward**
Brake horse power: **40**
Maximum speed: **35 mph**
Wheelbase: **10 ft 0 ins (3.04 m)**
Suspension: **front: semi-elliptic leaf-springs; back: elliptic leaf-springs**

ing to the desired speed, thus effecting the change of gears.

One part of the vehicle that saw the most modifications and changes were the seats—not so much their shape as their covering, the object being always to reduce the price.

Another major innovation brought about by Ford was the chain-production line. He realised that it would be much simpler, more practical, and quicker if, when

assembling the vehicle, the workers could draw the various components from suitable containers placed beside the production line, rather than going to the various storerooms for them, which meant they had constantly to be moving from place to place. In this way he managed to reduce the assembly time from 12 hours to an hour and a half.

The Model T was first marketed in 1908, but the models produced after April 1909 were so different from the original that they may be thought of almost as different cars. In the end Ford officially declared that there were were 2,500 vehicles of 1909 vintage. The first thousand were placed in a separate category. They differed from the others in having two external levers (brake and reverse). These levers were abandoned in

Car: **Ford Model T**
Year: **1908**
Engine: **4 cylinders in line**
Bore and stroke: **95 × 102 mm**
Cylinder capacity: **2890 cc**
Gears: **2 forward**
Brake horse power: **22**
Maximum speed: **45 mph**
Wheelbase: **8 ft 4 ins (2.54 m)**
Suspension: **front and back: transverse leaf-springs**

February 1909, in favour of the three-pedal system. Ford invited the owners of the first thousand vehicles to have them brought up to date for the very reasonable sum of $15, on condition that they returned the parts that were replaced. Basically, therefore, the true 1908 models, extremely rare today, are those carrying a serial number of under a thousand. With the outbreak of war and the need to reduce all gasoline consumption,

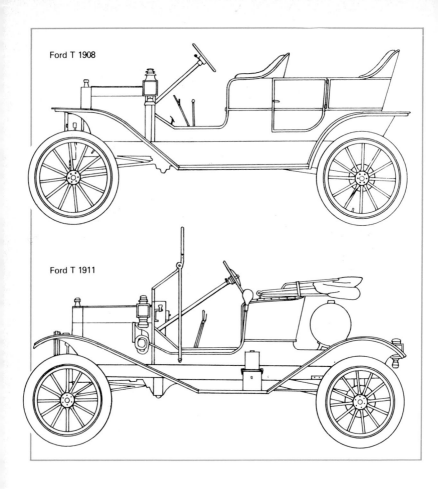

Ford T 1908

Ford T 1911

production of the T was hit. The original 22 bhp was reduced progressively in 1917 to 20. The engine speed was 1,500 revs, and the maximum speed of the vehicle about 36 mph. With the occasional rare exceptions, up until 1911 the bodywork was made of wood. After 1911, sheets of metal on a wooden frame were used. Two new models went into production in 1915, the 2-door sedan and the coupelet, the first convertible. That same year quite major stylistic and other more essential changes were introduced: an electrical ignition system, fenders (straight at the front, and curved at the back), a lower hood, and a horn. In 1917 it acquired a regular 'new look': the fenders, both

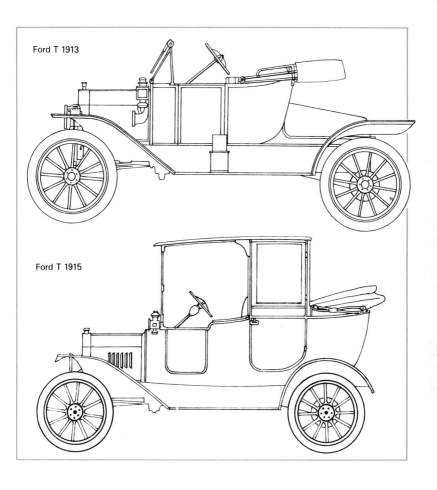

Ford T 1913

Ford T 1915

front and back, became curved, the hood was widened, and the brass radiator was replaced by a black-painted one. In 1919 there were important technical alterations (choke and removable wheel-rims). In 1923 the body was lowered, and the 4-door model was introduced.

Henry Ford always stubbornly resisted changes by insisting that, 'so far as I can see, the only trouble with the Ford car is that we can't make it fast enough'. Prices varied considerably: in 1910 the cheapest model cost $900, in 1912 $590, in 1913 $525, in 1914 $440, in 1915 $390, in 1916 $345, and the same in 1917. In 1918 the same model rose to $500, remaining the same in 1919, and going down again in 1920 to $440. In 1925 it was

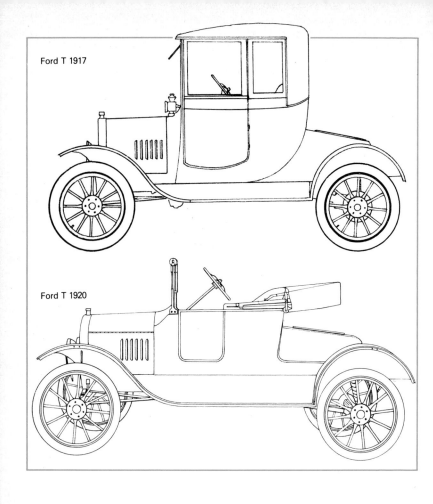

Ford T 1917

Ford T 1920

selling for $260, but in 1926 rose back to $360, where it stayed during 1927 which was its last year of production.

In June 1927, after 19 years, the T went out of production. The last one bore the serial number 15007033. It is said that on the day the T was taken off the assembly lines, Ford left the factory in a rage. He still believed in the car, although the market response showed that it was outdated.

In fact, looking at production figures throughout its whole lifespan, it can be seen that the peak year was 1923, with 2,055,309 cars made (as compared with only 380,741 in 1927).

The T was replaced by the A, thus going back to the beginning of the alphabet. It had a 4-cylinder engine, developing 40 bhp at 2,300 revs, and

the cheapest version cost $495. By now, however, the threatening shadow of Chevrolet was appearing on Ford's horizon.

In 1927 the Model A certainly represented a step forward from the T, but Ford's personal aversion to the 6-cylinder engine kept the A in 4-cylinder class. It was converted to 8-cylinder V in 1932, when Ford devised a method of building such an engine cheaply, in a single cast-iron block, with aluminium pistons. The 3-speed gearbox became synchronised, and safety glass was incorporated into the more expensive models.

Many parts of the V8 were interchangeable with parts on the Model B, a more advanced car than the A. The V8 had splash lubrication, like most Fords, and the mechanical

Car: **Ford V8 Model 18**
Year: **1932**
Engine: **8 cylinders V**
Bore and stroke: **77.8 × 95.2 mm**
Cylinder capacity: **3612 cc**
Gears: **3 forward**
Brake horse power: **65**
Maximum speed: **75 mph**
Wheelbase: **8 ft 10 ins (2.69 m)**
Suspension: **front and back: transverse leaf-springs**

brakes were designed to bring the car to a halt from 60 mph within a few yards. It was an instant success and was also built in England, France (by Matford), Germany, Hungary (by Mavag), and in Austria. The engine was bought by Chenard-Walcker in France and Allard in England among many small manufacturers. The engine was extensively used in American army vehicles during the Second World War.

47

The main feature of Franklins (the firm founded by Herbert H. Franklin, Syracuse, New York) was their air-cooled engines, which were built into every car. John Wilkinson in 1902 designed an air-cooled engine with 4 cylinders and overhead valves. The absence of a radiator, and the use of light metals made the Franklin both light and manageable, as well as reliable. The company demonstrated the reliability of its cars by organising, and winning, a rally across the whole continent.

Franklin started thinking about a 12-cylinder V engine in 1928, with the assistance of Glen Shoemaker. In building the assembly line he contracted debts of $5,000,000; the economic crisis led to the failure of the company in 1932, and the Series 17 was sold by the receivers. In fact,

Car: **Franklin Series 17**
Year: **1933**
Engine: **12 cylinders V, air-cooled**
Bore and stroke: **82.5 × 107.5 mm**
Cylinder capacity: **6810 cc**
Gears: **3 forward**
Brake horse power: **150**
Maximum speed: **95 mph**
Wheelbase: **12 ft 0 ins (3.65 m)**
Suspension: **front and back: semi-elliptic leaf-springs**

the car was not very well suited to the times. It weighed about 3 tons (3,000 kg)—as if to compensate for the lightness of the previous models—and although it could reach 95 mph, its gasoline consumption was in the region of 5 to 7 miles per gallon, and it cost $4,200. Franklin himself was an interesting person, having been editor of a newspaper, and then a match manufacturer, before becoming involved with the manufacture of motor cars.

This firm was started in Detroit in 1927 by three brothers (Joseph, Robert and Ray Graham) in conjunction with Paige-Detroit. They combined their name with that of the old firm, but only until 1931. For the next ten years they used the name Graham.

Car: **Graham Streak**
Year: **1932**
Engine: **8 cylinders in line**
Bore and stroke: **79.4 × 101 mm**
Cylinder capacity: **3998 cc**
Gears: **3 forward**
Brake horse power **90**
Maximum speed: **80 mph**
Wheelbase: **10 ft 3 ins (3.12 m)**
Suspension: **front and back: semi-elliptical leaf springs**

Grahams were distinctive above all for the look of their bodywork. It was quite a new style and came to be adopted by almost all other manufacturers, with Ford leading the way. These innovations included skirted fenders and a low windshield.

Mechanically the Streak was more or less conventional. Its 8-cylinder in-line engine, mounted on 5 bearings, developed just over 90 bhp, and the head was particularly subject to corrosion. It had hydraulic brakes and a maximum speed of about 80 mph.

Although a success, at least as a curiosity, stylistically it did not sell especially well (around 13,000 in 1932 and 11,000 the following year). The inclusion of a centrifugal compressor as used in airplanes increased the maximum speed to 90 mph (135 bhp), but did not greatly improve the car's fortunes. The unsatisfactory sales forced the Graham brothers to cease production in 1941. After the war the company was absorbed into Kaiser-Frazer.

Hudson was a typical American car company, started more out of financial than technical intrests. It was founded by Joseph L. Hudson and seven associates in 1908. In 1909 it was already operating in Detroit. Its cars were almost exclusively made up of standard components. It was intended to be a slightly up-market sedan. It did not figure prominently in the market until a six-cylinder car was built with counter-balanced crankshaft and special combustion chambers. This car became known for its quietness and comfort when travelling: it was the classic American middle-class car. The single-block engine with side valves proved very robust. Equipped with choke and lights, it cost $1,600. The body was popular, not only because of its daringly streamlined shape, but also

Car: **Hudson 37**
Year: **1913**
Engine: **4 cylinders in line**
Bore and stroke: **101.6 × 133.4 mm**
Cylinder capacity: **4323 cc**
Brake horse power: **—**
Maximum speed: **—**
Wheelbase: **9 ft 6½ ins (2.90 m)**
Gears: **3 forward**
Suspension: **front: semi-elliptic leaf-springs; back: ¾ elliptic leaf-springs**

because it was closed. In those days this was quite a rarity. The 37 came in four models, including a sports version advertised with the slogan 'a mile a minute', an obvious allusion to its maximum speed.

The Hudson Company found itself in deep waters in 1954, and amalgamated with Nash, creating American Motors. This company still operates today, although it has encountered, and continues to encounter, many obstacles.

Throughout the long and successful production life of this company (founded by W. L. Kissel in Hartford, Wisconsin), the 8 75 represents one of its most successful cars. Together with the 6-cylinder model built along the same lines, it remained in production longer than any of their other cars. Kissel had begun by making farm implements and agricultural machinery. In 1906 he went into car-production.

In 1914 Kissel brought out a big 6-cylinder car, which achieved fame partly through the Los Angeles-New York rally held just before the war.

The 8 75 had illustrious predecessors in the 6 45 (6-cylinder 4700 cc engine developing over 60 bhp at 3,200 revs) and the 6 55, which continued to be made until 1928. The 8 75 had a Lycoming engine

Car: **Kissel 8 75**
Year: **1927**
Engine: **8 cylinders in line**
Bore and stroke: **84 × 120 mm**
Cylinder capacity: **5317 cc**
Gears: **3 forward**
Brake horse power: **71**
Maximum speed: **75 mph**
Wheelbase: **10 ft 11 ins (3.32 m)**
Suspension: **front and back: semi-elliptic leaf-springs**

developing 71 bhp at 3,000 revs, and in turn gave way to a whole series of de luxe models (8-cylinder) including the White Eagle, which was one of the great cars of the period. In 1917, alongside Kissel Kar, there appeared another name, Silver Special (Conover T. Silver was Kissel's agents in New York, and he designed the body-work of the Special series). The firm was hit by the 1929 crisis, and in 1931 it merged with Moon. This last attempt at survival was, however, unsuccessful.

1912—K.R.I.T. 25/30 HP

K.R.I.T. did not survive long enough in the turbulent early years of the American car industry. Built by Kenneth Krittenden between 1909 and 1916, these cars were thoroughly orthodox, the one exception being the 1912 model illustrated here, which had elliptic rather than semi-elliptic leaf-spring rear suspension. Another distinguishing sign was a certain richness of colour on the body. The 1914 Touring Car L came in blue with grey wheels. It cost $1,050, including top, lights, choke, windshield, speedometer, and detachable wheels, and this was thus a strong selling feature. Punctures were by no means uncommon! Strangely enough, one of the characteristics specified by the company was the steering-wheel positioned on the left. The controls (gears and brakes) were also on the

Car: **K.R.I.T. 25/30HP**
Year: **1912**
Engine: **4 cylinders in line**
Bore and stroke: **95 × 102 mm**
Gears: **3 forward**
Cylinder capacity: **2890 cc**
Brake horse power: **30**
Maximum speed: **42 mph**
Wheelbase: **9 ft 0 ins (2.74 m)**
Suspension: **front: semi-elliptic leaf-springs; back: elliptic leaf-springs**

left. Not all manufacturers followed the same criteria at this stage, and the position of the steering-wheel and controls was probably a decisive element in the prospective purchaser's mind.

The 25/30 was made throughout the period 1912 to 1915. Although the company tried to make headway in the difficult and highly competitive cheap car market, not surprisingly it was defeated in the battle with the giant manufacturers.

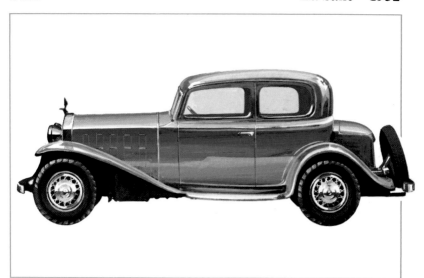

The La Salle was not just another model from General Motors. It was a series created strategically by the biggest car manufacturing firm in the world to fill a gap in the market between the Buick and the Cadillac. It started well in 1927, with 27,000 vehicles being made. The price was tempting ($3,000), and the bodywork was attractive, being along the lines of the Hispano-Suiza. Apart from anything else, these cars, together with the Cadillacs, were the first to have wholly synchronised gears. In the end, however, rather than being halfway between the Buick and the Cadillac, the La Salle finished up as a poor imitation of the Cadillac, unable to vie with it even in price. At the same time, the economic depression had forced General Motors to produce two commercially distinctive

Car: **La Salle**
Year: **1932**
Engine: **8 cylinders in V**
Bore and stroke: **85.4 × 125.4 mm**
Cylinder capacity: **5743 cc**
Gears: **3 forward**
Brake horse power: **115**
Maximum speed: **85 mph**
Wheelbase: **10 ft 10 ins (3.30 m)**
Suspension: **front: independent with spiral springs; back: semi-elliptic leaf-springs**

vehicles whilst keeping them as similar as possible on the engineering side. In 1931 both cars shared the same 5784 cc engine developing 115 bhp. The La Salle had a servo-assisted clutch, mechanical feed-pump, and servo-brakes. Yet despite these qualities, and a price difference of $400, sales of Cadillacs were more than double those of La Salles. The 1934 model had straight-8 engines, unlike any Cadillac. A return to V-8s came in 1937, and the La Salle was discontinued after 1940.

Lincoln Zephyr Fastback
Lincoln KV 12

Of the makes still on the American market, Lincoln, founded in 1920, is one of the most recent. It resulted from irreconcilable differences of opinion between the former Cadillac designer Henry Leland and the president of the company, William Crapo Durant. Although 65 years old, Leland left General Motors and founded Lincoln, named after the American president. In 1922 Henry Ford bought the company, intending himself to enter the de luxe and prestige section of the market. Ford took full advantage of Leland's acknowledged expertise, and Leland immediately started to produce cars for the top end of the market, with 8-cylinder V engines, slightly different from those he had designed for Cadillac in having a V angle of 60° rather than 90°. This engine was so successful that it remained practically unchanged for over ten years. Going straight to the best body designers of the time, they created a car that combined both elegance and mechanical excellence.

The Zephyr Fastback was one of the big attractions of the 1936 New York motor show. Its chief characteristic was its 4387 cc, 12-cylinder engine, with seven bearings, and hydraulic tappets. It developed 110 bhp and had a maximum speed of about 90 mph. An unusual feature was the position of the headlights which were built into the fenders.

Unlike the Ford V-8, the Lincoln V-12 engine was not fitted to many European makes of car, but one company which did use it was Brough

Superior. In late 1937 they announced a beautiful sedan with underslung chassis and body by Charlesworth. Three chassis were laid down, but only one Brough Superior V-12 was completed.

Lincoln used more 12-cylinder engines than any other make (over 150,000 between 1932 and 1948). Later, however, 12 cylinders were abandoned; from 1948 onwards Lincoln used only 8-cylinder V engines, and after 1952 one with overhead valves. In 1955 a model was offered at $10,000—the most expensive in absolute terms, this being a way of making the car into a luxury article, as it had in fact always been, to rival the Cadillac. This car was called the Continental Mark II and is sometimes thought of as a separate make from Lincoln.

Car: **Lincoln Zephyr Fastback**
Year: **1936**
Engine: **12 cylinders V**
Bore and stroke: **69.8 × 95.2 mm**
Cylinder capacity: **4369 cc**
Gears: **3 forward**
Brake horse power: **110**
Maximum speed: **90 mph**
Wheelbase: **10 ft 2 ins (3.09 m)**
Suspension: **front and back: transverse leaf-springs**

Car: **Brough Superior V-12**
Year: **1938**
Engine: **12 cylinders V**
Bore and stroke: **69.8 × 95.2 mm**
Cylinder capacity: **4369 cc**
Gears: **3 forward**
Brake horse power: **110**
Maximum speed: **90 mph**
Wheelbase: **10 ft 8½ ins (3.21 m)**
Suspension: **front and back: semi-elliptic leaf-springs**

1925—Locomobile Junior Eight

Of all this Company's output, the Junior Eight is considered one of its most important cars, and in fact was the last model still in production when the firm closed down in 1929.

Locomobile started in 1899 in Westboro, Massachusetts, under two partners, Barber and Walker, who began production with steam vehicles under a Stanley licence. Barber and Walker did not share the same confidence in the future of this form of locomotion, however, and eventually they separated. Walker continued with steam cars, which he sold under the name Mobile, while Barber set up a motor manufacturing business, which he continued to call Locomobile, in Bridgeport, Connecticut. He did not totally abandon steam propulsion, but in 1904 he moved over to the combustion engine. His

Car: **Locomobile Junior Eight**
Year: **1925**
Engine: **8 cylinders in line**
Bore and stroke: **71.4 × 101.6 mm**
Cylinder capacity: **3254 cc**
Gears: **3 forward**
Brake horse power: **63**
Maximum speed: **68 mph**
Wheelbase: **10 ft 4 ins (3.14 m)**
Suspension: **front and back: semi-elliptic leaf-springs**

cars were varied and covered a wide range, including racing cars.

The first signs of crisis came in 1920, but William Crapo Durant saved the company from ruin.

The Junior Eight came out in 1925, and its reception encouraged greater hopes for the future. Durant planned it to be a medium-class car, halfway between popular and de luxe models, which is why an 8-cylinder engine with five bearings, was chosen. It had two heads, pump lubrication, dry clutch, and expanding brakes.

Founded as a bicycle factory in 1880, the Lozier Manufacturing Company began to interest itself in engines for tricycles in 1897. In 1903 the death of Henry Abram Lozier, the founder, left his son Harry in the difficult position of carrying on the company, and possibly expanding it. This he did so successfully that a motor car was produced in 1904. Other models followed, all with 4-cylinder engines. All the models sold well.

With the building of a 6-cylinder engine, Lozier became actively involved in races, coming second in the 1911 Indianapolis 500 Miles, and winning the Vanderbilt Cup the same year at about 70 mph average speed with Ralph Mulford driving.

The 50 bhp dates from this period, and the bodywork reveals its dual purpose for sport and touring.

Car: **Lozier 50 HP**
Year: **1913**
Engine: **6 cylinders in line**
Bore and stroke: **117.5 × 140 mm**
Cylinder capacity: **9104 cc**
Gears: **4 forward**
Brake horse power: **55**
Maximum speed: **70 mph**
Wheelbase: **10 ft 11 ins (3.32 m)**
Suspension: **front and back: semi-elliptic leaf-springs**

The 72, with driver's seat on the left, launched in 1912, consolidated Lozier's position and prestige. Yet this company also felt the blight of the economic crisis. It tried to adapt, producing a cheap 4-cylinder model, but without success. In 1915 the company went into liquidation and was taken over by others. However, in 1917 it closed down for good. Basically it shared the fate of most firms making de luxe and racing cars; they were too expensive.

1931—Marmon V-16 USA

Another of the great American car manufacturing companies was Marmon, founded in Indianapolis in 1902 by the brothers Walter and Howard Marmon. Their cars rivalled the most famous of the time, including Duesenberg, in elegance, refinement, and performance. The Marmon brothers' first cars were a success. The first engine had 4 cylinders in V, an air-cooled system, and overhead valves. Then came 6 and 8-cylinder engines, still with an air-cooling system. The first Indianapolis 500 Miles (1911) presented an immense opportunity for publicity, especially as it was on their doorstep. Indeed the race was won by a Marmon (the Wasp).

Marmon followed, and often anticipated, the developments in car manufacture, using aluminium both

Car: **Marmon V-16**
Year: **1931**
Engine: **16 cylinders V**
Bore and stroke: **79 × 101 mm**
Cylinder capacity: **7917 cc**
Gears: **3 forward**
Brake horse power: **200**
Maximum speed: **95 mph**
Wheelbase: **12 ft 1 in (3.68 m)**
Suspension: **front and back: double leaf-springs**

in the engine and the bodywork. But its *pièce de résistance* was the legendary V-16, which developed 200 bhp at 3,400 revs (overhead valves, and camshaft in the engine block). This car won the Marmon brothers first prize from the Society of Automobile Engineers in 1930 for its technical excellence, but it had little market success, and was only produced for two years. The company turned to a prototype 12-cylinder car, but in 1933 they ceased production.

This company, founded in 1904 in Newcastle, Indiana, and absorbed into Chrysler in 1925, operated for less than 20 years. It was started by Jonathan Maxwell and Benjamin Briscoe; the latter left in 1912 to set up a company under his own name. Up until then, the cars they had produced were called Maxwell-Briscoes. Maxwell at first concentrated on the poorest sector of the market, but twin-cylinder engines, in which he was most interested, were soon abandoned in favour of 4 cylinders. The 50-6 was a de luxe model, aimed at the top of the market.

The 50-6 had wooden wheels, dual ignition, and electrical gear-change. Its qualities were undeniable, but it was costly compared with other vehicles in the same category. Hudson was offering a 7-seater model for $100

Car: **Maxwell 50-6**
Year: **1914**
Engine: **6 cylinders in line**
Bore and stroke: **104.8 × 120.7 mm**
Cylinder capacity: **6246 cc**
Gears: **3 forward**
Brake horse power: **41**
Maximum speed: —
Wheelbase: —
Suspension: **front: semi-elliptic leaf-springs; back: ¾ elliptic leaf-springs**

less than the Maxwell 50-6, and the engine, developing barely 41 bhp, was not the best available to the public. Although it was sold for a couple of years, Maxwell returned to 4-cylinder engines. But by then it was too late, and Chrysler took the company over in 1925. Nevertheless the name did not disappear—Chrysler used it for one of its own models, the 3044 cc 21 bhp with side distribution valves and 3-speed transmission.

The name Mercer enjoyed great prestige for some years in the U.S.A. because of its sports cars which were also used for racing. Founded in 1911 in Trenton, New Jersey, Mercer was backed by Washington August Roebling, son of the designer of the Brooklyn Bridge.

The 35 T was, for some time, the company's most successful car. Initially powered by a twin block T-head engine, in 1915 it was changed to a single-block L, the new model being called the Series 22. It had a 4-speed transmission, compared with three on the Type 35. It now developed 58 bhp at 1,700 revs, with a maximum speed of around 75 mph. Its total weight was less than a ton (1,016 kg).

Already in 1911, its first year of production, Mercer participated in the Indianapolis 500 Miles. The twin-

Car: **Mercer 35 T**
Year: **1912**
Engine: **4 cylinders in line**
Bore and stroke: **110 × 126 mm**
Cylinder capacity: **4789 cc**
Gears: **3 or 4 forward**
Brake horse power: **58**
Maximum speed: **75 mph**
Wheelbase: **9 ft 0 ins (2.74 m)**
Suspension: **front and back: semi-elliptic leaf-springs integrated with Hartford friction shock absorbers**

block engine was pepped up for the occasion to give 60 bhp at 2,000 revs. Placed 12th and 15th, the company saw its efforts amply rewarded. In the 1912 500 Miles, a Mercer came third, and in the 1913 race, second. Although the company also made classic touring vehicles (with a certain loss of character as a result), it fell on hard times and was unable to recover. Production ceased in 1925, though the name was revived five years later on two cars made by the Elcar company.

The first cars to appear with the name Nash were introduced in 1918, but Charles W. Nash himself had already had considerable experience of the car business. Previously vice-president of General Motors, in 1916 Nash had bought control of the Thomas B. Jeffery Company, well-known makers first of bodywork, then of cars such as Rambler and Jeffery.

With this company at this disposal, Nash suddenly found himself in a particularly advantageous position, being able to manufacture the bodywork he needed.

The Nash Four came on the market in 1921, at $1,395, reduced to $985 the following year. It was advertised as a good value 'sister car' to the 6-cylinder, as if already in 1921 Nash had the two-car family in mind. It was orthodox in many respects—splash

Car: **Nash Four**
Year: **1922**
Engine: **4 cylinders in line**
Bore and stroke: **85.7 × 127 mm**
Cylinder capacity: **2929 cc**
Gears: **3 forward**
Brake horse power: **36.75**
Maximum speed: **55 mph**
Wheelbase: **9 ft 4 ins (2.84 m)**
Suspension: **front and back: semi-elliptic leaf springs**

lubrication, coil ignition, and disc clutch.

In April 1922 the firm celebrated production of its 100,000th car. Meanwhile it continued to incorporate interesting details in its vehicles such as a device for checking the fuel level, shuttering on the front windows, two spare wheels, and a thermometer on the radiator cap. In 1954 Nash merged with Hudson, thus creating American Motors.

Oakland was founded in 1907 by Edward M. Murphy, and it started production with certain important technical innovations, such as a counter-balanced crankshaft and coil suspension. Commercially it was a failure, but after producing a moderately successful twin-cylinder car in 1908, the company gained the public's attention and respect with a 4-cylinder car developing 40 bhp. William Durant, who was working out his plans for creating the biggest motor car manufacturing group in the world, was impressed by Oakland's progress, and in 1909 invited Murphy to join him.

The 6-54 (the first figure indicating the number of cylinders, the second the engine brake horse power) was one of Oakland's most successful models. After joining General Motors

Car: **Oakland 6-54**
Year: **1924**
Engine: **6 cylinders in line**
Bore and stroke: **71.4 × 120.7 mm**
Cylinder capacity: **2898 cc**
Gears: **3 forward**
Brake horse power: **54**
Maximum speed: **58 mph**
Wheelbase: **9 ft 2 ins (2.79 m)**
Suspension: **front and back: semi-elliptic leaf-springs**

the company advanced both in terms of quantity and quality. The 6-54 was an exception in America at the time in having brakes (detachable disc) on all four wheels and pressure lubrication. Another characteristic, introduced when the 6-54 came on to the market, was the special scratch resistant paint on the bodywork.

In 1926 Oakland launched the Pontiac as a cheaper line, and within a few years this car outsold Oakland models to such an extent that the parent make was dropped in 1932.

Oldsmobile is one of the oldest American car firms still surviving today (as part of General Motors), and still produces successful cars. It was founded in Lansing, Michigan, in 1897 by Ransom Eli Olds, who had inherited from his father, a factory manager, a passion for engineering. In 1899 Oldsmobile, or rather the Olds Motor Vehicle Company, became Olds Motor Works, and in 1908 it became part of General Motors—of which, however, it only became Oldsmobile Division in 1942.

Olds could boast that it was the first company in the world to have entered mass production. The curved Dash was launched in 1900, and in production by 1901. This had a single cylinder engine (7 bhp), with gear transmission and 2-speed gearbox. It met with immediate success, and

Car: **Oldsmobile 43 A**
Year: **1921**
Engine: **4 cylinders in line**
Bore and stroke: **93.66 × 133.5 mm**
Cylinder capacity: **3677 cc**
Gears: **3 forward**
Brake horse power: **44**
Maximum speed: **62 mph**
Wheelbase: **9 ft 7 ins (2.92 m)**
Suspension: **floating axles**

today is one of the most highly prized veteran cars. The 1921 43 A was the last car produced by Oldsmobile to have a 4-cylinder engine. They also made a V8 from 1916 to 1923, but in 1923 the company moved exclusively to 6 cylinders.

The 43 A's 4-cylinder engine developed around 44 bhp. It incorporated a pump cooling system, splash lubrication, and disc clutch. A total of 13,867 43 As were manufactured; nine (43B) were built with 8-cylinder V engines.

The company was born in 1902 in Terre Haute, Indiana, under the name Standard Wheel Company, and became Overland Company when it moved its premises to Indianapolis in 1905; it took the name Willys-Overland Company after John North Willys, who had made his fortune selling first bicycles, then cars. The company began to make headway with a series of 4-cylinder models, adding two with 6 cylinders in 1909. These, however, were not a success.

After moving to Toledo, Ohio, into the former Pope premises, the company was among the first to put its faith in the Knight sleeve valve engine. The introduction of the Whippet in 1926 brought Overland into the top few names in the sales leagues: of 315,000 vehicles produced in 1928, half were Whippets. In 1929,

Car: **Overland Whippet Four**
Year: **1926**
Engine: **4 cylinders in line**
Bore and stroke: **79.4 × 111.1 mm**
Cylinder capacity: **2199 cc**
Gears: **3 forward**
Brake horse power: **30**
Maximum speed: **55 mph**
Wheelbase: **9 ft 4 ins (2.84 m)**
Suspension: **front and back: semi-elliptic leaf-springs**

190,000 were sold. Launched in June 1926 as the 1927 model, it was given the name Overland Whippet; but after the first 30,000 the name changed to Willys Whippet. The engine had side valves and dry disc clutch, pressure lubrication, and brakes on all four wheels. It was also the first car to combine choke and lights and horn controls on the steering column, thus within hand's reach. On the first models the door opened from the front, but this was immediately changed.

Packard Twin Six
Packard Super Eight
Packard Twelve

Packard was the creation of an enterprising and enlightened industrialist, James Ward Packard, who had taken an interest in electrical gadgets before he turned to cars. The turn of the century saw the rise and fall of many car companies, but Packard, which produced its first car in 1899, developed and grew until it became one of the most successful companies on the American market. Apart from anything else, Packard was responsible for certain technical innovations, including the steering-wheel (1901)—being one of the first American manufacturers to incorporate this equipment. Another characteristic of the firm was its reputation for quality.

Even when a middle-of-the-range model was being designed in 1935, half of the technical personnel were still kept engaged on designing and building de luxe 8- and 12-cylinder vehicles. Another, and perhaps the main, point in its favour, was that Packard did not follow the fashion current in Detroit for changing models every year. A 1931 Packard was not very different stylistically from one built ten years previously. The wisdom of this policy was borne out by the number of extremely distinguished clients who dealt with the

Car: **Packard Twin Six**
Year: **1916**
Engine: **12 cylinders V**
Bore and stroke: **76.2 × 127 mm**
Cylinder capacity: **6946 cc**
Gears: **3 forward**
Brake horse power: **88**
Maximum speed: **80 mph**
Wheelbase: **10 ft 5 ins (3.17 m)**
    or **11 ft 3 ins (3.42 m)**
Suspension: **front and back: semi-elliptic leaf-springs**

1928—Packard Super Eight USA

firm, including kings, presidents, and sheikhs. The notable rise in standard effected by the adoption of the 12-cylinder engine in favour of the 4- was due to a Detroit industrialist, Henry B. Jay, who in 1901 acquired possession of the Packard Motor Car Company shares. (James Packard continued as president of the company until 1909, however, and as administrative head until 1912.) In 1903 the company moved to Detroit, which was to become the car capital of America. But James Packard stayed in Warren, where he had kept his electrical company going all this time (later this firm became part of General Motors).

The 1916 Twin Six was the first 12-cylinder car to be mass-produced. Above all it drew the crowds: 25,000 people came to see it when it was first

Car: **Packard Super Eight**
Year: **1928**
Engine: **8 cylinders in line**
Bore and stroke: **88.9 × 127 mm**
Cylinder capacity: **6306 cc**
Gears: **3 forward**
Brake horse power: **106**
Maximum speed: **85 mph**
Wheelbase: **11 ft 11 ins (3.63 m)**
Suspension: **front and back: semi-elliptic leaf-springs**

put on show in San Francisco. The salient feature of the Twin Six was the extremely flexible engine, which could develop 88 bhp (there was also a 110 bhp racing version); it had aluminium pistons, pressure lubrication, and two water pumps. As well as having a maximum speed of about 80 mph (in itself quite impressive), it could accelerate from 0 to about 30 mph in 12 seconds.

Strangely, the gear lever and brake were positioned to the left of the

steering column, which was itself on the left. The Twin Six was famous too because President Warren G. Harding, the first president of the United States to use a car in an official ceremony, chose one in 1921.

The 1927-1928 Super Eight was also a refined car, incorporating central-ised semi-automatic lubrication, gearbox with three forward speeds, and nine bearing crankshaft. It developed 106 bhp, and had a maximum speed of about 80 mph. There were mechanical brakes on all four wheels, and the tires were of the 'balloon' type. There were three series of this model, the third having a 6300 cc 100 bhp engine.

The Twelve, as its name indicates, again had a 12-cylinder engine, with ferrous alloy cylinder block, side valves, removable head, centrifugal

Car: **Packard Twelve**
Year: **1933**
Engine: **12 cylinders V**
Bore and stroke: **87.3 × 101.6 mm**
Cylinder capacity: **7294 cc**
Gears: **3 forward**
Brake horse power: **180**
Maximum speed: **100 mph**
Wheelbase: **11 ft 7 ins (3.53 m)**
Suspension: **front and back: semi-elliptic leaf-springs**

forced water cooling, ventilator and thermostat, pressure lubrication, twin coil distributor ignition, twin disc dry clutch, semi-floating rear axle, pressed chassis and side-members, and drum brakes on all four wheels, with a handbrake acting on the back wheels.

In June 1954 Packard and Stude-baker merged, combining vehicles. However, the venture failed, and in 1958 production of Packard models ceased. Studebaker shared the same fate in March 1966.

1904—Peerless 24 HP

Founded in 1870, Peerless made its name in various spheres before turning to cars. It started with mangles for wringing out washing, then went on to produce bicycles and, in 1900, cars.

The first cars to be produced by Peerless, which were not overly successful, had single-cylinder engines; these became twin-cylinder with shaft transmission; and from 1903, a 4-cylinder engine was used. The 24 HP was the first car to have a 4-cylinder engine; it had a T-head and honeycomb radiator. The following year the company introduced a model with a similar design of 4-cylinder engine, but with a cylinder capacity of 6000 cc and limousine bodywork. That same year one of these took part in the New York-St Louis race, making it, so it is claimed, the first limousine to participate in a rally.

Car: **Peerless 24 HP**
Year: **1904**
Engine: **4 cylinders in line**
Bore and stroke: **108 × 102 mm**
Cylinder capacity: **3736 cc**
Gears: **4 forward**
Brake horse power: **25**
Maximum speed: **50 mph**
Wheelbase: **8 ft 8 ins (2.64 m)**
Suspension: **front and back: semi-elliptic leaf-springs**

First 6- and then V8-cylinder engines were developed, but the bodywork kept its austere elegance—which, whilst it was liked by the regular customers, did not win it new enthusiasts. The prestige model was a luxurious 16-cylinder car. It was introduced, however, in the middle of the slump, when the situation hardly augured well for such a model, beautifully designed and built as it was. In 1931, the firm's premises were bought by Carling Brewery.

George Pierce opened a small factory for household articles in Buffalo in 1870. In 1900 the company produced its first car, powered by a single-cylinder De Dion engine. Pierce only changed to twin-cylinder engines in 1903. In 1904 it was already making a 4-cylinder 4400 cc car called the Great Arrow 24/28, which was very successful. At this point George Pierce decided it would be a good idea to compete in motor racing, and was successful in rallies. The word 'Arrow' perfectly illustrated the look of Pierce cars, and from 1909 the firm became officially Pierce-Arrow Motor Car.

The 1915 48 Roadster is typical of the Pierce-Arrow range. Its powerful engine developed 70-75 bhp at 2,500 revs, and consisted of three blocks of 2 cylinders with side valves, having

Car: **Pierce-Arrow 48 Roadster**
Year: **1915**
Engine: **6 cylinders in line**
Bore and stroke: **114.3 × 139.7 mm**
Cylinder capacity: **8596 cc**
Gears: **4 forward**
Brake horse power: **75**
Maximum speed: **70 mph**
Wheelbase: **11 ft 2½ ins (3.41 m)**
  or **11 ft 10 ins (3.60 m)**
Suspension: **front: semi-elliptic leaf-springs;**
  back: ¾ elliptic leaf-springs

two spark plugs per cylinder, dual ignition, pressure lubrication, forced water cooling, and radiator; surprisingly, it had a cone clutch. A characteristic of the car was the headlights built into the fenders. Pierce-Arrow was one of the companies to use this design. It was forced to merge with Studebaker due to financial problems in 1928, but it regained its independence in 1933. It struggled on until 1938, when finally it closed down.

Plymouth was the creation of Walter Chrysler, in Detroit. Founded in 1928, it was intended to be a rival to General Motors and Ford at the lower end of the market. The imaginative and enterprising Chrysler thought of Plymouth as a 'fighting' company—an image which it still, to a certain extent, retains. Its first car (4 cylinders) came out in June 1928, and by the end of the year 58,000 had already been built.

The 1931 PA rėpresents one of the milestones in the company's history, in incorporating engine mountings using rubber bearings. This innovation was adopted by all other manufacturers, as it solved one of the major problems of comfort. The man responsible, Fred Zeder, one of the most versatile of American engineers at the time, and who, together with

Car: **Plymouth**
Year: **1928**
Engine: **4 cylinders in line**
Bore and stroke: **92.75 × 104.77 mm**
Cylinder capacity: **2844 cc**
Gears: **3 forward**
Brake horse power: **45**
Maximum speed: **60 mph**
Wheelbase: **9 ft 1 ½ ins (2.78 m)**
Suspension: **front and back: semi-elliptic leaf-springs**

Owen Skelton and Carl Breer, provided the technical expertise with which Walter Chrysler was able to start his company. His faith in the future of the car persuaded Chrysler to build a factory specially for Plymouths in 1929. Such a decision appeared folly at the time, but in the event proved justified. It celebrated production of its millionth car in August 1934, only six years after its foundation, thanks essentially to its very sensible price policies.

This firm operated from 1902 to 1913. After 1957 the name Rambler was taken up by Nash Motor Car Company.

The company started under Thomas B. Jeffery in Kenosha, Wisconsin, in 1901. It began with small-cylinder capacity engines and progressed to both higher cylinder capacities and greater numbers of cylinders. The 38 HP belongs to the period when the company was still called Rambler: a solid car, but essentially conventional. In 1904 the firm went from twin-cylinder engines to 4 cylinders; the engine in the car illustrated here had the distinctive feature of having equal bore and stroke. It was thus known as a 'square' engine, a type adopted by many makers after the Second World War. Rambler's early cars were all

Car: **Rambler 38 HP**
Year: **1912**
Engine: **4 cylinders in line**
Bore and stroke: **114 × 114 mm**
Cylinder capacity: **4652 cc**
Gears: **3 forward**
Brake horse power: —
Maximum speed: —
Wheelbase: —
Suspension: **front: semi-elliptic leaf-springs; back: ¾ elliptic leaf-springs**

built along certain lines (lightness, cheapness, twin-cylinder front-mounted engine), which earned it a good reputation.

In 1914 the name Rambler was changed to Jeffery (after the Firm's founder), but in 1917 the whole concern was taken over by Nash, which fifty years later revived the name Rambler. At first it was to be the name of a single model, but later it was used for many others, including Hudsons (Hudson had also become part of Nash in 1954).

1927—Reo Sedan A

USA

Reo was started by the energetic and idiosyncratic industralist Ransom Eli Olds (after whose initials these cars were named from 1904 on). Olds had already founded Olds Motor Vehicle Company in 1897, which later became Oldsmobile.

Olds began with two popular models, one single and one twin-cylinder. The latter had the engine in the middle, under the seat. 4-cylinder engines were adopted several years later, in 1911 (3700 cc), then 6 cylinders were introduced after that.

The 1927 Sedan A was the product of another period of change, its most noteworthy feature being the hydraulic brakes on all four wheels (although this was by no means a novelty in the American market). The engine had side valves with removable head, radiator and pump cooling, and

Car: **Reo Sedan A**
Year: **1927**
Engine: **6 cylinders in line**
Bore and stroke: **82.55 × 127 mm**
Cylinder capacity: **4078 cc**
Gears: **3 forward**
Brake horse power: **65**
Maximum speed: **74 mph**
Wheelbase: **10 ft 1 in (3.07 m)**
Suspension:**front and back: semi-floating**

multi-disc dry clutch. The decision to move into the de luxe car market, taken in the uncertain period before the 1929 crash, put Reo in difficulties, from which it tried to extricate itself with a hurriedly-constructed car in the middle-of-the-market range again. In 1936 Reo turned solely to production of commercial vehicles.

Simplex was another American firm which only operated for a short time (1907 to 1917), but which nonetheless left favourable memories because of the very high quality of its cars.

Founded by Herman Broesel, it began by importing foreign cars into the United States, but in 1907 it started making them itself. In 1907 Broesel took over Smith and Mabley, who also imported foreign cars.

The first Simplex was the 1912 model illustrated here. Certain features were new: the aluminium crank case, two side camshafts (the camshaft for the exhaust valves had an axial movement to regulate normal running or, with reduced compression, to facilitate moving off). The gearbox and differential were contained in a box separate from the engine. It had dual ignition, forced

Car: **Simplex 50 HP**
Year: **1912**
Engine: **4 cylinders in line**
Bore and stroke: **146 × 146 mm**
Cylinder capacity: **9772 cc**
Gears: **4 forward**
Brake horse power: —
Maximum speed: —
Wheelbase: —
Suspension: **front and back: semi-elliptic leaf-springs**

cooling, electric generator and gear-change, and removable wheel rims, but no windshield.

The Holbrook (New York) body-work was deceptive and made the car look smaller than it was (its exceptional cylinder capacity made it a powerful car). In 1914 the 46 HP came out, with 100 bhp, twin-block 6-cylinder engine. Although built exactly along the lines of the more popular Simplex models it had no impact on the fluctuating American market.

Stanley was the brainchild of twin brothers, Francis and Freelan, who after various industrial ventures, including manufacture of photographic equipment, decided to try making cars in 1897. They were so successful that they have earned a prominent place in the history of American car production. Surprisingly, they remained faithful to steam propulsion; indeed their cars were always known by the name Stanley-Steamer. The classic 'coffin-shaped' hood also remained virtually unchanged from 1906 to 1917.

Despite their intelligence and enterprise, however, the Stanley brothers failed to patent their inventions. Some of their key features were copied by Locomobile.

Their vehicles almost always bore the same characteristics: horizontal

Car: **Stanley 10 HP**
Year: **1911**
Engine: **twin-cylinder, steam**
Bore and stroke: —
Cylinder capacity: —
Gears: —
Brake horse power: **10**
Maximum speed: **50 mph**
Wheelbase: **8 ft 8 ins (2.64 m)**
Suspension: **front and back: semi-elliptic leaf-springs**

twin-cylinder double-acting engine and both longitudinal and transverse suspension. The available engines were basically of 10, 20, or 30 bhp, with maximum speeds of between about 30 and 50 mph.

Two events strengthened Stanley's reputation: the ride up Washington Hill in 28 minutes, in 1905, by Francis Stanley; and the world speed record of 127.66 mph set on January 26, 1906 by Fred Marriott on Ormond Beach. After the Stanley brothers had retired the company soon closed.

The story of this company, founded in Cleveland, Ohio, in 1896, is similar to that of many American car manufacturing companies of the time. It started modestly, with inexpensive vehicles, and progressed to de luxe cars inspired by Mercedes.

From single, twin, and 3-cylinder engines, in 1906 Stearns began using 6 cylinders, the chief feature of which was the enormous cylinder capacity, unusual in the U.S.A. even in those days. On the other hand the 45-90 HP could exceed 85 mph, and was considered the fastest American car of its time.

In 1912 the company went over to using Knight sleeve valve engines, and took the name Stearns-Knight; it was taken over by Willys Overland (Toledo). It still kept its 4-, 6-, and 8-cylinder models—the last of these

Car: **Stearns 45-90 HP**
Year: **1908**
Engine: **6 cylinders in line**
Bore and stroke: **136.5 × 149 mm**
Cylinder capacity: **13075 cc**
Gears: **4 forward**
Brake horse power: **90**
Maximum speed: **88 mph**
Wheelbase: **10 ft 8 ins (3.25 m)**
Suspension: **front and back: semi-elliptic leaf-springs**

mounted on 9 bearings. The variety of models and the support of Willys were not able to save it from the 1929 slump, however. The following year the company ceased production. Before the adoption of the sleeve valve engine Frank B. Stearns had left the company, but his successors carried on the basic ideas that had made Stearns cars truly original. Stearns was faithful to the Knight sleeve valve engine to the last, and used it in its final model in 1930, the 6500 cc 8-9.

Studebaker Four Touring Car
Studebaker Erskine

Studebaker is one of the oldest names in the history of transport, going back to 1736, when Peter Studebaker first arrived in the United States from Holland. He set the path for future generations of his family, building carriages. This business was consolidated by two great-grandchildren, Henry and Clem, who started a coach factory at South Bend, Indiana. A third grandchild, John, joined them, and during the Civil War the firm supplied military wagons to the Union army.

From wagons (the famous Conestogas) Studebaker began to build chassis for the first car manufacturers, and eventually they started thinking about making cars themselves. Studebaker thus became a car firm, but did not stop making horse-drawn vehicles until 1921. It began in a small way in 1902 with electric cars, and in 1904 progressed to 4-cylinder engines, in collaboration with Garford. They also had agreements with E.M.F. of Detroit, Northern, Wayne, and Flanders, which gives some indication of how cautiously they turned to car manufacture.

With the absorption of E.M.F. in 1910 the Studebaker Corporation was formed, that being the name given to all subsequent designs. In 1914 it became a car company in the full sense, producing cars under the name Studebaker only. There were basically two models, 4- and 6-cylinders, both cheap, and thus in direct competition with the most common makes of the day. The Four Touring Car sold for $1,050. The water cooled 4-cylinder engine was rated at 35 bhp. It had shaft transmission. As all American companies used to specify, the price included hood, trunk, lights, windshield, speedometer, and removable

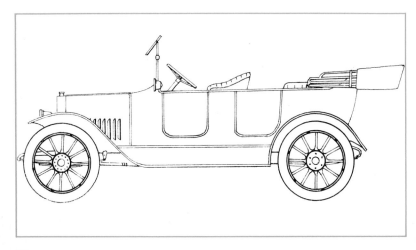

wheel rims. The listing of such details leads one to suppose that not all car manufacturers at that time considered these accessories as standard.

The Erskine had a 6-cylinder in-line engine rated at 40 bhp, crankshaft on four bearings, pump cooling, and single-disc dry clutch. Among the car's innumerable features, included in the price, was a device for locking the steering-wheel and at the same time disconnecting the ignition. Car thefts were thus already considered a problem.

In 1928 Studebaker took over Pierce-Arrow, makers of de luxe cars. In 1933, however, Pierce-Arrow became independent again. In 1966, after many ups and downs, the company announced that it was going to cease production

Car: **Studebaker Erskine**
Year: **1927**
Engine: **6 cylinders in line**
Bore and stroke: **66.67 × 114.3 mm**
Cylinder capacity: **2395 cc**
Gears: **3 forward**
Brake horse power: **40**
Maximum speed: **60 mph**
Wheelbase: **8 ft 11 ins (2.71 m)**
Suspension: **front and back: semi-elliptic leaf-springs**

Car: **Studebaker Four Touring Car**
Year: **1914**
Engine: **4 cylinders in line**
Bore and stroke: **89 × 127 mm**
Cylinder capacity: **3150 cc**
Gears: **3 forward**
Brake horse power: **35**
Maximum speed: **44 mph**
Wheelbase: **9 ft 0 ins (2.74 m)**
Suspension: **front and back: semi-elliptic leaf-springs**

This famous name is almost exclusively connected with racing, the story of its performances beginning in 1911, when it came 11th in the first 500 Miles Race at Indianapolis. That success put the company on a right footing to begin production on a small scale, using 4-cylinder 5000 cc Wisconsin engines.

One of the models that brought Stutz most publicity in the pre-war period was the Bearcat, a typical racing-car, with very high cylinder capacity and guaranteed 60 bhp. The Bearcat was an imitation of the Mercer, its great rival. The company entered the Indianapolis 500 Miles several times, without ever winning, although it distinguished itself in numerous other races held in America. In 1919 Harry Stutz left the company he had founded, and in 1921

Car: **Stutz Bearcat**
Year: **1914**
Engine: **4 cylinders in line**
Bore and stroke: **121 × 140 mm**
Cylinder capacity: **6436 cc**
Gears: **3 forward**
Brake horse power: **60**
Maximum speed: **75 mph**
Wheelbase: **10 ft 0 ins (3.04 m)**
Suspension: **front and back: semi-elliptic leaf-springs**

the Bearcat became a sports car, in a category of its own. Its 1917 6-cylinder engine acquired a removable head in 1921, and in 1923 it was further modified. Later, there was a Superbearcat, with an 8-cylinder in-line engine with double overhead camshaft and four valves per cylinder, two inlet and two exhausts. It had a cylinder capacity of 5277 cc, and developed 156 bhp at 3,900 revs as against the 131 bhp 6-cylinder version.

The 6-60 owes its fame to its victory in the 1908 New York-Paris race. It remained in production until 1912. The engine developed 72 bhp, and in 1907 it cost $4,500. The New York-Paris race was created by the Paris newspaper *Le Matin* and announced immediately after the Peking-Paris rally. Six cars set off at the start, including a Thomas Flyer. The almost 21,000 miles (34,000 km) journey westwards was completed in 170 days by George Schuster driving the Thomas Flyer; this was three days faster than a German Protos. The enterprise cost Thomas Flyer $100,000.

Thomas (the name Flyer was added later) was initially founded by Erwin Ross Thomas as a bicycle company. In 1897 the company was building engines, in 1900 motorcycles, and in

Car: **Thomas Flyer 6-60**
Year: **1907**
Engine: **6 cylinders in line**
Bore and stroke: **140 × 140 mm**
Cylinder capacity: **12924 cc**
Gears: **4 forward**
Brake horse power: **72**
Maximum speed: **70 mph**
Wheelbase: **11 ft 8 ins (3.55 m)**
Suspension: **front and back: semi-elliptic leaf-springs**

1902 cars were produced. From twin-cylinder engines it went to 3, then 4, then finally 6 cylinders. The New York-Paris winner was a 6-cylinder car with shaft transmission. After 1909 the firm's fortunes declined and it was bought by Eugene Meyer. Despite the introduction of new models, Meyer could not save the company.

1908—White 30 HP　　　　　　　　　USA

Although White started as a car manufacturer in 1901, it now makes trucks. Rollin H. White began in business making sewing-machines, but he soon became interested in cars, especially steam-cars (based on the French Serpollets).

From making a two-seater buggy (with a double-acting twin-cylinder engine situated at the back and with flash-boiler with superheater) the firm progressed to more sophisticated models equipped with condenser, which considerably reduced the consumption of water in the boiler.

Like almost every manufacturer of the time, Rollin White realised how much publicity could be gained through races, and he won a reputation for himself by the excellent performance of his cars.

The 1908 30 HP was one of White's

Car: **White 30 HP**
Year: **1908**
Engine: **twin-cylinder, steam**
Bore and stroke: —
Cylinder capacity: —
Gears: **2 forward**
Brake horse power: **30**
Maximum speed: **50 mph**
Wheelbase: **8 ft 8 ins (2.64 m)**
Suspension: —

last steam-cars. It had a pressure regulator and a device for measuring the temperature of the superheated steam. White saw in time that steam propulsion would be replaced by gasoline-driven engines, and so in 1910 he turned to internal combustion engines.

His new cars were distinguished for their quality and the care taken in their construction. After the First World War, White struck out in a new direction again, concentrating exclusively on heavy goods vehicles.

There are two aspects of the Wills Sainte Claire Company which make it one of the most interesting and original 'characters' in the story of the American car industry. The first is the founder of the company and designer of the car, Childe Harold Wills, who was the chief designer of the famous Ford Model T, and who collaborated with Ford up until 1919, when he set up on his own, using his own mechanical expertise. The second is the name of the firm which apart from recording the name of the founder, is taken from Lake Saint Clair near which the firm was based.

The Wills Sainte Claire was original above all in its engine (8 cylinders V), which was clearly inspired by the Hispano-Suiza, with overhead camshaft for each bank of cylinders, and cast-iron rather than metal alloy

Car: **Wills Sainte Claire**
Year: **1922**
Engine: **8 cylinders V**
Bore and stroke: **82.55 × 101.6 mm**
Cylinder capacity: **4350 cc**
Gears: **3 forward**
Brake horse power: **67**
Maximum speed: **80 mph**
Wheelbase: **10 ft 1 in (3.07 m)**
Suspension: **front and back: semi-elliptic leaf-springs**

engine block, as in the Spanish-French engine. The car appeared rather later than scheduled, due to the meticulous attention to detail. It was priced at $3,000. In 1922 4,300 vehicles were made, but sales figures dropped rapidly in following years, due to the difficulties of ensuring an efficient maintenance service. In 1924 a single plate clutch and hydraulic brakes were added. A more simple 6-cylinder model was unsuccessful and the company ceased production in 1927.

1911—Winton Tourer 17 B

Winton, founded in Cleveland in 1890 as a bicycle firm, had already changed to the production of motor cars by 1897. Its founder, Alexander Winton, was a Scottish naval engineer. His first car had a single-cylinder engine and wooden chassis.

Winton understood the importance of races, and for the 1900 Gordon Bennett he built a car of almost 4000 cc, with single-cylinder engine (165.1 × 177.8), battery and coil ignition, 2-speed gears, and chain transmission. Winton himself drove in the race, but did not finish.

The single-cylinder was followed by a twin-cylinder engine. 4-cylinder engines made their appearance in standard cars in 1904, and 6-cylinders in 1908. The engine in the Tourer 17 B was in three blocks of 2 cylinders, and had side valves, dual ignition (with

Car: **Winton Tourer 17 B**
Year: **1911**
Engine: **6 cylinders in line**
Bore and stroke: **114.3 × 127 mm**
Cylinder capacity: **7819 cc**
Gears: **4 forward**
Brake horse power: **48**
Maximum speed: **65**
Wheelbase: **10 ft 10 ins (3.30 m)**
Suspension: **front and back: semi-elliptic leaf-springs**

high-tension magneto and coil), forced water cooling, and honeycomb radiator. It developed 48 bhp, and the brakes acted only on the back wheels.

It had a folding canvas top, and two occasional back seats. It also came with a compressed air system which, apart from helping to start the engine, served to inflate the tires. The company continued to produce the same models. It realised too late that times had changed, and in 1924 began producing diesel marine engines.

Woods Mobilette was one of the many firms to prosper in Detroit with the production of light cyclecars. At one time these vehicles were quite popular because of cheap running costs and easy handling. The Woods company boasted that its car was the size of a kitchen table.

After starting life in Chicago, in 1914, it moved to Harvey, Illinois, where a proper production-line was set up. The 1914 model, priced at $380, was less than 3 feet (1 m) across, which explains why the two seats were placed in tandem. The two-speed transmission was of the epicyclic type, with selection lever positioned centrally. The brakes acted on the rear wheels. It could travel at around 35 mph. The extras included top and windshield ($15) and acetylene headlights. The rear of the vehicle

Car: **Woods Mobilette**
Year: **1914**
Engine: **4 cylinders in line**
Bore and stroke: **65.3 × 88.9 mm**
Cylinder capacity: **1190 cc**
Gears: **2 forward**
Brake horse power: **12**
Maximum speed: **35 mph**
Wheelbase: **8 ft 0 ins (2.43 m)**
Suspension: **front: semi-elliptic leaf-springs; back: elliptic leaf-springs**

could be removed to create a surface suitable for carrying a load.

After 1915 its production resembled more that of higher cylinder capacity cars (longer wheelbase, 3 forward speed transmission, but still not a standard top), while the price remained $380. The power of the engine was increased to 22 bhp.

Lights

Even the terminology saw a development here, going from 'lanterns' to 'beacons' and finally to 'headlights'. They first appeared on coaches around 1859; the years 1905-1910 saw acetylene lamps, and in 1912 (Cadillac) headlights as we know them. Other cars very soon adopted these.

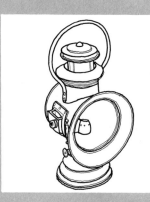

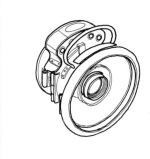

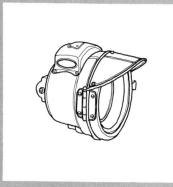

The first car wheels were wooden, reinforced with metal and with detachable rims. Then the metal 'artillery' type was developed, and subsequently those consisting of spokes, sheet metal discs, and light alloys. Solid tires were replaced by pneumatic rubber tires.

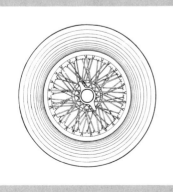

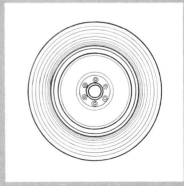

ROLLS-ROYCE
THE WORLD'S BEST CAR

Great Britain

Together with France, Great Britain led the field in the development of steam propulsion. In 1781 James Watt patented his revolutionary steam engine and by the early 19th century Britain had entered the age of motorisation. Despite being heavily taxed it was not long before steam propelled vehicles were in regular service on English roads.

Ironically, however, the laws of the land seemed to have been designed to discourage the development of motorised vehicles, and 1865 saw the introduction of the notorious 'Red Flag Act' which limited the speed of mechanical vehicles by stipulating that each one should be preceded by a man carrying a red flag. The speed of vehicles had to correspond with the speed of the man bearing the red flag; This was fixed at 4 mph on country roads and 2 mph in populated areas. Later, the law was amended, so instead of walking 60 yards (54.86 m) in front of the vehicle, the man now had to walk only 30 yards (18.28 m) in front of it. Such a minimal change to the law obviously had little or no effect at a time when there were vehicles in the country which were capable of reaching speeds of 15 mph in 1890.

The anachronistic 'Red Flag Act'

was finally abolished in 1896 and the results of its withdrawal were soon evident. The Daimler Motor Company was established in Coventry in the same year, and F. W. Lanchester began to design his first motor cars.

The years between 1900 and 1914 saw the emergence of many famous automobile manufacturing companies in Britain: Rolls-Royce, Napier, Albion, Crossley, Austin, Morris, Standard, Ford and Vauxhall. Many of these companies had already been in existence for some time in areas relating to mechanical engineering, while others had started life as bicycle manufacturers. The Lancashire Steam Motor Company (later Leyland) had been producing steam-propelled vehicles since 1896. By 1913 there were approximately 198 different makes of motor car available in Britain. At the same time, the motorised heavy transport industry was also beginning to develop and in 1902 Napier produced a 3-ton truck for the transport of flour.

At the beginning of this century, however, the British authorities still tended to treat the motor car as an intrusive and hostile element in the transport world and the passing of various laws still limited its freedom of use. Severe penalties were imposed for driving without proper care and attention, or at a 'dangerous' speed. The official speed limit was 20 mph, or 10 mph where the local authorities considered it necessary. Hyde Park was forbidden to motor vehicles from 4 am to 7 pm (a restriction which remained in force until 1910). In July 1905 alone, 903 motorists were fined for exceeding the 20 mph speed limit, while another 250 were penalised for driving in the Royal Parks at over 10 mph. The fine for such offences was normally over £3 and could rise to a maximum of £10, or even £20 in the case of further offences. The great number of accidents led to the formation of an association for the protection of the highways (Highway Protection League), its promoters claiming that the league was not so much directed against the motor car as against reckless drivers. In 1905 a child was knocked down and killed by a motor car, and this terrible scandal was featured by the whole of the British national press.

However, though impeded in various ways, the advance of the motor car could not be stopped. The 1913 Motor Show was attended by 156,000 people, while 227,000 visited that held in 1919. Membership of the Automobile Association, which was 100,000 in 1914, had more than doubled by 1924. In 1918 the price of a brand-new American car costing £250 rose to £500 within a few months. The average price for a small car was £185-195 in 1914, but by 1918 the same used car could cost £300-400.

The American-style production methods introduced by William Morris (later Lord Nuffield) did much to stabilise prices. A Morris Cowley 2-seater, which had cost a little over £165 in 1915, cost just over £142 in 1928. The 4-seater Cowley went from £465 in 1920 to £225 in 1922. A Morris Minor sold for £125 in 1929, but by 1931 it had been reduced to £100.

It is worth noting that the first true mass-produced motor car was the Ford Model T. Ford had opened a plant at Old Trafford, near Manchester, as early as 1911, and assembly of the Model T began there three years after its appearance on the American market. Mass-production, in the modern sense of the term, only really began, however, just before the outbreak of the First World War. The total of 19,000 vehicles, including motor cars and commercial vehicles, produced in 1911, rapidly became 34,000 in 1913, thanks chiefly to the output of the Ford plants. In 1920 there were some 187,000 motor cars on the road in Britain; 18 months later there were 242,500.

During the 1920s, British car manufacturers began to reorganise their production methods, with the intention of building light, standardised cars in large quantities. The first make of car to compete directly with Ford in this area of the market was Morris, followed almost immediately by Austin. In spite of the appearance of new makes, the number of motor cars competitive in a commercial sense rapidly grew smaller; by 1929, Morris, Austin and Singer produced seventy-five per cent of all the cars built in Great Britain. Morris and Ford were also the major manufacturers of commercial vehicles. The British car industry, as a whole, was able to produce 239,000 vehicles in 1929; but in the United States figures reached 5,380,000.

By 1931 there were only 31 makes on the British market, as opposed to 88 in 1922. The 1929 general depression in world trade hit the British car industry much less hard than it did that of other countries. In 1933 the joint production of motor cars and commercial vehicles had reached 286,000 units. Increases in production continued throughout the 1930s and by 1937 the industry was producing 379,000 motor cars and 114,000 commercial vehicles a year, making it the second largest in the world after the United States.

The progress of the British motor car industry during those years has been attributed to various factors: production levels had previously been relatively low; there had been considerable increases in *per capita* income; motor taxation and the price of fuel were low; and the British industry had always concentrated on engines with a high number of revs but a low fuel consumption.

There was also a relatively large increase in the number of medium-priced, medium-engined cars. In 1938 there were 20 independent manufacturers in the country, six of which accounted for ninety per cent of the production. In order of importance, these were: Morris, Austin, Ford, Vauxhall, Rootes and Standard. Vauxhall, bought by General Motors in 1925, had also become the chief manufacturer of light commercial vehicles, followed by the Rootes Group.

A considerable proportion of the production was exported: 3,800 cars were exported in 1923; 25,000 in 1929; 43,000 in 1934 and 68,000 in 1938. The British motor industry thus strengthened its manufacturing base at home and enjoyed increasing success in many important markets overseas.

A.C. Sociable
A.C. 10 HP
A.C. Six

The A.C. Company had a rather curious origin in that it was the brainchild of a London butcher, John Portwine, and an engineer, John Weller, who soon proved himself a person of great abilities. In 1904 John Portwine's business had been doing very well, but Portwine believed that it could do even better if he had motorised transport for making deliveries. He mentioned his needs to John Weller, who then designed a three-wheeled vehicle, powered by a single-cylinder engine (631 cc). This was very successful, and Portwine urged Weller to adapt the vehicle for transporting people. Thus, in 1910 the 'Sociable' was born. The mechanical parts were identical to those of Portwine's butcher's vehicle, but the space for goods was reduced and replaced by another seat. This was placed near that of the driver, so that the vehicle could now be used for the transport of people. The air-cooled engine being placed transversally.

The 10 HP model of 1913 used a French engine, the Fivet, which had a very good weight/power ratio. After the war this was discarded in favour of the English Anzani engine, and the price of the car rose to £560. The first models incorporated a cone clutch, which proved very unsuitable for such a light vehicle. This problem was solved, however, when Weller became one of the first men, if not the first, to

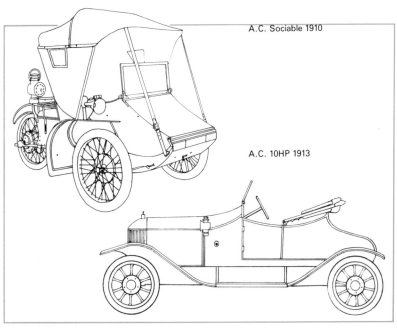

A.C. Sociable 1910

A.C. 10HP 1913

use a disc clutch in a motor car, although it should be noted that the A.C. Company never claimed that it was the first to do this. The speed of the 10 HP model was about 45 mph.

The 6-cylinder model made its debut at the London Salon of 1919. The overhead camshaft engine, with its overhead valves, remained in production until 1963, a unique case in the history of the automobile. Its main advantage was its relative quietness. From its original 40 bhp the power of the engine was gradually increased to 85 bhp. A.C. changed its name four times during its history, though always keeping those initials, which stood for Auto Carrier at the time of the company's creation. In 1904 it became Autocars and Accessories, changing in 1911 to Auto-carriers Ltd, and in 1922 to A.C. Ltd.

Car: **A.C. Six**
Year: **1922**
Engine: **6 cylinders in line**
Bore and stroke: **65 × 100 mm**
Cylinder capacity: **1991 cc**
Gears: **3 forward**
Brake horsepower: **40**
Maximum speed: **53 mph**
Wheelbase: **9 ft 3 ins (2.81 m)**
Suspension: **front and back: semi-elliptic leaf-springs**

Car: **A.C. Sociable**
Year: **1910**
Engine: **single-cylinder**
Bore and stroke: **89 × 102 mm**
Cylinder capacity: **631 cc**
Gears: **2 forward**
Brake horse power: **8**
Maximum speed: **43 mph**
Wheelbase: **6 ft 2 ins (1.87 m)**
Suspension: **front and back: ¼ elliptic leaf-springs**

Car: **A.C. 10 HP**
Year: **1913**
Engine: **4 cylinders in line**
Bore and stroke: **59 × 100 mm**
Cylinder capacity: **1094 cc**
Gears: **3 forward**
Brake horse power: **10**
Maximum speed: **45 mph**
Wheelbase: **8 ft 5½ ins (2.57 m)**
Suspension: **front: transverse leaf springs; back: elliptical leaf-springs**

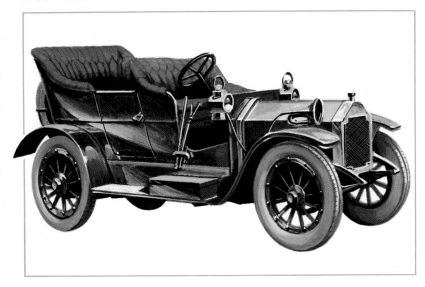

The A6 was a very solid de luxe car in keeping with the style of this Glasgow firm run by Blackwood Murray and Norman Fulton. As its name indicates, it was the sixth production model, and was technically very conventional. This betrays the firm's desire to sell abroad, with a model that would give as little trouble as possible. The A1 and A2 had twin-cylinder centrally positioned engines with low-tension magneto ignition and bodywork clearly derived from coaches. The A3 differed from the previous models in having the engine in the back. The A6 had chain transmission and low-tension magneto ignition. The engine could turn at a maximum of 1,200 revs. With the A3 and the A6 Albion had struck success. In 1906, the year the A6 came out, the company (with almost 300 employees)

Car: **Albion A6**
Year: **1906**
Engine: **4 cylinders in line**
Bore and stroke: **108 × 114 mm**
Cylinder capacity: **4180 cc**
Gears: **4 forward**
Brake horse power: **24**
Maximum speed: **40 mph**
Wheelbase: **10 ft 2 ins (3.09 m)**
Suspension: **front: semi-elliptic leaf-springs; back: elliptic leaf springs**

produced over 200 chassis. In 1911 came the A14, with shaft transmission. Albion continued car production until 1914, when it turned exclusively to trucks. It made these up to 1972, as part of the British Leyland group. In some ways it is comparable to the Italian company O.M., which went from cars to trucks, continuing making these today as part of the great Fiat empire.

In the history of any car company there is always one model that stands out from the others and is remembered—for Alvis this model was the 12/50, which went into production in 1923 and continued to be produced until 1932. Alvis was founded in 1920, when Thomas George John took over Holley Brothers Company Ltd, and started making motorcycles and cars. In 1921 it took the name Alvis Car and Engineering Company Ltd. As the result of financial difficulties in 1922, the company worked at assembling twin-cylinder V, air-cooled Buckingham engines, but in 1936 the company became simply Alvis Ltd.

Today, the 12/50 is one of the cars most highly prized and jealously guarded by collectors of vintage cars. It had a successful racing career, both with professional and amateur

Car: **Alvis 12/50 S**
Year: **1923**
Engine: **4 cylinders in line**
Bore and stroke: **68 × 103 mm**
Cylinder capacity: **1496 cc**
Gears: **4 forward**
Brake horse power: **50**
Maximum speed: **67 mph**
Wheelbase: **9 ft ½ in (2.75 m)**
Suspension: **front and back: semi-elliptic leaf-springs**

drivers, and was the winner of the 1923 Brooklands 200 Mile Race. The 12/50 was nicknamed the 'duck's back', because of its odd shape at the back. This version, with a maximum speed of about 80 mph, was very popular in racing circles at the time. The sports version, distinguished by the letter S (the T was for Touring, and F for front-wheel drive, which was tried in 1925 and incorporated on a production model after 1928), had almost the same engine as the touring (1645 cc) but with smaller capacity.

93

Like so many car factories operating at the start of the century, Argyll had a difficult time, due to mistaken commercial tactics and a lengthy law case with the American company Knight over the rights on the so-called single-sleeve-valve engine. An engine of this kind had been invented by Peter Burt at Argyll, and Argyll had patented it under the name Burt McCollum. Argyll won the case, but at such cost that in 1914 it had to sell out.

Founded by Alex Govan in 1899, it was known at first as Hoziers Engineering Company, and only became Argyll Motors Ltd in 1905. The success of the company led to its transferring its premises from Glasgow to Alexandria, Strathclyde.

The 15-30 had brakes on all four wheels (one year after the Isotta-Fraschini, therefore). Front brakes

Car: **Argyll 15-30 HP**
Year: **1913**
Engine: **4 cylinders in line**
Bore and stroke: **80 × 130 mm**
Cylinder capacity: **2614 cc**
Gears: **4 forward**
Brake horse power: **32**
Maximum speed: **45 mph**
Wheelbase: **9 ft 8 ins (2.94 m)**
Suspension: **front: semi-elliptic leaf-springs; back: ¾ elliptic leaf-springs**

first appeared on the 1911 12 HP, then as standard on the 15-30 and 25-50. In 1914 an Argyll 15-30 HP cost £495. Argyll offered more than ten models at once, and this turned out to be a serious commercial miscalculation. The 15-30 had limited success on the racing circuits: one car ran for 14 hours at Brooklands at an average of around 80 mph. The engine power had been considerably increased, and with it also the engine speed (2800 revs).

This was the prestige car of this Scottish firm founded in 1897 by William Arrol and George Johnston. At first called Mo-Car Syndicate Ltd, from 1905 it changed its name to New Arrol-Johnston Car Company Ltd. Its early cars had much in common with coaches, but gradually they became more modern, acquiring a certain name for themselves through race results. In a twin-cylinder model J. S. Napier won the first Tourist Trophy (1905) with an average speed of over 30 mph. The 15-9 HP was the brainchild of T. C. Pullinger, director of Arrol in 1909. The engine had side valves, with L-head and shaft transmission. Detachable wheels and dashboard radiator made it an original car. The front brakes were standard, but were abandoned due to malfunctioning. In 1927 it merged with the

Car: **Arrol-Johnston 15-9 HP**
Year: **1911**
Engine: **4 cylinders in line**
Bore and stroke: **80 × 120 mm**
Cylinder capacity: **2411 cc**
Gears: **4 forward**
Brake horse power: **34**
Maximum speed: **45 mph**
Wheelbase: **9 ft 6 ins (2.89 m)**
Suspension: **front: semi-elliptic leaf-springs; back: elliptic leaf-springs**

Aster Engineering Company Ltd and for four years cars were made under the name Arrol-Aster. The decision to reduce production, in 1929, did not have the results that had been hoped for and the company closed down in 1930.

Aston-Martin

Throughout its history Aston-Martin has had six changes of ownership, and has passed through periods of relative good fortune and (more commonly) periods of crisis. The main reason for this fitful progress has been the desire on the part of all its various owners to produce beautiful cars, even at the risk of reduced profits. The company has never compromised quality for lucre.

The company started, almost accidentally, in the 1920s under Lionel Martin and Richard Bamford, London agent for Singer. It was named Aston Martin after a hill-climb at Aston Clinton, which Martin had won in 1913. The idea of building cars themselves came to Martin and Bamford when they were adapting the Singer Ten for racing (calling it the B.M.). The vehicle in which Martin won the Aston Clinton was made up from a Coventry-Simplex engine (about 1500 cc) and an Isotta-Fraschini chassis. In its early manufacturing days Aston-Martin invariably used this same engine, but between 1921 and 1925 only 69 cars were built. The Coventry-Simplex had a fixed head on an alloy single block, similar in design to Bugattis of the same period. In 1920 Richard Bamford left the firm, and was replaced by Count Louis Zborowski, a gifted young man of Polish-American descent, who had made racing his life. Famous for the numerous 'specials' he had made, Zborowski was persuaded to finance the creation of an Aston-Martin car dear to Lionel Martin's heart— sparkling as a Bugatti and dignified as a Rolls-Royce. From 1921 to 1925 Martin continued to use the Coventry-Simplex engine with side valves, which had an important record to its credit—that set by Kensington Moir at Brooklands in 1921 for the 1500 category. Martin developed an engine

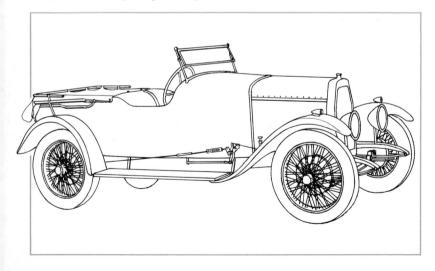

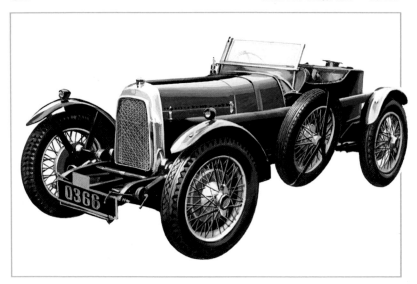

with the same cylinder capacity especially for Zborowski, but with 16 valves (4 per cylinder). It was in a car of this type that Zborowski took part in the Strasbourg G.P. in 1922.

With the death of Zborowski on the track at Monza in 1924, Aston-Martin entered a new crisis. On this occasion it was saved by another foreigner, an Italian, Augusto Cesare Bertelli, who struck lucky on the race-track. In the early 1930s it was taken over by R. G. Sutherland. The fifth owner was David Brown, and his arrival (1947) recorded by the addition of his initials to the firm's name. In 1976 a Canadian-American consortium bought the company. The models reproduced here, though similar both in looks and mechanically, are historically important in that they were the first the company built,

Car: **Aston-Martin**
Year: **1922**
Engine: **4 cylinders in line**
Bore and stroke: **65 × 112 mm**
Cylinder capacity: **1486 cc**
Gears: **4 forward**
Brake horse power: **50**
Maximum speed: **100 mph**
Wheelbase: **8 ft 2 ins (2.48 m)**
Suspension: **front and back: semi-elliptic leaf-springs**

Car: **Aston-Martin**
Year: **1925**
Engine: **4 cylinders in line**
Bore and stroke: **66.5 × 107 mm**
Cylinder capacity: **1486 cc**
Gears: **4 forward**
Brake horse power: **35**
Maximum speed: **80 mph**
Wheelbase: **8 ft 7 ins (2.66 m)**
Suspension: **front and back: semi-elliptic leaf-springs**

in the full sense of the word, in its early pioneering days. After 1927 it used 4-cylinder engines with overhead valves and removable heads.

Austin 7 HP
Austin Seven Baby

Herbert Austin founded the company that bears his name in 1906, after being director-general of Wolseley. The firm started with a sturdy and reliable model that was very simple in its general conception. The 15 HP came into production in 1908. It was typical of the early period, and as often happened at that time, various parts, especially the gearbox and ignition, were quickly modified. Thus, by 1922 a small, truly popular car had evolved. In the meantime, Herbert Austin had been knighted for his contribution to the war effort. The Great War had in fact been both favourable and unfavourable to Austin: on the one hand a war machine had had to be built; on the other, factories had sprung up and prospered everywhere in the building

of it. At the end of the war this was an embarrassment. The administrative board's refusal to subsidise the equipment necessary for production of the Seven induced Sir Herbert Austin to work on his small car plan not in the official workshops, but at home, in the evenings, with the help of a designer. Although the Seven could thus have been built by another firm, under a different name as it turned out, the car, when it appeared, bore the name of the Birmingham firm.

Some 300,000 were produced. With the Baby, Austin was in effect doing what Peugeot had already done with the Bébé and Quadrilette, and Citroën with the 5 HP Type C. The Seven was also known as the Chummy—the 'sociable' 4-seater. Between 1921 and 1929 Austin made 100,000 Sevens, and roughly twice as many again in the next ten years.

First produced in 1922, in 1924 the engine of the Seven was enlarged

(from 54 × 76.2 mm, 696 cc). In 1922 the standard Tourer version cost £165. This obviously lucky name (seven) crops up four times in Austin's history: first in 1908 by events probably dictated by strong commercial pressures.

Between 1909 and 1911 there was another, single cylinder, 7 HP, though this time built by the Swift Motor Co. Ltd under Austin's name (this car appeared in the Swift catalogue). It had a water-cooled, single-cylinder 1087 cc engine. In 1952, the name Seven was given to another series of low cylinder capacity cars, which remained in production for seven years—proof that this too had been spot-on in meeting market demand. Finally the first Austin Minis, announced in 1959, were called Austin Sevens.

Car: **Austin Seven Baby**
Year: **1924**
Engine: **4 cylinders in line**
Bore and stroke: **56 × 76.2 mm**
Cylinder capacity: **750 cc**
Gears: **3 forward**
Brake horse power: **10.5**
Maximum speed: **52 mph**
Wheelbase: **6 ft 3 ins (1.90 m)**
Suspension: **front: semi-elliptic leaf-springs; back: ¼ elliptic leaf-springs**

Car: **Austin 7 HP**
Year: **1911**
Engine: **Single cylinder**
Bore and stroke: **105 × 127 mm**
Cylinder capacity: **1100 cc**
Gears: **4 forward**
Brake horse power: **7**
Maximum speed: **32 mph**
Wheelbase: **6 ft 0 ins (1.82 m)**
Suspension: **front: semi-elliptic leaf-springs; back: elliptic leaf-springs**

Bean only had a short life as a car company (from the end of the First World War to 1931), but its origins date back to 1826, when A. Harper Sons and Bean Ltd started doing hot forging and foundry work. The first modern Bean vehicle dates from 1919. It had a 11.9 bhp engine with side valves, designed and built in modest numbers by Perry, of which Bean had bought the manufacturing rights.

The 14 HP, first produced in 1924, had an engine with detachable head and three main bearings, and could do 50 mph. In 1925 the standard production model was equipped with brakes on all four wheels. Bean also collaborated with Fiat England, supplying it with bodywork for imported Fiat 501 chassis.

Rather than relying on traditional races, the company concentrated

Car: **Bean 14 HP**
Year: **1926**
Engine: **4 cylinders in line**
Bore and stroke: **75 × 135 mm**
Cylinder capacity: **2385 cc**
Gears: **4 forward**
Brake horse power: **32**
Maximum speed: **50 mph**
Wheelbase: **9 ft 2½ ins (2.80 m)**
Suspension: **front and back: semi-elliptic leaf-springs**

more on rallies to advertise its cars. Its most successful venture was in 1927 when Francis Birtles crossed Australia in a 14 HP. The drive began in London, and also took in India and Indo-China, which caused considerable difficulties and stress for both car and driver. The solidity of Bean cars can quite justifiably be attributed to the work of one of the founders in 1826. The only Bean sports car was the 1929 Hatfield Bean 14/70 HP.

The 10/12 HP was one of the last successful cars built by this Manchester-based company dating from 1897. In 1924, after a turbulent life typical of the period, Belsize went bankrupt. Another typical aspect of the company's history was its development from a bicycle concern, through manufacturing under licence from a foreign firm (in this case the French Hurtu), to being a fully-fledged car-manufacturing company. It is worth noting also that Hurtu in turn developed its cars from the German firm Benz.

In 1903 Marshall and Company became the Belsize Motor and Engineering Company, and it straight away tried to change its production. However, it could not give up foreign engines that quickly, and it improved and developed those that it used from

Car: **Belsize 10/12 HP**
Year: **1912**
Engine: **4 cylinders in line**
Bore and stroke: **69 × 130 mm**
Cylinder capacity: **1945 cc**
Gears: **3 forward**
Brake horse power: **12**
Maximum speed: **34 mph**
Wheelbase: **8 ft 0 ins (2.43 m)**
Suspension: **front and back: semi-elliptic leaf-springs**

the Paris Société Buchet. Almost immediately after becoming independent, Belsize was offering single-, twin-, 3-, 4-, and 6-cylinder cars. This variety of engines shows again how Belsize faithfully reflected the uncertainty of the market. Mass-produced small cylinder capacity cars became the order of the day, however, and those firms that could not cope with the new market requirements ceased production.

Bentley 3 litre
Bentley 4 1/2 litre

This is without question one of the most prestigious English makes of car, not only by virture of its quality and racing results, but also of the character of the founder and chief designer of the firm, Walter Owen Bentley himself. A contemporary of Ettore Bugatti, Bentley was an expert mechanic, having attended a mechanical engineering course with the Great Northern Railway. During his formative years he was first attracted to trains, and then motorbikes. He finally discovered his true vocation when he and his brother took over an agency for French cars (D.F.P. and La Licorne) in England.

Born in London in 1888, Bentley joined the Navy in the war, and met F. T. Burgess, the designer of the Humber. The first, authentic Bentleys were mechanical jewels, but their designer-maker had no real factory and was dependent on various suppliers, and his name became associated not only with high quality, but also with late deliveries.

He was one of the first people to believe in races as a form of advertising, and in fact his cars raced with considerable success. Suffice it to mention the five victories at Le Mans, in the 24 Hours—four of those victories consecutive (1927-1930). The first Bentley, a 3-litre, was delivered to its owner in 1921. It had a five-year guarantee. The 3-litre stayed in production until 1939, and 1,630 were built in all. Despite the high cylinder capacity, the engine had 4 cylinders and 4 valves (2 inlet, 2 exhaust), with overhead camshaft, and magneto ignition. It only acquired front wheel brakes in 1924, which was the year that Duff and Clement won for the first time at Le Mans.

The fame of the company, which lasted only 12 years as originally constituted, was largely due to the famous 'Bentley Boys', the group of top-class drivers (like Woolf Barnato) who offered the firm their services and also gave financial support. Unfortunately racing alone was not enough to sustain Bentley's enterprise, however modest in scale it might be, and his finances began to totter. The company announced production of an 8-litre 6-cylinder model. This alarmed Rolls-Royce, which saw the threat of a competitor to its Phantom. Thus when Bentley was offered for sale in 1931, Napier, which had made some of the proposed series, was pipped at the post by Rolls-Royce, who (it is claimed) wanted to take over the rival firm in order to eliminate its competitor, the

Car: **Bentley 4 1/2 litre**
Year: **1929**
Engine: **4 cylinders in line**
Bore and stroke: **100 × 140 mm**
Cylinder capacity: **4396 cc**
Gears: **4 forward**
Brake horse power: **100**
Maximum speed: **92 mph**
Wheelbase: **10 ft 10 in (3.30 m)**
Suspension: **front and back: semi-elliptic leaf-springs**

Car: **Bentley 3 litre**
Year: **1921**
Engine: **4 cylinders in line**
Bore and stroke: **80 × 149 mm**
Cylinder capacity: **2996 cc**
Gears: **4 forward**
Brake horse power: **70**
Maximum speed: **80 mph**
Wheelbase: **9 ft 9½ in (2.98 m)**
Suspension: **front and back: semi-elliptic leaf-springs**

8-litre; in fact, no more of that model were produced. When it appeared in 1933, the new 'Rolls-Bentley' shared many components with the Rolls-Royce 25/30 HP.

Calcott was another small English car firm of humble origins (it first made bicycles, then motorcycles). It went over to 4-wheelers in 1913, but production was hampered by over-elaborate manufacturing processes. In fact, having neither foundry nor bodywork department, Calcott was engaged only in assembling engines. The chassis came from Glasgow, the bodywork from Coventry. Despite this the 10.5 HP was a highly technical car: it weighed some 1,300 pounds (600 kg), had a maximum speed of 45 mph, and was guaranteed to do around 40 miles to the gallon. In 1915 it acquired an electrical system; was modified in 1919, and in 1925 was given brakes on all four wheels—a novelty of which many people were still distrustful. A. Alderson, the original designer, was replaced by L.

Car: **Calcott 10.5 HP**
Year: **1913**
Engine: **4 cylinders in line**
Bore and stroke: **65 × 110 mm**
Cylinder capacity: **1460 cc**
Gears: **3 forward**
Brake horse power: **16**
Maximum speed: **45 mph**
Wheel base: **7 ft 9 ins (2.36 m)**
Suspension: **front and back: semi-elliptic leaf-springs**

Shorter, from Humber. Shorter helped modernise the line, designing a larger car (1954 cc) with removable head. The transmission acquired four speeds. Then a 6-cylinder model went into production, but by now the fierce competition among the larger companies, who could afford to wage bitter price wars, forced Calcott into liquidation. Its reputation still lived on, however. The 1920s saw the end of many small firms, unable to make a living from their small clientele.

The Morris Minor, a triumph of the rising star Alec Issigonis (the first English car of which over a million were made), had an illustrious predecessor in the Calthorpe, which shared the same name. Introduced in 1913, the Minor was very well received: the (for the times) very modest cylinder capacity was backed up by easy handling and a respectable maximum speed of around 50 mph.

At the same time it was in line with the general policy of the newly-founded firm (Birmingham, 1904), which considered racing in the 'voiturette' or, as these vehicles were known in England, 'cyclecar' category an excellent form of publicity. A special version of this same model averaged 68 mph in the 1914 Cyclecar Grand Prix. Calthorpes also ran successfully in many tough rallies in the 1920s.

Car: **Calthorpe Minor**
Year: **1914**
Engine: **4 cylinders in line**
Bore and stroke: **62 × 90 mm**
Cylinder capacity: **1087 cc**
Gears: **3 forward**
Brake horse power: **25**
Maximum speed: **50 mph**
Wheelbase: **7 ft 3 in (2.20 m)**
Suspension: **front and back: semi-elliptic leaf-springs**

After the war the Minor was called the Sporting Four, and its cylinder capacity increased to 1261 cc.

In 1921 the founder of Calthorpe, G. W. Hands, left the company to found another under his own name, but in 1924 he returned with some of his new models, which he inserted into the old firm's line, causing a certain degree of confusion. The name Calthorpe remained alive until 1932, though very few were made in the company's last years.

This firm was founded by G. H. Wait in 1901. In 1932, after producing some 260 vehicles, it shut down. During that time, however, it also made a certain number of motor-cycles and bicycles. After first using Simms and Aster engines, Clyde in 1905 turned to White and Poppes, though only in the higher cylinder capacity models. The Clyde 12/14 HP had a White and Poppe water-cooled engine, with dual ignition, cone clutch, rear gearbox, acetylene lights, and chain transmission. The price, £250 in 1906, was far from expensive, and included windshield and hood in the Tourer version.

The First World War produced a long hiatus in the car business. Clyde made a comeback around 1920, and again sold its cars remarkably cheaply. Leaving aside the rear gear-

Car: **Clyde 12/14 HP**
Year: **1906**
Engine: **White and Poppe, 3 vertical cylinders**
Bore and stroke: **80 × 90 mm**
Cylinder capacity: **1416 cc**
Gears: **3 forward**
Brake horse power: —
Maximum speed: —
Wheelbase: **6 ft 10 ins (2.08 m)**
Suspension: **front and back: semi-elliptic leaf-springs**

box, one change was in the engine: though still brought in from else-where, ready-made, they were now 1000 cc, vertical twin-cylinder Coventry-Simplex engines and 1500 cc, 4-cylinder Dormans—both water-cooled. It is worth noting that the 3-cylinder model illustrated here has run in several modern vintage-car rallies with the founder of the firm at the wheel.

Daimler started in 1893 under the name Daimler Motor Syndicate, in order to make use of the Daimler Motor Gesellschaft patent (in practice it began making cars only in 1896). The 20 HP is one of the smallest cars ever made by the firm as regards the cylinder capacity of the engine (the Silent twin sleeve-valve engine, manufactured under licence from the Anglo-American Charles Yale Knight). Daimler acquired the production rights on this engine in 1908. A characteristic detail of the Daimler was the strip of wood on the fuel tank. Daimler began making cars with smaller cylinder capacity only after the war: but alongside this new 1500 (6 cylinders), it also offered an 8500 cc model (also 6 cylinders). Edward VII, when Prince of Wales learnt to drive on a Daimler, and always remained

Car: **Daimler 20 HP**
Year: **1914**
Engine: **4 cylinders in line**
Bore and stroke: **90 × 130 mm**
Cylinder capacity: **3300 cc**
Gears: **4 forward**
Brake horse power: **25**
Maximum speed: **40 mph**
Wheelbase: **10 ft 3½ ins (3.13 m)**or
   11 ft 0 ins (3.35 m)
Suspension: **front and back: semi-elliptic leaf-springs**

fond of this make. George V, Edward VIII, and George VI all continued the tradition, and Daimler thus became the Royal Family Car. In 1960 it was taken over by Jaguar, and it now produces cars identical in every respect to Jaguars, except for the radiator, which remains its one distinguishing feature. This continuity, however superficial, makes Daimler one of the oldest car firms still in business.

This company was named after its founder, H. H. Deasy (1906), until 1912, when it became Siddeley-Deasy Motor after the arrival of John Davenport Siddeley, one of the most outstanding personalities in the English car world. Siddeley began his career as a manufacturer of cars in 1903 with a model inspired by the Peugeot, which he imported into England. His agreement with the French company stipulated that their imported cars should sell under the importer's name.

One distinctive feature of the 12 HP was the radiator mounted behind the engine, a fashion of the day. A 4-speed transmission rather than 3- could be incorporated if desired. The name Deasy disappeared completely in 1919 when Siddeley joined up with Armstrong-Whit-

Car: **Deasy 12 HP**
Year: **1910**
Engine: **4 cylinders in line**
Bore and stroke: **75 × 110 mm**
Cylinder capacity: **1944 cc**
Gears: **3 forward**
Brake horse power: **12**
Maximum speed: **35 mph**
Wheelbase: **9 ft 3 ins (2.81 m)**
Suspension: **front: semi-elliptic leaf-springs; back: ¾ elliptic leaf-springs**

worth, thus creating Armstrong-Siddeley, which closed down in 1960.

John Davenport Siddeley also had other concerns: he was director-general of Wolseley (replacing Herbert Austin) who had been building his cars for him. He influenced Wolseley to adopt the vertically (rather than horizontally) mounted 2-, 4-, and 6-cylinder engines. This was a complete novelty for Wolseley.

Ford crossed the Atlantic for the first time in 1911, with the creation of a base at Old Trafford Park (Manchester). It had actually begun exporting cars to Britain in 1903, with the Model A. The steady success of these vehicles persuaded Ford to start up a small factory, which for some years produced the same models as those being made in America. In 1931 the factory moved to Dagenham and began producing its own models.

1935 saw the sedan Ten, with a 34 bhp engine. The battery was situated under the hood, rather than under the front seat. The extremely low price (£145) for the 4-door sedan version was less than that being asked for Fords in America. The Ten was quite fast (70 mph), was economical on fuel (about 35 miles to the gallon), and had good acceleration: 18.2 seconds

Car: **Ford Ten**
Year: **1936**
Engine: **4 cylinders in line**
Bore and stroke: **63.5 × 92.5 mm**
Cylinder capacity: **1172 cc**
Gears: **3 forward**
Brake horse power: **34**
Maximum speed: **65 mph**
Wheelbase: **7 ft 6 ins (2.28 m)**
Suspension: **front and back: transverse leaf-springs**

to reach 50 mph from standstill. 97,000 were produced in the first year. An equivalent to the Ten was produced also in Germany and called the Eifel. In 1937 the Ten was lengthened slightly, to allow access to the trunk from the outside. The modification was accompanied by small aesthetic changes, but the car's greater height and weight, and the fact of its being narrower had an adverse effect on its road-holding ability and on its maximum speed, which was reduced to around 60 mph.

The 1921 G.N. was considered one of the most interesting and popular cyclecars among the many built in England. In an attempt to keep the price low the cars were made as light and simple as possible. The air-cooled engine was mounted at the front; the chassis was made of wood.

There were three available versions of this vehicle: the standard, the 3-seater (the third fitted into the distinctive 'tail'), and the Vitesse, a sports version of the 2-seater, with overhead camshafts and metal alloy pistons.

The G.N. racing model was for many years the heroine of the celebrated hill climb at Shelsey Walsh. It was also widely used on the race track, reaching extremely high averages (over 66 mph in a race at Boulogne in 1921).

Car: **G.N.**
Year: **1921**
Engine: **V-twin**
Bore and stroke: **84 × 98 mm**
Cylinder capacity: **1087 cc**
Gears: **3 forward**
Brake horse power: **17**
Maximum speed: **48 mph**
Wheelbase: **8 ft 6 ins (2.59 m)**
Suspension: **front and back: ¼ elliptic leaf-springs**

The founders of G.N. were H. R. Godfrey and Archie Frazer-Nash (the G stood for Godfrey, and the N for Nash). Later Godfrey started HRG, and Frazer-Nash another firm under his own name.

The partnership between Godfrey and Frazer-Nash, without which British motor sports would never have seen cars of the highest quality, was destroyed by an incredible flooding of the cyclecar market, even by established firms such as Rover. The two partners broke up in 1922.

This firm, which still produces trucks as part of British Leyland, built no more than 150 cars between 1919 and 1925. And yet it has left an indelible impression, especially with its 1919 model, the first standard-produced 8-cylinder V engine car to be made in England. The 1919 Guy engine had inclined side-valves and removable head.

Another interesting feature of this car was the way in which the chassis was lubricated with the excess engine oil. Such details made the 8-cylinder Guy seem one of the most advanced and intelligently designed cars of its time. The following year the company also produced a 4-cylinder 1700 cc car with splash lubrication, but this was not particularly successful. In view of the difficulties that faced many English car manufacturers during the

Car: **Guy**
Year: **1919**
Engine: **8 cylinders V**
Bore and stroke: **72 × 125 mm**
Cylinder capacity: **4072 cc**
Gears: **4 forward**
Brake horse power: **53**
Maximum speed: **70 mph**
Wheelbase: **10 ft 10 ins (3.30 m)**
Suspension: **front and back: semi-elliptic leaf-springs**

1920s, Guy was fortunate that it was able to turn to the heavy goods sector of the market.

Humber is another English car company, and one of the most famous, whose origins went back to the mid-nineteenth century (1868) when they produced bicycles. Based in Beeston, in Nottinghamshire, the firm later transferred its cheap car section to Coventry (continuing to manufacture de luxe cars at Beeston), from where the first cars came out in 1901. A similar experiment had already been tried between 1896 and 1900, but without any concrete outcome. The company's subsequent success (in 1964 it was absorbed into Chrysler UK) was largely due to its designer, Louis Coatalen, one of the most inventive men of his time, who then went on to build up a reputation at Sunbeam. The first 'creation' of Coatalen's to catch the attention of both engineers and public was the

Car: **Humber 8 HP**
Year: **1909**
Engine: **twin-cylinder, vertical**
Bore and stroke: **90 × 120 mm**
Cylinder capacity: **1525 cc**
Gears: **3 forward**
Brake horse power: **8**
Maximum speed: **40 mph**
Wheelbase: **7 ft 6 ins (2.28 m)**
Suspension: **front and back: semi-elliptic leaf-springs**

Humberette, with a single-cylinder 613 cc engine with shaft-transmission. After the Humberette, Coatalen turned to 4-cylinder engines, but in 1908 the company began to take a fresh interest in medium-to-small capacity engines, coming up with the 8 HP, which was manufactured from 1909 on. Its light-weight 1,500 pounds (700 kg) makes the declared maximum speed of around 40 mph seem quite believable. Other features were dual ignition and removable wheels.

This is one of Invicta's best-known models. The company had many endurance records to its credit with the intrepid Miss Violet Cordery driving a 3-litre. These records were intended to show the toughness and reliability of the firm's cars, rather than their speed, which in fact in the early models was rather limited (little over 60 mph) given their cylinder capacity. The 4½-litre S derived from the 4½-litre Standard, but had a much lower chassis. Its Meadows engine had a compression ratio of 1:6.8 or 1:7.1. The car's success was compromised by an accident in 1931, at Brooklands, in which the driver 'Sammy' Davis was hurt. It was attributed to the car's bad road-holding ability, due to an incorrect weight-distribution, or too low centre of gravity. Davis, a journalist, denied

Car: **Invicta 4500 S**
Year: **1931**
Engine: **6 cylinders in line**
Bore and stroke: **88.5 × 120.6 mm**
Cylinder capacity: **4448 cc**
Gears: **4 forward**
Brake horse power: **110**
Maximum speed: **90 mph**
Wheelbase: **9 ft 10 ins (2.99 m)** *or*
    10 ft 6 ins (3.20 m)
Suspension: **front and back: semi-elliptic leaf-springs integrated with hydraulic shock-absorbers**

that the motor car had any faults, and blamed the accident entirely on himself. The S won a brilliant victory at the Monte Carlo Rally that same year, with Donald Healey driving. Founded by Noel Macklin in 1924, Invicta closed down in 1950. Apart from the misfortunes of the Model S, this company's cars were considered some of the most sophisticated of the time.

SS1
SS Jaguar

The two cars illustrated here have been specially chosen as they emphasise the rather curious beginnings of the Jaguar organisation.

Jaguar's origins go back to 1920, when William Walmsley and William Lyons met, almost by chance, in Blackpool. William Lyons helped his father sell pianos, while Walmsley was renovating old motorbikes left over from the war. Walmsley also built aluminium sidecars, and it was when Lyons came to buy one of these that the two met. Their shared enthusiasm for motorbikes and sidecars led them to join forces and found a company called the Swallow Sidecar Company. This was in 1922. In 1927, though business was thriving, Swallow started to turn to cars, modifying the bodywork of the most popular models of the day. They began with the Austin Seven and continued with the Standard, the Fiat 509A, and the Wolseley Hornet, restricting themselves to aesthetic alterations only. In 1928 Swallow moved to Coventry, but the year before it had already changed its name to Swallow Sidecar and Coachbuilding Company. In 1930 side-cars were shelved, thus indicating that the company had resolved to turn to cars. The first car with bodywork by Swallow and mechanical parts made (by Standard) expressly for the company was called the SS. In general it seemed like a car for the rich driver. In fact it sold for £310. The SS 1 was such a

success that 776 were sold in the first year of production, and 1,500 in the next. Adaptation of the Standard engine, first to 2143 cc, then to 2664 cc, enabled Swallow (who in 1934 had once again changed names to SS Cars Ltd) to expand their line (sedan, sports tourer, and cabriolet). The name Jaguar appeared for the first time in 1936, apparently as the personal choice of William Lyons, who by now was on his own, Walmsley having left the partnership to build trailers and mobile homes.

The SS Jaguar of 1936 also had a Standard engine. It was only in 1945 that the company finally became Jaguar Cars Ltd, and began to produce engines itself. The step from graceful swallow to voracious jaguar might seem bold, if not impossible: William Lyons (later Sir Wiliam

Car: **SS1**
Year: **1934**
Engine: **6 cylinders in line**
Bore and stroke: **65.5 × 101.6 mm**
Cylinder capacity: **2025 cc**
Gears: **4 forward**
Brake horse power: **48**
Maximum speed: **65 mph**
Wheelbase: **9 ft 4 in (2.84 m)**
Suspension: **front and back: semi-elliptic leaf-springs**

Car: **SS Jaguar**
Year: **1936**
Engine: **6 cylinders in line**
Bore and stroke: **73 × 106 mm**
Cylinder capacity: **2664 cc**
Gears: **4 forward**
Brake horse power: **104**
Maximum speed: **90 mph'**
Wheelbase: **10 ft 0 in (3.04 m)**
Suspension: **front and back: semi-elliptic leaf-springs**

Lyons) succeeded completely. Automobile history cannot boast many makers of coachwork (which was basically how he started) who became manufacturers of de luxe sedans and racing cars.

Jowett has gone down in history for the solidity of its flat, twin-cylinder, water-cooled car, which was in production from 1911 to 1939.

The brothers Benjamin and William Jowett went from bicycles to cars, building first a 3-cylinder model, then a twin-cylinder engine like the one in the car illustrated here. Although light, weighing around 716 pounds (325 kg) and economical (about 60 miles to the gallon), the 1911 Jowett was in other respects an antiquated vehicle, as the tiller steering indicates (a wheel was adopted only after 1914).

By emphasising its cars' reliability in its advertising, Jowett survived the crisis that shook all small car firms in Britain in the 1920s. In 1946 it brought out the Javelin which had a flat, 4-cylinder opposed 1485 cc

Car: **Jowett**
Year: **1911**
Engine: **twin-cylinder**
Bore and stroke: **72 × 102 mm**
Cylinder capacity: **830 cc**
Gears: **3 forward**
Brake horse power: **12**
Maximum speed: **40 mph**
Wheelbase: **7 ft 0 ins (2.13 m)**
Suspension: **front and back: semi-elliptic leaf-springs**

engine (50 bhp). The bodywork was sturdy, and it had torsion bar suspension. Some 30,000 were built. At the London Motor Show in 1953 Jowett launched a lighter version of the Jupiter Sports, but it was a complete failure. The company disappeared when International Harvester and Ford, England took over its premises.

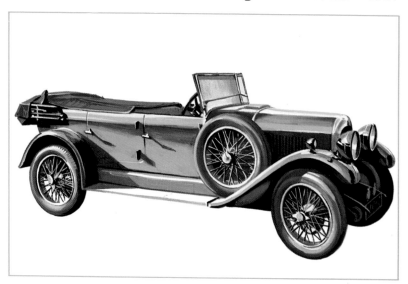

Lagonda was founded towards the end of the last century by an American, Wilbur Gunn, who began with motorbikes, and went on to de luxe cars. In one sense therefore the tradition has been continued, since in 1947 the firm was bought by David Brown, which already owned Aston-Martin.

The 1927 2-litre model (officially launched at the 1925 London Motor Show) had double overhead camshaft and hemispherical combustion chambers. The engine developed around 60 bhp. Its maximum speed was somewhat over 60 mph. There was also a sporting version of the 14-60, the Speed Model, which could reach close to 80 mph. This came as a 4-seater coupé, or 2 or 4-door sedans. The failure of the Rapier in 1935 brought Lagonda into difficulties. Alan Good rescued it, putting the technical side

Car: **Lagonda 14-60 HP**
Year: **1927**
Engine: **4 cylinders in line**
Bore and stroke: **72 × 120 mm**
Cylinder capacity: **1954 cc**
Gears: **4 forward**
Brake horse power: **60**
Maximum speed: **65 mph**
Wheelbase: **10 ft 0 ins (3.04 m)**
Suspension: **front and back: semi-elliptic leaf-springs**

under the charge of Walter Owen Bentley, to whom he entrusted the design of new models. In 1937 V-12 engines with double overhead camshaft were introduced, and these produced a car that was fast (maximum speed of over 100 mph), silent, comfortable, and elegant.

117

Lanchester 20 HP
Lanchester 40

The Lanchester 20 HP is one of the most typical cars of this firm, which throughout its lifespan earned a justifiable reputation for excellence and precision craftsmanship. It first made a name for itself with the 10 and 12 HP models, with horizontal opposed cylinders, which stayed in production from 1900 to 1908. It had already introduced a series of 4-cylinder models, including that illustrated here, the bodywork of which was completely original, but which found no imitators perhaps because it was not aesthetically very pleasing. Together with the 20 HP there was a 6-cylinder 28 HP model. The steering tiller of the 20 HP was situated on the left. It was a popular car with connoisseurs because of its mechanical refinements (there was a preselector for the gears, self-changing clutch in an oil bath, and two lubrication pressure pumps, one for the engine, one for the gears). The company also produced a number of sports models, notably the 38 HP, which developed 68 bhp and had a maximum speed of 68 mph.

The 40 HP was introduced at the 1919 London Motor Show. Its comfort and luxuriousness, as well as its engine-power (90 bhp) placed it alongside the Rolls-Royce of the time (indeed they cost much the same). About 500 were built altogether. A special version of the 40, a single-seater with lighter bodywork, set a new world 24 hour record in 1924, covering a thousand miles at an average of around 95 mph.

The firm was founded in 1893 by the Lanchester brothers, Frank, Frederick William, and George. At first they built only engines; but in 1896 they started making cars as well. Frederick was the brains behind the firm. He was considered one of the most brilliant, versatile, and imaginative engineers ever to have been involved with cars. Everything the company produced reflected his outstanding design-work. However, like all who give themselves up totally to one thing, he was not much of a businessman, and in 1904, when Lanchester found itself in serious difficulties, he did not hesitate to resign as director-general, although he remained the company's designer.

Lanchester were taken over by Daimler in 1931, and ceased production in 1956.

Car: **Lanchester 20 HP**
Year: **1908**
Engine: **4 cylinders in line**
Bore and stroke: **102 × 76 mm**
Cylinder capacity: **2485 cc**
Gears: **3 forward**
Brake horse power: **30**
Maximum speed: **50 mph**
Wheelbase: **9 ft 5 ins (2.87 m)** *or*
   10 ft 5 ins (3.17 m)
Suspension: **front and back: cantilever**
   leaf-springs

Car: **Lanchester 40**
Year: **1923**
Engine: **6 cylinders in line, in two blocks**
   of three
Bore and stroke: **101.6 × 127 mm**
Cylinder capacity: **6175 cc**
Gears: **3 forward**
Brake horse power: **90**
Maximum speed: **70 mph**
Wheelbase: **11 ft 9 ins (3.58 m)**
Suspension: **front: semi-elliptic leaf-springs;**
   back: cantilever leaf-springs

This was one of the first English road-going cars to have a supercharger. The engine was a Meadows. The Ulster derived from the Hyper, which had been longer and less easy to handle. The crankshaft came from Germany. The name of this model came from the famous Irish circuit, on which Kaye Don had that year won the Tourist Trophy, just beating a front-wheel-drive Alvis, at an average of over 70 mph.

Like so many English car companies of the period, Lea-Francis saw many hard times. Initially founded as a bicycle factory in 1897 by R. H. Lea and G. J. Francis, it went over to cars in 1904—though without much conviction. A 3-cylinder design was adopted, and a few cars built; the design was then sold to Singer, for whom Lea had once worked as an

Car: **Lea-Francis Ulster**
Year: **1928**
Bore and stroke: **69 × 100 mm**
Cylinder capacity: **1496 cc**
Gears: **4 forward**
Brake horse power: **61**
Maximum speed: **90 mph**
Wheelbase: **9 ft 3 ins (2.82 m)**
Suspension: **front and back: semi-elliptic leaf-springs**

engineer. The firm returned to cars in 1920 (having started to produce motorbikes in 1911). Another break in 1935, and another new start in 1938—this time under two different associates, G. H. Leek and R. H. Rose. In 1953 the firm was again foundering, and it suspended car production, to start up again, though unsuccessfully, in 1960, with a 2500 cc model with a Ford engine. It then sank for ever. Lea-Francis cars are still held in high esteem by collectors of vintage vehicles.

MG was the creation of William Richard Morris (the founder of the company of that name) and Cecil Kimber (the managing-director of the Oxford Morris Garages Ltd). The letters MG stand for Morris Garages. Kimber's idea was to produce low-cost sports cars using, as far as possible, standard production components and publicised by racing.

Everything began simply at first; Kimber realised that it would be worthwhile making certain modifications to the bodywork of some models. To begin with these were more aesthetic than mechanical. The thought of starting a new company was far from Kimber's mind, but things developed almost of their own accord. By 1927 the Morris Garage had become too small, and Kimber moved to the outskirts of Oxford, and

Car: **MG Midget M Type**
Year: **1930**
Engine: **4 cylinders in line**
Bore and stroke: **57 × 83 mm**
Cylinder capacity: **847 cc**
Gears: **4 forward**
Brake horse power: **20**
Maximum speed: **64 mph**
Wheelbase: **6 ft 6 ins (1.98 m)**
Suspension: **front and back: semi-elliptic leaf-springs**

later to Abingdon. At the London Motor Show of 1928 substantially new models were introduced—new in that, though they were Morris cars, they had been modified both aesthetically and mechanically. One of these, derived from the Minor, was the Midget M Type. It was the first of a lucky series. In a supercharged version, but with its reduced engine (750 cc) to qualify it for the class, the Midget was the first car of that cylinder capacity to top 100 mph.

From railways, H. F. S. Morgan went over to cars, opening a business selling Wolseleys and Darracqs. Then, with his father's help, he started a car manufacturing company, whose first vehicle was launched at the London Motor Show of 1910. It was disconcertingly simple (the outer tubes of the chassis were also the exhaust pipes), but its most striking feature was its front suspension. At £89 it was extraordinarily cheap.

The 1914 Cyclecar had a twin-cylinder air-cooled engine, with overhead valves operated with push-rods and rockers, magneto ignition, pressure lubrication, and cone clutch. The car's 8 bhp was sufficient to give it a respectable speed. Drive was by chain to the rear wheels.

The ban on three-wheel vehicles at

Car: **Morgan Cyclecar**
Year: **1914**
Engine: **Jap V-twin**
Bore and stroke: **85.5 × 85 mm**
Cylinder capacity: **976 cc**
Gears: **2 forward**
Brake horse power: **8**
Maximum speed: **40 mph**
Wheel base;. **6 ft 0 ins (1.82 m)**
Suspension: **front: vertical telescopic mountings and coil springs; back: cantilever leaf-springs**

Brooklands put an almost complete stop to production of any Morgan racing models. In 1936 it was able to adapt, quickly changing to 4-wheelers powered by 4-cylinder Ford engines.

Morris Oxford
Morris Cowley
Morris Minor

With William Richard Morris, later created Lord Nuffield for his services to industry, the car took a definite step forward. No longer was it reserved for the few. Though he had no technical qualifications, he combined mechanical instinct with that of a far-sighted industrialist, setting up a large-scale, complex, and well articulated production system; bringing together the products from various suppliers and adapting his own vehicles, at least to begin with, to other goods on the market.

The Oxford, named after the city where his business grew up, typifies its creator's philosophy. The engine, with T valves, was supplied by White and Poppe; the rear axle by Wrigley, and the chassis from a third source. The car weighed around 1,380 pounds (625 kg). Within a year after it had first been introduced, 40 were being made each week.

Continuing his policy of making as cheap a car as possible, when the Cowley was being designed, Morris did not think twice about using an American engine, the Continental. This at first had a cylinder capacity of 1495 cc (69×100 mm), but later grew to 1547 cc through an increase in the 'stroke' of the piston (103.5 mm).

The Cowley was designed in 1915, but, except for some 1,500 built before hostilities really began, was mainly produced after the war.

Morris's intuitive foresight, and his certainty in the future of cars were fully confirmed in the Cowley. The

Car: **Morris Oxford**
Year: **1912**
Engine: **4 cylinders in line**
Bore and stroke: **60×90 mm**
Cylinder capacity: **1018 cc**
Gears: **3 forward**
Brake horse power: **15**
Maximum speed: **50 mph**
Wheelbase: **7 ft 0 ins (2.13 m)**
Suspension: **front: semi-elliptic leaf-springs; back: ¾ elliptic leaf-springs**

list price of this car in fact saw a continuous drop, from £465 in 1920 to £375 in 1921, to £225 in October 1922.

The Cowley was made up also of components from different sources. Apart from the engine, supplied by Continental, then later produced in Coventry by Hotchkiss; the gearbox, axles, and magneto also came from the United States. In 1926 its appearance changed substantially: the characteristic 'bullnose' radiator disappeared, to be replaced by one a different shape, and brakes on all four wheels became the norm. The price went down to £142.

The success of the car can be amply illustrated by the production figures: over 55,000 in 1928, over 63,000 in 1929. The attempt at every level to rival Austin found concrete expression in the Minor, which appeared in 1929. From the technical point of view, the overhead camshaft and forced lubrication represented a double advance on the Seven (it was also more roomy and faster: around 55 mph). The sedan version was priced at £140, but the 2-seater cost barely £100. Morris realised, however, that the success of his two basic models so far (the Oxford and the Cowley) could not go on for ever.

Whilst starting off designs for a 'Baby', he still did not neglect American-style large cylinder capacity engines, for which he claimed the English market was ripe.

From 1923 onwards he experimented with a series of 6-cylinder engines, and in 1928 his first six went into production as the 2.4-litre Isis. With the Oxford, the Cowley, and now the Minor, William Morris had

offered the public what he maintained was the logical fruit of a sane, far-sighted industrial policy. After 1928 things changed. He now had to adapt to what the market demanded. His enlightened administrative abilities enabled him to ride the 1929 slump without great loss, and by the constantly balancing costs against profits, his company became the largest not only in Great Britain, but in the whole of Europe.

William Morris, Viscount Nuffield, died in 1963. In 1952 the merger of his firm with Austin had given rise to the British Motor Corporation. He did not live to see that other great industrial operation—the grouping into a single entity (1969) of Austin-Morris and Leyland, to create British Leyland, now one of the major car manufacturers in Britain.

Car: **Morris Cowley**
Year: **1920**
Engine: **4 cylinders in line**
Bore and stroke: **69 × 103.5 mm**
Cylinder capacity: **1550 cc**
Gears: **3 forward**
Brake horse power: **24**
Maximum speed: **55 mph**
Wheelbase: **8 ft 6 ins (2.59 m)**
Suspension: **front: semi-elliptic leaf-springs; back: semi-cantilever leaf-springs**

Car: **Morris Minor**
Year: **1929**
Engine: **4 cylinders in line**
Bore and stroke: **57 × 83 mm**
Cylinder capacity: **847 cc**
Gears: **3 forward**
Brake horse power: **20**
Maximum speed: **50 mph**
Wheelbase: **6 ft 6 ins (1.98 m)**
Suspension: **front and back: semi-elliptic leaf-springs**

The debate as to whether Montague Napier was the first to design a 6-cylinder in-line engine, or the engineers at the Dutch firm Spyker has gone on for many years. There is no doubt, however, that Spyker was the first to incorporate it in a car (1903), but, more than anyone else, Napier can take the credit for its spread in popularity.

The 40-50 was designed by A. J. Rowledge. The engine had overhead camshaft, removable head, and crankshaft mounted on 7 bearings, and developed 82 bhp at 2,000 revs. The engine block, head, and pistons were of aluminium alloy, a technique applied by Napier during the First World War to aircraft engines, including the famous 12-cylinder Lion, which was later used on land in attempts to break records. The

Car: **Napier 40-50**
Year: **1922**
Engine: **6 cylinders in line**
Bore and stroke: **102 × 127 mm**
Cylinder capacity: **6246 cc**
Gears: **4 forward**
Brake horse power: **82**
Maximum speed: **70 mph**
Wheelbase: **11 ft 5 ins (3.48 m)**
  or **12 ft 1 in (3.68 m)**
Suspension: **front: semi-elliptic leaf-springs;**
  back: cantilever leaf-springs

Napier 40-50, which after 1924 had brakes on all four wheels and balloon tires, was destined for an élite market, so no expense was spared in its construction.

The history of the company was, to begin with, closely linked with the name of Selwyn Francis Edge, one of the most outstanding figures in the English car world. A first-rate test-driver, Edge was also a good publicity man for Napier. The association of Edge with Napier ended in 1912.

In retrospect Perry can be seen to have traced the progress of many other English companies in the first twenty years of this century. It began in 1912 with a cyclecar powered by a twin-cylinder 875 cc engine. However it had previously earned a reputation as a steel producer, and as a bicycle manufacturer. Before 1912, as experiments, it had built a tricycle and a carriage, both motor-powered.

Only a few hundred (700, it is estimated) cars of the kind illustrated here were built—but this does not mean it was unsuccessful. Built together with a twin cylinder 875 cc model (with water-cooled engine in block, a 3-speed transmission, magneto ignition, and maximum speed of around 35 mph) it was considered one of the toughest cars of its time. Perry always proceeded with great caution

Car: **Perry**
Year: **1914**
Engine: **4 cylinders in line**
Bore and stroke: **69 × 120 mm**
Cylinder capacity: **1796 cc**
Gears: **3 forward**
Brake horse power: **28**
Maximum speed: **55 mph**
Wheelbase: **8 ft 6 ins (2.59 m)**
Suspension: **front and back: semi-elliptic leaf-springs**

in its car manufacture, and the decision to sell the production rights of this model to Bean Cars Ltd illustrates its fear that it could never compete with Austin and Morris. Its relationship with the 1919 Bean can be seen by the almost identical shape of the radiator. Bean had different ideas about the car's potential. It intended, after slight modifications and of course rechristening, to make 50,000 a year. These plans turned out to be somewhat over-ambitious, however.

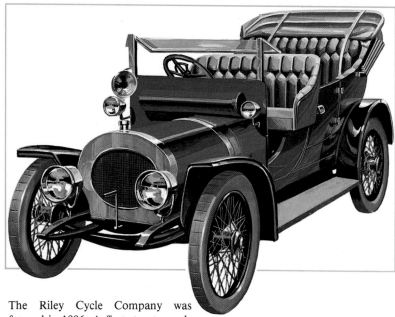

The Riley Cycle Company was formed in 1896. A first step towards the production of pedal 2-wheelers had been made in 1890, when the Riley brothers (Allan, Percy, and Victor) took over Bonnick and Company of Coventry, who also specialised in bicycles. The firm approached powered vehicles through tricycles, quadricycles, and motorcycles. In 1903 the 'cycle' was completed with the creation of the Riley Engine Company. The engine of the 10 HP was also 'home-made', from drawings by Percy Riley.

The 1909 10 HP had the engine at the front, whilst in the 9 HP, from which it was derived, it had been mounted in the middle. The 9 HP, introduced in 1905, was the company's first four wheeled car.

From 1912 production was concen-

Car: **Riley 10 HP**
Year: **1909**
Engine: **V-twin**
Bore and stroke **96 × 96 mm**
Cylinder capacity: **1388 cc**
Gears: **3 forward**
Brake horse power: **15**
Maximum speed: **38 mph**
Wheelbase: **8 ft 0 ins (2.43 m)**
Suspension: **front and back: semi-elliptic leaf-springs**

trated almost exclusively on cars, and this policy dictated important changes. The Riley Cycle Company turned to production of removable wheels, already patented in 1907, whilst a new company, Riley (Coventry) Company, was responsible for building cars. Mass-production, which the Riley brothers had foreseen and been in favour of, ironically spelt the end for their company. In 1969 it too became part of British Leyland.

Rolls-Royce 20 HP
Rolls-Royce Silver Ghost
Rolls-Royce Twenty
Rolls-Royce Phantom I
Rolls-Royce 20-25 HP

Henry Royce's first cars, 1904, consisted of one twin-cylinder and one 3-cylinder model, of which 16, and 6 respectively were built. The first 4-cylinder model was the 20 HP.

With this car Henry Royce, an electrical engineer who had started a small crane and winch manufacturing firm in Manchester, began to show his talents as a designer. The meticulousness with which he designed the various parts of the vehicle, and the precision he demanded from his workforce, was at the basis of his success—a success unique in the

history of cars. The 4-cylinder model was also the first to carry the famous trademark of almost superimposed Rs, which recorded the partnership of Henry Royce and Charles Stewart Rolls. The latter, an agent for foreign firms in England (Panhard, Mors, and Minerva), was not only a great sportsman and an intrepid aviator, but also a good businessman. For two years he refrained from associating his name with that of Royce, simply selling the cars. Only in 1906 did Rolls-Royce Ltd come about, with £60,000 capital.

Car: **Rolls-Royce 20 HP**
Year: **1905**
Engine: **4 cylinders in line**
Bore and stroke: **100 × 127 mm**
Cylinder capacity: **3994 cc**
Gears: **4 forward**
Brake horse power: **20**
Maximum speed: **50 mph**
Wheelbase: **8 ft 10 ins (2.69 m)**
  or **9 ft 6 ins (2.89 m)**
Suspension: **front: semi-elliptic leaf-springs;**
  back: semi-elliptic leaf springs with
  auxiliary transverse leaf-springs

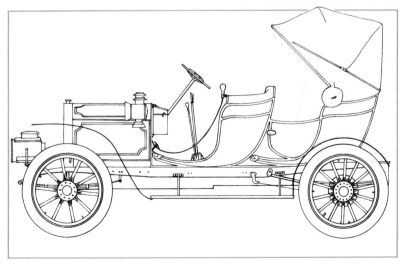

1906 was also important because a 20 HP driven by Charles Rolls won the Tourist Trophy; in 1905 Percy Northey, also driving a Rolls-Royce, had come second.

After the 20 HP Royce set to work on an 8-cylinder 3½ litre engine, arranged in a V, in two groups of four. Four of these were produced, together with the components for a fifth which was never assembled.

Royce's first real masterpiece was the Silver Ghost (1907-1925), first known as the 40-50 HP. This sealed the success of the 6-cylinder in-line engine. But apart from the forced lubrication, which was very rare at the time, and the luxury finish, there was nothing to distinguish it from other cars in the same category in that period. The admiration which the engine aroused (according to unofficial specifications, it developed 48 bhp at 1250 revs) was due not so much to its technical features as to its manner of construction. Royce furthermore never claimed to have invented, nor even to have applied anything really new in his engines.

The Ghost, with a maximum speed of just over 60 mph, underwent an important change in 1909, when the cylinder capacity of the engine was increased to 7428 cc by means of alteration of the piston stroke (from 114 to 120.7 mm). The suspension was also modified: ¾ elliptic leaf-springs at the rear in 1908, then cantilever leaf-springs; 1908 also saw the introduction of shock-absorbers (Hartford friction type).

6,173 Silver Ghosts were produced, in 19 distinct series. In 1911 a winged figure representing 'the spirit of ecstasy' appeared on the radiator cap.

The 20 was heralded by many, often inaccurate, rumours of its various features. With its relatively modest cylinder capacity, it was at once nicknamed the Baby Rolls. First produced in 1922, it continued in production until 1929, 2,940 being built altogether. During these years there were no great modifications, apart from the adoption of a 4-speed gearbox, which several clients had requested. Royce remained against having four speeds, because the great flexibility of his engines meant that the driver could go up any hill in third. In 1926 hydraulic shock-absorbers were added to the front suspension and in 1928 also to the back.

The Phantom I, which differed from the Ghost only in cylinder capacity and having overhead valves had a relatively short lifespan (1925-1929), and a total of 2,212 were built. It saw few modifications, and all there were were in the suspension (hydraulic shock-absorbers on the front wheels in 1926, and on the back in 1927).

1929 saw the Phantom II series, with various modifications from the Phantom I (different engine block and bearings); in many people's opinion it gave the model back its traditional flexibility and silence. Opinions were divided, however. Some described it as a truck, others compared its smooth running to a 'velvet carpet'. Progress had been made in that the mechanical components lasted longer, and it was less

Car: **Rolls-Royce Silver Ghost**
Year: **1907**
Engine: **6 cylinders in line**
Bore and stroke: **114 × 114 mm**
Cylinder capacity: **7035 cc**
Gears: **4 forward**
Brake horse power: **48**
Maximum speed: **63 mph**
Wheelbase: **11 ft 2 ins (3.40 m)**
Suspension: **front: semi-elliptic leaf-springs; back: semi-elliptic leaf-springs with auxiliary transverse leaf-springs**

expensive to run (though still very far from cheap: less than 15 miles to the gallon).

The chassis of the vehicle was quite new, with centralised lubrication system, semi-elliptic leaf-spring suspension, and final drive through bevel gears. The engine had the same cylinder capacity as the Phantom I, but the combustion chambers and manifolds were completely different, and both inlet and exhaust positioned on opposite sides of the engine. The

131

▲

Car: **Rolls-Royce 20**
Year: **1922**
Engine: **6 cylinders in line**
Bore and stroke: **76.2 × 114.3 mm**
Cylinder capacity: **3127 cc**
Gears: **3 forward**
Brake horse power: **50**
Maximum speed: **65 mph**
Wheelbase: **10 ft 9 ins (3.27 m)**
Suspension: **front and back: semi-elliptic leaf-springs integrated with friction shock-absorbers**

Car: **Rolls-Royce Phantom I**
Year: **1925**
Engine **6 cylinders in line**
Bore and stroke: **107.95 × 139.7 mm**
Cylinder capacity: **7688 cc**
Gears: **4 forward**
Brake horse power **95**
Maximum speed: **90 mph**
Wheelbase: **12 ft 0 ins (3.65 m)**
or **12 ft 6 ins (3.81 m)**
Suspension: **front: semi-elliptic leaf-springs; back: cantilever leaf-springs**

▼

maximum speed was around 80 mph. In 17 seconds it could go from about 10 mph to around 50. 1,767 Phantom IIs were built. A third Phantom series appeared in 1935, the main innovations being in the engine: no longer 6 cylinders in line, but 12 cylinders V, at an angle of 60°, overhead valves, and cylinder capacity of 7340 cc (bore and stroke: 82.5 × 114 mm), developing 165 bhp at 3000 revs. Other details included: aluminium head, dual ignition, and twin electric feed pump, 4-speed synchromesh transmission, and independent front suspension with coil springs; its speed was 85 mph. 710 of these were built.

The 20-25 in 1929 saw a return to a smaller cyinder capacity engine; this car was also designed to bring the Bentley back on the scene (Rolls-Royce had taken over Bentley in 1931). The Bentleys had the same

Car: **Rolls-Royce 20-25 HP**
Year: **1929**
Engine: **6 cylinders in line**
Bore and stroke: **82.55 × 114.3 mm**
Cylinder capacity: **3670 cc**
Gears: **4 forward**
Brake horse power: **62**
Maximum speed: **68 mph**
Wheelbase: **11 ft 0 ins (3.35 m)**
Suspension: **front and back: semi-elliptic leaf-springs**

engine as the 20-25 HP, although overall they were more sporting cars. A total of 3,827 20-25 HPs were built, as against 1,191 Bentley 3½ litres. In 1936 the 20-25 HP became 25-30 HP (engine enlarged to 4257 cc), and another 1,201 were added to the 3,827 of the previous model. The Bentley became 4¼ litre, and 1,241 were made.

Henry Royce died on April 22, 1933, and thereafter, as an expression of respect, the two Rs of the trademark became black.

The Twelve is one of the most interesting of the cars made in the early days of Rover's long lifespan, in as much as it consolidated the good name the company had already made for itself. On the technical level, production at Rover was given a boost by the arrival of a staff of designers headed by Owen Clegg from Wolseley. It is to them that the Twelve owed its existence. It had single-block engine with L-head, and was one of the first to feature a dip-stick for measuring the level of the oil. Its success can be gauged by the fact that 1,600 cars had been produced just one year after its appearance on the market. In 1914 it was Rover's only model, and it continued in production up until 1924, though under the name Fourteen. Later the Twelve also inspired the 16 HP—further proof of

Car: **Rover 12**
Year: **1912**
Engine: **4 cylinders in line**
Bore and stroke: **75 × 130 mm**
Cylinder capacity: **2297 cc**
Gears: **3 forward**
Brake horsepower: **22**
Maximum speed: **45 mph**
Wheelbase: **9 ft 2 ins (2.79 m)**
Suspension: **front and back: semi-elliptic leaf-springs**

its soundness of design.

Known first of all as bicycle manufacturers, then for their cars with single-cylinder water-cooled 1300 cc engines, Rover is one of the few car firms founded before the turn of the century still in existence in England. In 1906 it drew public attention to itself by the London-Istanbul rally, in which R. K. Jefferson drove a single-cylinder 1300 cc model; and again after the war, when it entered a turbine car at Le Mans two years running.

In 1876 George Singer began making bicycles and then became interested in cars in 1901.

In his first cars he used various engines: Edwin Perks's Auto Wheel, the Lea-Francis, and the White and Poppe. In 1912 Singer built its own engine, with 4 cylinders and thermo-siphon cooling, and the car in which it was incorporated was a great success thanks to its robustness and graceful lines. In 1913 an electrical system was added. It had a maximum speed of around 40 mph, but, with lighter bodywork and a few suitable modifications, it broke the Light Car circuit record at Brooklands, averaging over 70 mph. It also distinguished itself in the Alpine Trial. The 10 HP was supplied for army use during the First World War, and this enabled Singer, after the armistice, to resume

Car: **Singer 10 HP**
Year **1912**
Engine: **4 cylinders in line**
Bore and stroke: **63 × 88 mm**
Cylinder capacity: **1096 cc**
Gears: **3 forward**
Brake horse power: **15**
Maximum speed: **40 mph**
Wheelbase: **7 ft 6 ins (2.28 m)**
Suspension: **front and back: semi-elliptic leaf-springs**

production immediately, introducing numerous modifications as it went along (rear-mounted fuel tank, adoption of the feed pump, ¼ elliptic suspension, gearbox in the middle, 6-cylinder engine with side valves, then with overhead valves, plate clutch, and front brakes).

135

This firm was founded in 1903 in Coventry by R. W. Maudslay, and its first few years of activity produced a considerable number of models. These all had many components in common, and were, therefore, interchangeable and standardized. Hence the name Standard.

In 1913 Maudslay produced the 9.5 HP: the engine in this had side valves, with high-tension magneto ignition, worm drive, and removable wheels. This was a 2-seater known as the Rhyl with spare wheel, top, and windshield all included in the price of £185. The price went up £10 immediately the orders started coming in, because the standard accessories were too generous. The Rhyl's cheap running costs ensured its success, in competitions based on fuel consumption as well as on the market. In 1915

Car: **Standard 9.5 HP**
Year: **1913**
Engine: **4 cylinders in line**
Bore and stroke: **62 × 90 mm**
Cylinder capacity: **1087 cc**
Gears: **3 forward**
Brake horse power: —
Maximum speed: —
Wheelbase: **7 ft 6 ins (2.28 m)**
Suspension: **front and back: semi-elliptic leaf-springs**

50 were being built a week, which was a large number for the times. The subsequent models were also successful, and in 1945 Standard took over Triumph, and from then on was known as Standard-Triumph. However, in 1961, unable to compete with the big groups, it was absorbed into Leyland, which in 1963 completely did away with the models Standard had bequeathed them.

Stellite was a short-lived company, with modest production under the shadow of Wolseley. It specialised in cheap cars, which it began making in 1913: 4-cylinder engines with wooden chassis, 2- (then 3-) speed gearbox, cone clutch, magneto ignition, shaft transmission, and removable wheels. They were 2-seaters, with top and windshield, plus acetylene lights. The model illustrated here was introduced in 1913, and stayed in production until 1915. In 1914 it cost £158. It was very like the 1922 Wolseley, which is to be explained by the fact that the two firms co-operated closely together. The Stellite was made by one of Vickers's subsidiaries, as Wolseley was not able to satisfactorily fulfil even its own orders. The Wolseley that replaced the Stellite had a slightly greater cylinder capacity

Car: **Stellite**
Year: **1914**
Engine: **4 cylinders in line**
Bore and stroke: **62 × 89 mm**
Cylinder capacity: **1075 cc**
Gears: **3 forward**
Brake horse power: **—**
Maximum speed: **—**
Wheelbase: **8 ft 0 ins (2.44 m)**
Suspension: **front and back: semi-elliptic leaf-springs**

(bore and stroke: 65 × 95 mm), and a considerable number were built. A 2-seater sports version gave birth to a single-seater called a Moth (because of the quiet noise of the engine) which had a brief moment of glory. One of its drivers was Tony Vandervell, who many years later was to come up with the Vanwall, the British single-seater that toppled Italian Formula 1 supremacy.

Sunbeam 12-16 HP
Sunbeam 20 HP

The problem of just how useful racing is to technical progress has provoked much debate even as far back as 1913. Louis Coatalen, designer of the 12-16 HP, was convinced that competitions stimulated progress. Coatalen, however, owed his reputation to racing, thanks to the cars he designed and developed. The 12-16 HP was a good example of how racing necessitated modifications. In 1911, when it appeared on the market, it had a 2412 cc engine (bore and stroke of 80×120 mm), but for the *Coupe de l'Auto* in 1912 Coatalen adapted several engines, keeping the bore the same, but increasing the piston stroke to 150 mm for a total cylinder capacity of 3016 cc. Thereafter all cars in the 12-16 series incorporated this engine. Later, still because of competitions, the stroke was reduced again, to bring the car within the 3000 cc class. 1,700 vehicles were built by the company in 1913.

The 1925 Sunbeam marked the beginning of the end for the firm, precisely because it was too involved with racing—although the 20 HP was positive proof of the validity of the experiments carried out on the circuit. Yet while the racing engine developed almost 90 bhp, guaranteeing a maximum speed of around 90 mph (the car could do around 50 mph in second, and over 70 mph in third), the touring version could manage barely 55 bhp at 3,600 revs, a rather low amount in relation to the cylinder capacity even for those days. Record-breaking not just on the race-track, this version played an important part in the firm's history; but it was these sporting interests that in the end brought about the company's down-

fall. In 1920, after various kinds of difficulties, it merged with Clement-Talbot, and Darracq, and the consortium became known as S.T.D. (Sunbeam, Talbot, Darracq). In 1923 Coatalen was replaced by an Italian, Vincenzo Bertarione, who designed an engine with double overhead camshaft and spherical main bearings. The technical similarities between this and Fiat's current racing model (Bertarione had come from Fiat) prompted the suspicion that it had been taken straight from the Italian 804-404, which had been designed for the new formula imposed in 1922. In 1923 Segrave won the French Grand Prix in a car designed by Bertarione.

In 1935 S.T.D. was absorbed into Rootes, and Sunbeam ceased production. In 1938 the name was revived in a new firm created by Rootes called

Car: **Sunbeam 20 HP**
Year **1930**
Engine: **6 cylinders in line**
Bore and stroke: **75 × 110 mm**
Cylinder capacity: **2992 cc**
Gears: **4 forward**
Brake horse power: **55**
Maximum speed: **76 mph**
Wheelbase: **10 ft 4½ ins (3.16 m)**
Suspension: **front and back: semi-elliptic leaf springs**

Car: **Sunbeam 12-16 HP**
Year: **1914**
Engine: **4 cylinders in line**
Bore and stroke: **80 × 150 mm**
Cylinder capacity: **3016 cc**
Gears: **4 forward**
Brake horse power: **25**
Maximum speed: **42 mph**
Wheelbase: **10 ft 4½ ins (3.16 m)**
Suspension: **front and back: semi-elliptic leaf-springs**

Sunbeam-Talbot Ltd. Later Rootes cars with particularly high performance were given the name Sunbeam. In 1975 Chrysler, which had bought Rootes, abolished the name, only reinstating it in 1977.

This vehicle's curious and highly original bodywork is the result of the fenders, which continue uninterruptedly right along the whole length of the car. They were made of wood, as were the box-shaped chassis with weatherproofed fibreboard panels with plate reinforcements. The fenders also acted as supports. Another interesting feature of the Tamplin was the independent front suspension, which at the beginning of the 1920s was far from common.

The car's motorcycle origins are amply demonstrated by the lack of starter (until 1923) and reverse gear. The vehicle was set in motion by means of a pedal operated from the driving seat. The two seats were almost in tandem, and the passenger could stretch out his legs beside the driver. The JAP engine (mounted at

Car: **Tamplin**
Year: **1920**
Engine: **V-twin**
Bore and stroke: **85 × 85 mm**
Cylinder capacity: **900 cc**
Gears: **3 forward**
Brake horse power: **10**
Maximum speed: **42 mph**
Wheelbase: **7 ft 0 ins (2.13 m)**
Suspension: front: **independent with closed helical springs contained in tubes;** back: **¼ elliptic leaf-springs**

the front) and Sturmey-Archer gearbox also derived from the motorcycle. The wheel transmission operated by means of cables and pulleys, and as these were not covered, bad weather posed certain problems. There was only one pedal to work both clutch and brake, which acted on the rear wheel rim. The handbrake acted on the pulley of the gear-shaft. There was no electrical system. The car had acetylene lights and magneto ignition.

Triumph's involvement with cars stems from 1923, but it had been producing bicycles since 1890, the year the Triumph Cycle Company was founded in Coventry. The company later also produced motorbikes and these made it world famous.

The first 4-wheeler to raise Triumph to the same level of fame in cars as it had won in motorcycling was the 4-cylinder Super 7 of 1927 (it was presented at the London Motor Show of that year). Its very small engine size suggested that the Coventry firm intended it to rival the Austin Seven, as the time was ripe for the establishment of a cheap, light, 4-seater utility car. About 15,000 Super 7s were produced between 1927 and 1934. Two noteworthy features of the Super 7 were the three main bearings and its hydraulic brakes. However, it was

Car: **Triumph Super 7**
Year: **1928**
Engine: **4 cylinders in line**
Bore and stoke: **56.5 × 83 mm**
Cylinder capacity: **832 cc**
Gears: **3 forward**
Brake horse power: **20**
Maximum speed: **67 mph**
Wheelbase: **6 ft 9 ins (2.05 m)**
Suspension: **front and back: semi-elliptic leaf-springs**

never able to rival the Austin Seven's domination of its class of engine size, partly because of the greater industrial power wielded by Austin. A sports version of the Super 7 was also produced, with a shortened stroke (74.5 mm) and reduced engine capacity.

In 1961 Triumph became part of Leyland, which in turn became British Leyland in 1969.

The most original feature of this small car was its monobloc, 2-stroke, 4-cylinder engine. It was designed by Leslie Hounsfield and at least 15,000 were built by Leyland. Three pre-production cars were ready in 1913 and a further six were ready in 1921. The design was entrusted to Leyland for production and this began properly in 1923, but in 1928 Trojan took the design back.

Another of its original features was the positioning of the engine, which was mounted horizontally beneath the front seats. Initially Hounsfield thought of having it vertically between the two seats, yet another example of the imagination and boldness of the early motor engineers. The PB's 4-cylinder engine was also unusually flexible, delivering its 11 bhp at anywhere between 450 and

Car: **Trojan PB**
Year: **1923**
Engine: **horizontally-mounted 4 cylinder, two stroke**
Bore and stroke: **63.5 × 120.7 mm**
Cylinder capacity: **1523 cc**
Gears: **2 forward**
Brake horse power: **11**
Maximum speed: **34 mph**
Wheelbase: **7 ft 11½ ins (2.32 m)**
Suspension: **front and back: cantilever leaf-springs**

1,200 rpm and this enabled a gearbox with just two speeds to be fitted. The engine was particularly long lasting as it had only seven moving parts.

Aiming principally for cheapness, Hounsfield maintained that the car he had designed could do without pneumatic tires. This would be a significant saving of £4. To this end the PB had disc wheels. The excellent suspension gave quite a comfortable ride. It had neither a starter nor a crank; instead it was started by pulling a lever from the driver's seat.

This car took its name from the German Prince Henry Trials, in which it put up a good performance in 1910. This led to a series sports and also touring cars. The Prince Henry gave rise, in 1913, to another famous model, the 30/98; this had a larger engine with a capacity of 4525 cc. The Prince Henry was designed by Laurence Pomeroy, one of the most talented English designers of the time, and it was regarded as one of the best sports cars. Its engine had side valves, high tension magneto ignition, water cooling and it developed 75 bhp at 2,500 revs. It had a maximum speed of 75 mph. Neither its road holding nor its braking system (transmission and rear wheels) could claim to be the car's strong points. This was due to its high weight and relatively short wheelbase. The 30/98 was the logical

Car: **Vauxhall Prince Henry**
Year: **1914**
Engine: **4 cylinders in line**
Bore and stroke: **95 × 140 mm**
Cylinder capacity **3969 cc**
Gears: **4 forward**
Brake horse power: **75**
Maximum speed: **75 mph**
Wheelbase: **10 ft 0 in (3.04 m)**
Suspension: **front and back: semi-elliptic leaf-springs**

development of the Prince Henry; its engine developed about 100 bhp and the maximum speed rose to 90 mph.

Vauxhall was taken over by General Motors in 1925 and it ceased to be a make that specialised in sports cars. The policy of its new owners, the largest motor group in the world, required it to specialise in quite the opposite direction. This was the production of family cars and trucks (Bedford) and these are now the firm's main business.

143

Wolseley 16/20 HP
Wolseley 10 HP

Amongst the English makes of the past, Wolseley is one of the few that lasted until 1975. It was founded by Frederick York Wolseley who moved on to cars from sheep shearing machines in 1895. Design was entrusted to Herbert Austin who was later to become, in his turn, one of the great men of English motoring. Production began with engined tricycles along the lines of those then in fashion in France. In 1899 a 4-wheeler with a single-cylinder, front mounted engine was introduced. In 1901 Wolseley underwent its first substantial internal change when management of the factory passed to the Vickers brothers. Wolseley, under the direction of Herbert Austin, became intensely involved in racing.

The 16/20 appeared in a period of transition and changes. Herbert Austin had left in 1905 and had been replaced by John Davenport Siddeley (for a time the latter's name appeared with Wolseley's on the radiator), but in 1909 Siddeley left as well, having bought control of Deasy.

The departure of two engineers as talented as Herbert Austin and John Davenport Siddeley did not alter the course of the Birmingham firm's production. It continued to be known for the sturdiness of the cars which it built. If anything it became more conventional, though it retained a great variety of models with 4- and 6-cylinder engines with high tension magneto ignition and shaft drive. The 16/20 was produced from 1910 until 1915 and it was the best selling car in its category. The 10 HP of 1922 derived from the Stellite and became, in its turn, highly popular in Great Britain. Its engine had an overhead camshaft and overhead valves and it was suitable, with modifications for use as a racing engine. It did in fact

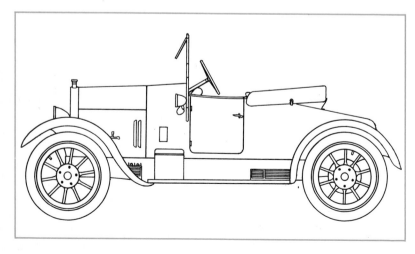

power single- and 2-seaters during the golden era of the Brooklands circuit. The top speed of the standard model exceeded 43 mph and in the sports versions it was about 65-68 mph.

The 10 HP was the first new car from Wolseley after the war and it gave rise to a logical progression of models, both technically and commercially. In the meantime the market was feeling the ever increasing impact of Austin and Morris, whose production was based on modern methods, as exemplified by the United States. In 1925 Wolseley declared itself bankrupt and it was absorbed by Morris. With the creation of the British Motor Corporation (a merger of Austin and Morris) and of British Leyland, Wolseley lost its identity and in 1975 the name was finally dropped. The large number of makes within British Ley-

Car: **Wolseley 16/20 HP**
Year: **1911**
Engine: **4 cylinders in line**
Bore and stroke: **90 × 121 mm**
Cylinder capacity: **3080 cc**
Gears: **4 forward**
Brake horse power: **20**
Maiximum speed: **38 mph**
Wheelbase: **10 ft 9 in (3.27 m)**
Suspension: **front: semi-elliptic leaf-springs; rear: ¾ elliptic leaf-springs**

Car: **Wolseley 10HP**
Year: **1922**
Engine: **4 cylinders in line**
Bore and stroke: **65 × 95 mm**
Capacity: **1260 cc**
Gears: **3 forward**
Brake horse power: **15**
Maximum speed: **43 mph**
Wheelbase: **8 ft 3 ins (2.51 m)**
Suspension: **front and rear: semi-elliptic leaf-springs**

land was one of the reasons for Wolseley being sacrificed. In any case, its role in recent years had been reduced to reworking of what were basically Austin and Morris models.

LORRAINE
10. RUE PERGOLÈSE. PARIS

France

France is regarded as the cradle of the car, because it produced the first self-propelled vehicle (Cugnot's Fardier), and the first manufacturers of cars on an industrial scale. Prominent amongst these were Panhard & Levasor who made an agreement in 1889 with Gottlieb Daimler for the French rights to his engine, and in 1891 put their first car on the road.

Count De Dion and an engineer, Georges Bouton, founded a company for the production of cars and in 1894 the company brought out a gasoline engine, an air-cooled, single-cylinder with a maximum power of ½ bhp. More than fifty car producers bought manufacturing rights to De Dion-Bouton engines.

In the meantime, Louis Renault, together with his brothers Marcel and Fernand, founded a firm that with time would become one of the largest car manufacturers in the world. Initially, the firm produced small-engined cars, but the three brothers quickly saw that the way to make a name for themselves abroad was to go into racing. They abandoned De Dion and Aster engines and successfully ventured into producing their own engines: a 1728 cc twin-cylinder and 3800 cc 4-cylinder. The latter powered the car with which Marcel Renault won the 1902 Paris-Vienna race.

In 1908 Fernand retired and the company changed its name to Société Anonyme des Usines Renault. By then it was a manufacturer of international standing, but the Second World War dealt it a serious blow. Renault passed entirely into the hands of the State and it became Regie Nationale des Usines Renault. Its recovery began with the 4 CV, and continued with a series of front-wheel-drive models. Peugeot's progress was very similar in small, gradual stages.

Possibly the most enterprising, imaginative and commercially gifted figure in the French car world was André Citroën. He was the first manufacturer to realize that the car was first and foremost a means of transport and his spartan cars were well received by the public.

Ettore Bugatti was a manufacturer for whom the car was synonymous with perfection, elegance and refinement. He has gained his place in history through his pearls of engineering, such as the legendary Royale.

Gabriel Voisin, on the other hand, was an innovator, delighting in this innovating ability, irrespective of the welcome that the public gave his machines.

At the end of the nineteenth century until 1930 Berliet was best known as a French car maker, but is nowadays known as a heavy vehicle manufacturer. Unlike many other manufacturers at that time, Berliet used to make his own engines rather than buy the finished product from one of the many specialist firms.

The 16 CV bore some resemblance to the Dodge, both in appearance and in technical features (a side valve engine, the lubrication system, the 3-speed transmission, the 12-volt electrical system, the rear cantilever leaf-spring suspension, the fixed wheel discs and the detachable rims). When it appeared in 1921, the 16 CV cost 9,500 francs.

Marcius Berliet, the founder, had ambitious aims. His experience as a military supplier during the First

Car: **Berliet VL 16 CV**
Year: **1921**
Engine: **4 cylinders in line**
Bore and stroke: **90 × 130 mm**
Cylinder capacity: **3308 cc**
Gearbox: **3 forward**
Brake horse power: **30**
Maximum speed: **52 mph**
Wheelbase: **10 ft 3 in (3.07 m)**
Suspension: **front: semi-elliptic leaf-springs; rear: cantilever leaf-springs**

World War, when he had succeeded in delivering 40 trucks and 40,000 bullets a day to the army, encouraged him to try to produce 100 cars a day.

A stream of models followed until 1939, the year in which a 2-litre car the Dauphine, with independent front suspension and synchromesh transmission entered production. After 1945 Berliet took over Rochet-Schneider and concentrated exclusively on trucks. In 1964 it was absorbed by Citroën-Michelin and, ultimately, by Renault.

Brasier Type VL—1908

The Brasier fame rests mainly on its renowned sporting feats which included two victories (1904 and 1905) in the celebrated Gordon Bennett Cup. At that time its cars bore the name of Richard Brasier, but in 1905 Georges Richard left the firm to found Unic.

The Gordon-Bennett of 1904 was won by Théry driving a 4-cylinder 9869 cc Richard Brasier with a maximum power of 80 bhp at an average speed of 54.214 mph. Théry also won in 1905 at an average of 48.735 mph. The 1905 Richard Brasier was even more powerful than the previous year's car (96 bhp at 1,200 revs) due to an increase in the engine's capacity (11259 cc). The Brasier Type VL was the last twin-cylinder to be built by the firm and remained in production until 1908. However, from 1905, with the

Car: **Brasier Type VL**
Year: **1908**
Engine: **vertical in line twin-cylinder**
Bore and stroke: **90 × 120 mm**
Cylinder capacity: **1526 cc**
Gearbox: **3 forward**
Brake horse power: —
Maximum speed: —
Wheelbase: —
Suspension: **front: semi-elliptic leaf-springs; rear: ¼ elliptic leaf-springs**

departure of Richard, the company's name was reduced to Brasier. It was managed by Henry Brasier.

In 1930 the company was overcome by the economic crisis. Between 1905 and 1930 Brasier did not completely give up racing, but apart from 4th, 7th and 9th place in the 1906 French G.P. it did not achieve any great success. Brasier models were also produced in Italy as Fides. They built three models (small, medium and large capacities), but these were unsuccessful.

Bugatti 5 Litres Roland Garros 'Black Bess'
Bugatti 50 T
Bugatti 57 S
Bugatti 41 Royale

The name Ettore Bugatti is immortal in motoring history. He had an extraordinary personality and his creations were highly original. He had a unique understanding of how to infuse art into a product that until then had lacked almost any artistic merit, expressing it itself only in the brute force of its engine. Ettore Bugatti's motto was, *'Un'opera tecnica non può essere perfetta se non è perfetta dal punto di vista estetico'*. (A piece of engineering cannot be perfect if it is not perfect from the aesthetic viewpoint.)

He was born in Milan on September 15, 1881 and died in the American hospital at Neuilly near Paris on August 21, 1947. He retained his Italian citizenship despite spending a large part of his life at Molsheim in Alsace where the Bugatti factory was situated. The make itself has, on the other hand, always been regarded as French although Molshiem was in fact German territory until 1918. In 1898 at the age of 18 he became a regular apprentice with Prinetti & Stucchi, after having designed a tricycle for them in 1895. In 1900, under the patronage of Count Gulinelli, he designed and built a proper 4-wheeler. This was unveiled at the first international exhibition of cars at Milan winning the prize offered by the city council for the best Italian design for a car. This car excited the interest of

Car: **Bugatti 5 Litres Roland Garros 'Black Bess'**
Year: **1913**
Engine: **4 cylinders in line**
Bore and stroke: **100 × 160 mm**
Cylinder capacity: **5027 cc**
Gearbox: **4 forward**
Brake horse power: **100**
Maximum speed: **90 mph**
Wheelbase: **8 ft 4 ins (2.84 m)**
Suspension: **front: semi-elliptic leaf-springs; rear: upside down semi-cantilever leaf-springs**

the French firm De Dietrich who wanted to buy it from Ettore Bugatti as well as offering him a job as their technical director. Bugatti accepted and he remained with De Dietrich until 1904. He collaborated briefly with Mathis and then he sold another of his designs to Deutz of Cologne of which he was also technical director.

At the age of 28, with the help of the Alsatian banker de Vizcaya (two of whose sons were later to become Bugatti drivers), Ettore founded his own factory at Molsheim near Strasbourg. The first cars to emerge from his factory were the 13, the 15 and the 17. These all had 4-cylinder 1327 cc engines and the differences between them were confined to the wheelbase. The mono-bloc engine had a single overhead camshaft, two valves per cylinder, magneto ignition, an oil

Car: **Bugatti 50 T**
Year: **1932**
Engine: **8 cylinders in line**
Bore and stroke: **86 × 107 mm**
Cylinder capacity: **4972 cc**
Gearbox: **3 forward**
Brake horse power: **200**
Maximum speed: **105 mph**
Wheelbase: **10 ft 2 ins (3.10 m)**
Suspension: **front: semi-elliptic leaf-springs;**
   rear: upside down ¼ elliptic leaf-springs

bathed (wet) multi-plate clutch, a 4-speed transmission and the hand brake acted on the rear wheels. The total production of the type 13 and its various derivatives up to the modified type Brescia was 2,400-2,500 cars, of which about 2,000 had 16 valves.

Between 1912 and 1913 five or six chassis were prepared at Molsheim intended for use on racing cars. These were the first large engined cars. The engine had a capacity of 5027 cc, three main bearings and three valves per cylinder (two inlet and one exhaust), a pattern that was to become standard on Bugatti products. The overhead camshaft was driven by a vertical shaft and this also drove the magneto and the water pump. The wheelbase of the chassis was 8 feet 4 inches (2.84 m) and its width (track) was 4 feet 1 inch (1.24 m). It had chain drive, a method that had by then been discarded by virtually every manufacturer and which suggests that Ettore Bugatti had designed this car much earlier. The brake pedal acted on the transmission and the hand brake acted on the rear drums. Of particular interest was the 5-litre pear-shaped radiator which it adopted a year in advance of the small capacity machines. One of these machines was given the nickname 'Black Bess'. Officially it was called Roland Garros after a French aviator who had ordered a machine with a 5000 cc engine from Bugatti.

The 50 T was modelled on the 46 and had the same chassis but with a shorter wheelbase, 10 feet 2 inches (3.10 m) as against 11 feet 6 inches (3.50 m). Sixty-five of them were built between 1930 and 1934, the majority of which had short chassis. It differed from the 46 only in the suspension and a few other details. The 50 did not enjoy much racing success and it seems that it was heavily criticised by its drivers for its poor road holding. It was not a successful model and stands as one of Bugatti's few failures. The type 57 appeared at the Paris Motor Show of 1933 and deliveries to customers began in 1934. It also had a 'personal' history, being to a great extent designed by Jean Bugatti, Ettore's son who died whilst testing a Type 57 G that was to race in the La Baule G.P. The engine had twin overhead camshafts and a dry single plate clutch. Below the semi-elliptic leaf-spring front suspension there was a flexible mounting to prevent the steering being jolted. Contrary to Jean's advice it had right hand drive.

In 1936, after 300 units had already been produced, the Type 57's engine was mounted on four rubber supports, the single body carburetor was replaced by a double body carburetor, hydraulic brakes were fitted (Lockheed) and the De Ram shock absorbers were replaced by Allinquant telescopic shock absorbers. The most important modification was the addition of a supercharger. Maximum power rose from 130 bhp at 4,500 revs to 160 bhp at 5,000 revs and the maximum speed increased from 90-93 mph to 102-106 mph. A total of 750 57s were produced.

The design of the Royale was absolutely unique and the actual number that were built still remains a mystery. Some chassis have had more than one body which has added to the uncertainty. The makers of the car knew it by its workshop designation, the Type 41, and it was named the Royale by Ettore Bugatti as he intended that its clientele would be royalty.

An English journalist, W. F. Bradley was a friend of Bugatti and knew a great deal about the career of the Royale. Bradley states that the name Royale comes from the fact that the reigning King of Spain, Alfonso XIII, wished to buy the first produc-

tion model. He had seen it at the San Sebastian G.P. at which Ettore Bugatti drove the prototype. Unfortunately, Alfonso XIII was deposed before the machine was finished. It is known that other monarchs such as the Kings of Albania and Romania visited Bugatti in order to buy the Royale, but again neither actually purchased the car. As Clifford Penn wittily wrote in 'Autocar', the Type 41 was one of the Queens of cars but it was never the car of a king. Andre Citroën was another potential customer, but all names of purchasers were kept as secret as possible.

Maurice Smith, editor of 'Autocar' visited the Molsheim factory and was able to ascertain that there were six Royales, including the prototype, in production. Paul Kestler, another Bugatti historian believes that there

Car: **Bugatti 57 S**
Year: **1936**
Engine: **8 cylinders in line**
Bore and stroke: **72 × 100 mm**
Cylinder capacity: **3257 cc**
Gearbox: **4 forward**
Brake horse power: **180**
Maximum speed: **110 mph**
Wheelbase: **9 ft 9½ ins (2.98 m)**
Suspension: **front: semi-elliptic leaf-springs;
  rear: upside down ¼ elliptic leaf-springs
  and hydraulic shock-absorbers**

are seven Royales because the six known cars all had a wheelbase of 15 feet (4.57 m), whereas the prototype had a wheelbase of 14 feet (4.27 m). Ettore Bugatti had an accident in one Royale, the four window Weymann, whilst travelling from Strasbourg to Paris. He hit a tree but did not receive any serious injuries. There is speculation as to whether the chassis was rebuilt and the car was transformed into a coupé Napoleon to a design of Jean Bugatti, or whether it was

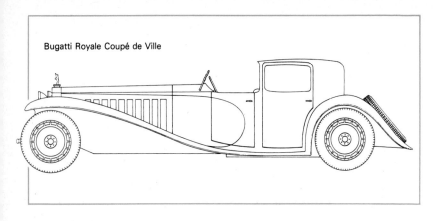

Bugatti Royale Coupé de Ville

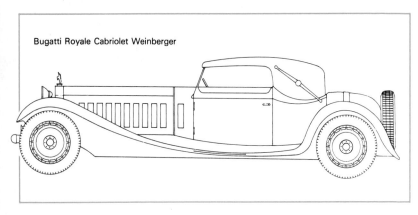

Bugatti Royale Cabriolet Weinberger

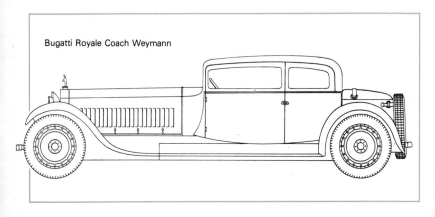

Bugatti Royale Coach Weymann

destroyed in the accident. Because the rebuilt car also had a wheelbase of 15 feet (4.57 m), Kestler deduces that the prototype that was involved in the accident was completely destroyed.

The first Royale was sold in 1932 to the French textile manufacturer Armand Esders. The body, a 2-seater roadster was personally designed by Jean Bugatti. It was later given a new body (coupé de ville). The second was sold, also in 1932, to the German gynecologist Joseph Fuchs as a 2-door cabriolet by the car body designer Ludwig Weinberger in Bavaria. The third was delivered to the English landowner W. Foster in 1933 who had it built as a 7-seater limousine by Park Ward of London. The three remaining Royales stayed with the Bugatti family. This included the prototype which had several dif-

Car: **Bugatti 41 Royale**
Year: **1926-1933**
Engine: **8 cylinders in line**
Bore and stroke: **125 × 130 mm**
Cylinder capacity: **12760 cc**
Gearbox: **3 forward**
Brake horse power: **300**
Maximum speed: **120 mph**
Wheelbase: **14 ft 2 ins (4.31 m)**
Suspension: **front: semi-elliptic leaf-springs; rear: ¼ elliptic leaf-springs, 2 cantilever leaf-springs and hydraulic shock absorbers**

ferent bodies: a torpedo inspired by a Packard of the time; a 2-door sedan by the Paris designer Kellner, which was displayed at the London Motor Show of 1932 and subsequently passed to Ettore's daughter Ebé Bugatti; a touring sedan with a partition which was built in the factory; and a sedan de ville or coupé Napoleon which is its present form. All six Royales have survived, two of which are in France and four are in the U.S.A., one Royale being on display

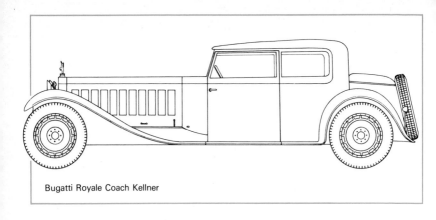

Bugatti Royale Coach Kellner

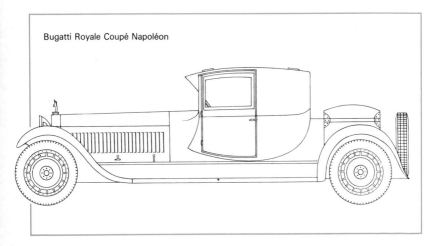

Bugatti Royale Coupé Napoléon

in the Ford Museum.

The Royale is still one of the longest cars that has ever been built with a length of 19 feet 8 inches (5.99 m). In the final version it was powered by a 12760 cc 8-cylinder in line engine but the prototype had an even larger capacity (14726 cc). Its maximum power was 300 bhp at 2,000 revs. The weight varied, depending on the type of body, between 4,970 pounds (2,250 kg) and 6,620 pounds (3,000 kg). The chassis cost F500,000 (the equivalent of £5,250 at that time) whilst a Rolls-Royce Phantom with body cost £2,000.

Ettore Bugatti was so convinced of the Royale's mechanical perfection that he guaranteed it for life provided that it remained in the hands of the owner. Its claimed maximum speed was 124 mph.

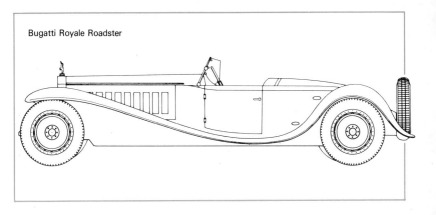

Bugatti Royale Roadster

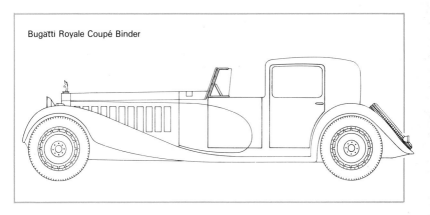

Bugatti Royale Coupé Binder

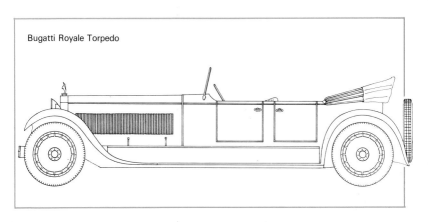

Bugatti Royale Torpedo

157

Chenard-Walcker has an important place in the history of racing through its victory with Lagache and Leonard in the first Le Mans 24 Hour race in 1923 though the firm did not concentrate solely on racing. It was founded in 1898 at Asnières and it latter moved to Gennevilliers taking the name of Société Anonyme des Anciens Etablissements Chenard & Walcker. The Chenard-Walcker car pictured here won its class in the 1925 Le Mans 24 Hour. In 1926 it was awarded the Coupe Boillot at Boulogne and its class in the Spanish G.P. of the same year. A feature of this car was its unattractive but functional tank shaped body which brought back memories of similar Bugatti and Voisin bodies. The tank's 4-cylinder engine had overhead valves, only two main bearings and it

Car: **Chenard-Walcker**
Year: **1926**
Engine: **4 cylinders in line**
Bore and stroke: **66 × 80 mm**
Cylinder capacity: **1095 cc**
Gears: **4 forward**
Brake horse power: —
Maximum speed: **93 mph**
Wheelbase: —
Suspension: **front and rear: semi-elliptic leaf-springs**

had oversized inlet valves. Some versions were also supercharged and this raised the maximum speed to more than 105 mph (more than 93 mph in a non-supercharged engine). This French firm gave up racing in 1927, returning to it ten years later in the 1937 Le Mans 24 Hour, but by then it had lost its individuality and its reputation of being unbeatable. Car production ceased in 1946 and in 1951 it was absorbed by Peugeot.

Citroën 10 HP Type A
Citroën 5 CV Type C
Citroën 7 A Traction Avant

The Citroën 10 HP Type A of 1919 was the first mass produced European car, and it was the first cheap car to be fully equipped (five tires with the spare one carried on the left side; an electrical system and starter and hood). It was also amongst the first to be fitted with left hand drive and disc wheels made of pressed sheet steel.

It was presented to the public on June 4, 1919 in the Champs Elysées show room of the manufacturer Fernand Charron which had been lent for the occasion to André Citroën. Deliveries began in July of that year at a lower price than similar models built by his competitors. Initial production was 30 units a day. Including utility versions a total of 28,400 were built.

The Citroën 10 HP Type A's maximum speed was 40 mph. The engine developed a maximum power of 18 bhp at 2,100 revs (maximum engine speed 2,400 revs). At 2,000 revs the *vitesse d'utilisation* (recommended speed) was 36.36 mph. It was also available in 4-seat three door torpedo, 3-seat torpedo, 3-seat coupé and sedan versions. The 4-seater torpedo weighed only 1,790 pounds (810 kg).

Citroën took a further step forward on its way to popularising the car and gaining the public's favour for its approach with the Type C of 1922. It developed 11 bhp at 2,100 revs and its

Car: **Citroën 10 HP Type A**
Year: **1919**
Engine: **4 cylinders in line**
Bore and stroke: **65 × 100 mm**
Cylinder capacity: **1327 cc**
Gearbox: **3 forward**
Brake horse power: **18**
Maximum speed: **42 mph**
Wheelbase: **9 ft 6 ins (2.89 m)**
Suspension: **front: inverted ¼ elliptic leaf-springs; rear: superimposed double elliptic leaf-springs**

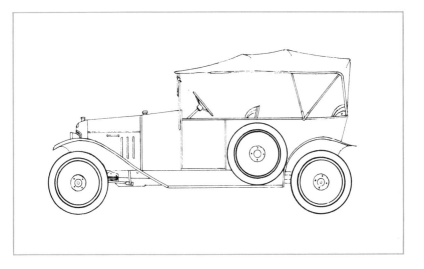

maximum speed was 38 mph. The torpedo weighed 1,300 pounds (590 kg).

Like Henry Ford, who for a while, offered the body of his famous Model T in a single colour (black), Citroën restricted it to yellow 'citron'. It is worth mentioning that from 1923 onwards Citroën made catalogues and price-lists for repair available to purchasers of the Type C with the obvious intention of *éviter toute surprise dans les factures* (to prevent any surprises in the bill). It was also possible to replace a part that was not working with a new or reconditioned part. This prevented the car from being off the road for a lengthy period.

In 1925 the Type C was given wrap around fenders and the spare wheel on the torpedo was moved from the left side to the back. In 1926

another important modification was made: the brake pedal now acted simultaneously on the differential gear and on the drums of the rear brakes. In May of the same year, though demand for it was continually increasing, production of the Type 5 was inexplicably stopped. By that date a total of 80,232 vehicles had been built.

Citroën's great novelty appeared in 1934. André Citroën's specifications

Car: **Citroën 7 A Traction Avant**
Year: **1934**
Engine: **4 cylinders in line**
Bore and stroke: **72 × 80 mm**
Cylinder capacity: **1303 cc**
Gearbox: **3 forward**
Brake horse power: **32**
Maximum speed: **62 mph**
Wheelbase: **9 ft 6 in (2.89 m)**
Suspension: **front: longitudinal torsion bars with friction shock absorbers; rear: transverse torsion bars with double action hydraulic shock absorbers**

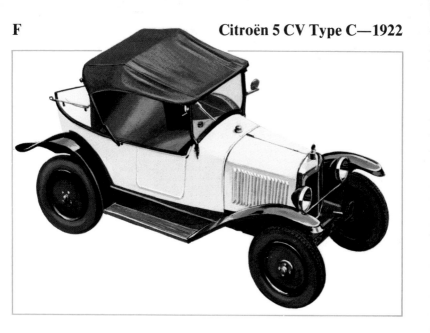

to his engineers were peremptory: the car was to be a light machine, revolutionary in concept, capable of reaching 62 mph and of carrying four people and economical with a fuel consumption of 28 miles per gallon. The two main features of the new car were front-wheel drive and its redesigned body. These innovations, particularly the front-wheel drive were not well received by the public and initially the 7 A was more criticised than praised. From then on all Citroëns have had front-wheel drive and because of this feature the 7 A, as the first in the line, and its followers simply bear the title 'traction'. The sheet (metal) monocoque body was very low, making it easy to get into and the inside was very roomy. It was, however, poorly received because there was no running board. The 7

Car: **Citroën 5 CV Type C**
Year: **1922**
Engine: **4 cylinders in line**
Bore and stroke: **55 × 90 mm**
Cylinder capacity: **856 cc**
Gearbox: **3 forward**
Brake horse power: **11**
Maximum speed: **38 mph**
Wheelbase: **7 ft 4½ ins (2.29 m)**
Suspension: **front and rear: 4 semi-cantilever leaf-springs**

A's engine developed 32 bhp at 3,200 revs and its maximum speed, in accordance with André Citroën's specifications, was 62 mph (recommended maximum: 58 mph at 3,800 revs). In the 7 C the capacity was increased to 1628 cc and its power to 36 bhp at 3,800 revs. A total of 83,789 of the 7 A and its derivatives (B, S, C) were built. The basic design remained in production until July 1957.

This model is renowned in France for its quality in relation to its small engine capacity and the roominess of its seating. A feature of this model was that the radiator was positioned behind the hood of the engine.

Clément-Bayard's production was characterized by a large number of models (eight in 1913) of various engine sizes. Amongst these, in 1906 there was a large 100 HP 'square' engine (160 × 160 mm), intended principally for racing. The 18 HP which distinguished itself in the 1903 Paris-Madrid race also had a 'square' engine (90 × 90 mm).

Adolphe Clément was more a business man than an engineer and he directed all his efforts towards establishing a consortium with foreign manufacturers to expand production with an international flavour. The

Car: **Clément-Bayard Type 4M**
Year: **1911**
Engine: **4 cylinders in line**
Bore and stroke: **60 × 120 mm**
Cylinder capacity: **1354 cc**
Gearbox: **3 forward**
Brake horse power: **18**
Maximum speed: **52 mph**
Wheelbase: **7 ft 5 ins (2.26 m)**
Suspension: **front and rear: semi-elliptic leaf-springs**

first fruit of this policy was the creation of Clément-Talbot in England. Adolphe Clément also attempted to produce a standardised type of taxi. In Italy he had business connections with Diatto. After the war Clément-Bayard had financial problems and its factories at Levallois were taken over by Citroën. The English Clément-Talbot company retained this name although the cars were always known simply as Talbots.

Besides being an engineer Alexandre Darracq was an able and open-minded business man who quickly saw the role that the car would play in the twentieth century. By 1900 he had already built 1,200 units of a 6½ bhp car. Darracq drew up agreements with other manufacturers in Great Britain, Germany and Italy.

His involvement with cars began when he bought the production rights to a vehicle designed by Leon Bollée, powered by a single horizontal cylinder engine. However, he became dissatisfied with this and in 1920 he bought the English firm of Clément-Talbot and later Sunbeam, creating S.T.D. (Sunbeam, Talbot Darracq); but this group made the mistake of producing cars that were very alike.

The 1920 Type 25 was obviously inspired by American cars of the

Car: **Darracq Type A 25 CV**
Year: **1920**
Engine: **V-8**
Bore and stroke: **75 × 130 mm**
Cylinder capacity: **4594 cc**
Gears: **4 forward**
Brake horse power: **80**
Maximum speed: **65 mph**
Wheelbase: **11 ft 5 ins (3.37 m)**
Suspension: **front: semi-elliptic leaf-springs; rear: cantilever leaf-springs**

period, with coil ignition, 4-speed transmission, cantilever leaf-spring rear suspension and a weight of approximately 3,970 pounds (1,800 kg). On the basis of its general characteristics it was presented as a compromise between the needs of American drivers and European motorists. Unfortunately the 25 was criticized for its road holding and high fuel consumption. Furthermore it cost almost as much as a Cadillac. A total of 500 cars were built but sales were very slow.

De Dion 10 CV
De Dion 25 HP

It was De Dion—enterprising, modern in outlook and fired by a sporting spirit—who promoted the car in France from the rank of an 'instrument of death' and an 'object of adventure' to a peaceful means of travel as well as sport. De Dion was a wealthy aristocrat (on the death of his father he would become a Marquis), but his partners, Boulton and Trépardoux, earned their living by building model steam cars. The spread of the car through France can be traced back to the meeting of these three men. For some time they built steam cars and De Dion (who was the only contestant) won the first car race in history. This took place on April 28th, 1887 and was organised by the newspaper *Le Vélocipède*. However, steam was strongly challenged by the internal combustion engine and the three

partners split up. Trépardoux remained faithful to steam whilst De Dion and Bouton chose the internal combustion engine. This happened in 1893 and in the same year the two partners patented a type of rear suspension based on a rigid axle that linked the two wheels and which reduced the unsprung weight as the differential was rigidly fixed to the chassis. This form of suspension is still in favour today.

De Dion resumed production of V-8 engines after the First World War. However, his interest in them went back to 1911, when the company produced highly refined models which show what the French firm had accomplished since the pioneering days of steam cars. Amongst the pre-war V-8s there was a coupé and a torpedo. The same engines, apart from a few modifications, reappeared immediately after the war but in 1923 they were abandoned.

The 10 CV of 1921 can already be

regarded, even in its shape, as a modern car but De Dion-Bouton had lost its elite clientele and its production was not numerically great enough to enable it to compete with Renault and Peugeot. After the war, during which De Dion-Bouton, like others, was occupied with orders for the military, it was unable to adjust itself to the new climate and to produce popular models. It returned to its old pre-war cars, including the 8-cylinders that had made it famous, but this was against the general trend. Three thousand cars a year was not enough to keep a car manufacturer alive. Perhaps one of the reasons for De Dion-Bouton's decline was that the two founders did not train and mould young engineers to continue their work. De Dion-Bouton ceased to make cars in 1933.

Car: **De Dion 25 HP**
Year: **1920**
Engine: **V-8 cylinder**
Bore and stroke: **70 × 120 mm**
Cylinder capacity: **3600 cc**
Gears: **4 forward**
Brake horse power: —
Maximum speed: —
Wheelbase: **11 ft 2 ins (3.40 m)**
Suspension: **front and rear: semi-elliptic leaf-springs**

Car: **De Dion 10 CV**
Year: **1921**
Engine: **4 cylinders in line**
Bore and stroke: **70 × 120 mm**
Cylinder capacity: **1847 cc**
Gears: **4 forward**
Brake horse power: —
Maximum speed: —
Wheelbase: **9 ft 9 ins (2.97 m)**
Suspension: **front: semi-elliptic leaf-springs
rear: cantilever leaf-springs**

Delage 4 Cylinder
Delage D8

Delage was a famous name in the second and third decades of the twentieth century due to its numerous sporting victories. Outstanding amongst these was the one gained by Thomas in the 1914 Indianapolis 500 setting a new record (at an average of more than 82 mph) for the celebrated American circuit. Another of its instant successes was the win in a race based on fuel consumption at the Sarthe circuit (Le Mans).

Racing activity absorbed a large part of the French firm's manufacturing resources but it also enjoyed an excellent commercial reputation. The 1913 4-cylinder is typical of Delage's touring products. These, to begin with, were powered almost exclusively by 4-cylinder engines, the standard models being built by Ballot. The 1447 cc 4-cylinder entered production in 1910 and continued until

1913. Its maximum speed was about 31-34 mph.

The 1929 8-cylinder was a luxury machine. Its straight-8 engine developed 120 bhp in the touring version and 145 bhp in the D8 S. The 4-speed gearbox was mated directly to the engine. The use of rubberised canvas flexible couplings made the transmission particularly quiet. It had wire wheels like almost all prestige cars of the period. The model pictured here weighed 3,180 pounds (1,440 kg) which was quite heavy. It was unveiled at the 1929 Paris Motor Show and it entered production in 1930. The D8 was the firm's largest model.

Delage's racing fortunes began to decline in 1923 and this was paralleled by a similar decline in touring production, despite the fact that Delage had secured the collaboration of a famous engineer, Albert Lory. After the Second World War he would be entrusted with the design of a national racing car which, with the participa-

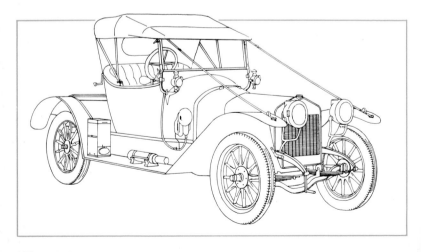

tion of the entire French motor industry, ought to have defended the national colours with credit in the classic races. It failed, however, just as the 16-cylinder BRM which was created for the same purpose failed.

A 12-cylinder engine was chosen for the 2-litre formula. This developed 120 bhp at 6,000 revs. This engine had been designed by Plancton and Lory who tried to make it more reliable and powerful by the addition of a supercharger. When the new 1½ formula came into force, Lory chose an 8-cylinder which in 1927 won a notable string of successes.

The 6-cylinder D6 marked the end of Delage. It was absorbed by Delahaye and lived on shakily until 1953—when they both ceased business. It is significant that both Delage's and Delahaye's brief spell of

Car: **Delage D8**
Year: **1929**
Engine: **8 cylinders in line**
Bore and stroke: **77 × 109 mm**
Cylinder capacity: **4060 cc**
Gears: **4 forward**
Brake horse power: **120**
Maximum speed: **98 mph**
Wheelbase: **10 ft 10 in (3.30 m)**
    or **11 ft 11 in (3.63 m)**
Suspension: **front and rear: semi-elliptic
    leaf-springs**

Car: **Delage**
Year: **1913**
Engine: **4 cylinders in line**
Bore and stroke: **65 × 110 mm**
Cylinder capacity: **1447 cc**
Gears: **3 forward**
Brake horse power: **—**
Maximum speed: **34 mph**
Wheelbase: **7 ft 8 ins (2.33 m)**
Suspension: **front and rear: semi-elliptic
    leaf-springs**

fortune was due to racing. When mass production swept the luxury models out of the market, Delage and Delahaye were unable to compete.

It is strange that the company name of Delahaye was perpetuated throughout its career from 1894 to 1953, because by 1901 Emile Delahaye had very little to do with the running of the company. Charles Weiffenbach, therefore, was given very little credit for guiding the company throughout those years. Weiffenbach was responsible for, amongst other things, the attempt to bring about mass production based on standardisation.

This was another company that was responsible for sporting triumphs. The 135 is a typical example of its large range of products. It had a 6-cylinder engine with the same bore and stroke as a 4-cylinder engine introduced at the same time, (this was one way of bringing about the standardisation that was Weiffenbach's object). The 135 was bodied in

Car: **Delahaye 135**
Year: **1934**
Engine: **6 cylinders in line**
Bore and stroke: **80 × 107 mm**
Cylinder capacity: **3500 cc**
Gears: **4 forward**
Brake horse power: **130**
Maximum speed: **100 mph**
Wheelbase: **9 ft 8 ins (2.94 m)**
Suspension: **front: independent suspension with transverse leaf-springs; rear: semi-elliptic leaf-springs**

a variety of ways by the French coachwork/designers, who at that time were the acknowledged masters of the art.

The Delahaye was regarded as a car for the elite and the preserve of a very select clientele. Streamlined bodies were built on Delahaye chassis even for models that were not strictly sporting and they were given winged fenders that were fashionable before the outbreak of the last war.

It is maintained that Delaunay Belle-villes, known for their elegance and robustness, formed part of the Russian Czar's fleet and that after him they served Lenin and Trotsky. It is certain, however, that this make was synonymous with elegance and refinement over a long period of time. It began at the 1904 Paris Motor Show, when three cars designed by the highly regarded engineer, Marius Barbarou were displayed.

The early models had side valves, T-cylinder heads and shaft drive. The Type HB of 1911 was one of the first 6-cylinders and its quietness, a quality much appreciated in those days, rapidly excited admiration. The bodies, built by the best French firms, added that touch of elegance and ex-clusiveness to the Delaunay Belleville.

During the war the French firm

Car: **Delaunay Belleville Type HB**
Year: **1911**
Engine: **6 cylinders in line**
Bore and stroke: **85 × 130 mm**
Cylinder capacity: **4426 cc**
Gears: **4 speed**
Brake horse power: **30**
Maximum speed: **50 mph**
Wheelbase: **10 ft 6 in (3.20)**
Suspension: **front: semi-elliptic leaf-springs**
    rear: semi-elliptic leaf-springs with trans-verse leaf-springs

assembled Hispano-Suiza airplane engines and at the end of the war it resumed activity with its old models, but these appeared rather outdated, especially as it had to compete with tougher, more modern manufac-turers. In 1933 it ceased to be a manu-facturer of luxury cars. It tried to win itself a new corner of the market with an assembled car (using chassis and engines from other makers) but this failed.

This was one of the most successful of Gregoire's models. Gregoire began by producing motorcycles and boat engines, moving on to cars in 1903. It produced small engined cars or 'voiturettes' as they were known in France, which were powered by twin-cylinder or twin block four-cylinder engines.

Gregoire's early years were characterised by an intense but rather unprofitable involvement in racing. In 1920 it entered a machine in the Indianapolis 500 Mile Race. The dividends that Gregoire failed to gain on the circuits came from its ordinary customers as it had won an enviable reputation for the handling and the sturdiness of its cars. The 13/18 CV gave rise to the 14/24 CV which was particularly successful. It had a 2212 cc 4-cylinder engine (80×110 mm)

Car: **Gregoire 13/18 CV**
Year: **1911**
Engine: **4 cylinders in line**
Bore and stroke: **80 × 110 mm**
Cylinder capacity: **2212 cc**
Gears: **3 forward**
Brake horse power: —
Maximum speed: —
Wheelbase: **9 ft 6 ins (2.89 m)**
Suspension: **front and rear: semi-elliptic leaf-springs**

and a 3-speed transmission. After two years it was increased to 3217 cc and a 4-speed gearbox was fitted. The latter had a certain impact on racing which was suitably appreciated by the public. Its most prominent features were a good top speed and its lightness in weight. Gregoire continued production after the First World War but to a lesser extent. In 1920 it supplied chassis to Bignan and in 1924 it went out of business entirely.

Like many other manufacturers Hotchkiss did not begin as a car factory. In its case it did not begin with bicycles or motor cycles but with heavy armaments, as the two crossed cannons that form its emblem clearly show. History tells that a certain Benjamin Berkeley Hotchkiss supplied Napoleon III with cannons.

The AL, which was considered to be the equivalent of the Lancia Theta or Kappa, was a direct descendant of the AF which had taken part in 1914 in the Austrian Alpine Trial. After the Armistice the AF became the AH with a cone clutch, a 4-speed gearbox, pressure (pumped) lubrication and an electric starter. The AL includes all the improvements made in the preceding models and it used for the first time an open shaft drive. This was known as Hotchkiss transmission and

Car: **Hotchkiss AL Torpedo**
Year: **1922**
Engine: **4 cylinders in line**
Bore and stroke: **95 × 140 mm**
Cylinder capacity: **3962 cc**
Gears: **4 forward**
Brake horse power: —
Maximum speed: —
Wheelbase: —
Suspension: **front: semi-elliptic leaf-springs
rear: cantilever leaf-springs**

was used in place of a shaft enclosed in the propeller tube. The car weighed 2,870 pounds (1,300 kg) and was capable of a top speed of about 60 mph. An interesting feature was the two piece windshield that protected the passengers in the rear seats.

The AL was a successful car; in 1919 and 1920 450 were sold. In 1922 overhead valves were fitted, the cylinder head was detachable whilst in 1923 brakes on the front wheels were added.

The little Le Zèbre was one of the first cars to be designed by Jules Salomon, who was later to be summoned by André Citroën to design the legendary 5 CV. This 4 CV had all the features of a normal car and despite its small engine capacity it appeared to the sceptical eyes of the public to be a normal 4-wheeler. The engine was water cooled, it had magneto ignition and shaft drive. The first version was a single-seater and could reach speeds of 31 mph. This version was progressively improved and updated. In 1913 a 3-speed transmission was fitted and it became a 4-seater. A third series, in a 2-seater torpedo version, had an increased engine capacity of 785 cc. A fourth series came out in 1918. The feature that distinguished this car from its predecessors was its 4-cylinder engine. This was

Car: **Le Zèbre 4 CV**
Year: **1911**
Engine: **single-cylinder**
Bore and stroke: **85 × 106 mm**
Cylinder capacity: **616 cc**
Gears: **2 forward**
Brake horse power: **10**
Maximum speed: **31 mph**
Wheelbase: **7 ft 0 ins (2.13 m)**
Suspension: **front and rear: semi-elliptic leaf-springs**

Salomon's last effort for Le Zèbre as in 1919 he moved to Citroën.

The company then improved the quality of their product, abandoning small engines and producing an engine of medium capacity: a 2000 cc 4-cylinder, the Z, which was designed by another talented engineer called Ricardo. This machine did not achieve the success of tiny and efficient utility cars and the firm had disappeared by 1932.

This make, which began in 1897 as Société De Dietrich et Cie (later becoming Société Lorraine des Anciens Etablissements De Dietrich et Cie de Luneville) was very successful in the sporting field. Its first car was designed by Amédée Bollée and another was designed by Ettore Bugatti. Convinced that racing would bring it great publicity, De Dietrich concentrated on racing. It began by competing in the Paris-Madrid race and then in the Gordon-Bennett cup, the Circuit of the Ardennes and the Moscow-St Petersburg race. The employment of Marius Barbarou as engineer increased the sporting character of Lorraine. It took second and third places in the 1924 Le Mans 24 Hour and won it in 1925. The engine had overhead valves (which were operated by rockers), water-

Car: **Lorraine-Dietrich 15 CV Sport**
Year: **1925**
Engine: **6 cylinders in line**
Bore and stroke: **75 × 130 mm**
Cylinder capacity: **3446 cc**
Gears: **3 forward**
Brake horse power: **70**
Maximum speed: **93 mph**
Wheelbase: **10 ft 3 ins (3.12 m)**
Suspension: **front: semi-elliptic leaf-springs; rear: cantilever leaf-springs**

cooling and pressure lubrication. It developed 70 bhp at 3,500 revs. weighed 2,380 pounds (1,080 kg) and had a maximum speed of 93 mph.

Lorraine-Dietrich attempted to expand internationally by buying half the registered stock of Isotta-Fraschini and by setting up an English Lorraine-De Dietrich in Birmingham. It was itself, however, taken over and was forced to become part of a Franco-Belgian financial group.

Emile Ernst Mathis, who began work as an apprentice, and Ettore Bugatti, who was also working for De Dietrich, found themselves free of commitments and for a time they collaborated together before each went his own way. Mathis and Bugatti had designed a large car, the 7500 cc Hermes-Simplex, later known as the Mathis-Hermes, the construction of which was entrusted to an outside firm. In 1906 there were four models in production but it was not until 1910 that Mathis itself built cars.

After the war activity was resumed and publicised by an intense involvement in racing. There was a forerunner of the PS 10 that had an even smaller engine (1080 cc) and a 3-speed gearbox. In 1923 it was fitted with a 4-speed transmission and the capacity was increased to 1140 cc. The engine

Car: **Mathis PS 10 CV**
Year: **1924**
Engine: **6 cylinders in line**
Bore and stroke: **55 × 80 mm**
Cylinder capacity: **1140 cc**
Gears: **4 forward**
Brake horse power: —
Maximum speed: **55 mph**
Wheelbase: **9 ft 0 ins (2.74 m)**
Suspension: **front and rear: semi-elliptic leaf-springs**

had a fixed cylinder head and there were brakes only on the rear wheels. There was also a sporting version with overhead valves and a maximum speed of more than 68 mph. In 1924 brakes were finally fitted on all four wheels and the wheelbase was lengthened to allow it to carry four people. There were then five models: 2-seater, tourer, cabriolet, 3-door sedan, and 4-door sedan. The lowest priced model cost 21,000 francs.

If it had not been absorbed by Citroën in 1965 and had its name totally suppressed, Panhard would have shared with Renault and Peugeot the record for being the oldest car companies still in business. The company was founded in 1889 but its origins go back to 1845 with a company for the manufacture of wood-working machines in Paris. In 1867 Réné Panhard joined, and in 1872 a school fellow of his, Emile Levassor, joined the company as well. The founder of the company, Perin, died but Panhard and Levassor continued together and they received the commission to build in France an engine designed by Gottlieb Daimler. In 1889 Panhard and Levassor began to design and manufacture cars.

The X17SS was one of the most up-to-date vehicles produced by the firm.

Car: **Panhard-Levassor X17SS**
Year: **1912**
Engine: **4 cylinders in line**
Bore and stroke: **80 × 130 mm**
Cylinder capacity: **2614 cc**
Gears: **4 forward**
Brake horse power: —
Maximum speed: —
Wheelbase: —
Suspension: **front: semi-elliptic leaf-springs; rear: elliptic leaf-springs consisting of two semi-elliptic ones, the upper being a cantilever leaf-spring**

It had a sleeve-valve engine under licence from Knight; this was a vertical twin block with fitted and flat cylinder heads and it was fed by a Panhard constant adjustment carburetor. It had magneto ignition, shaft drive, pressure lubrication and water cooling and an oil bath clutch. The Knight sleeve engine of four cylinders in line, was adopted by Panhard in 1911, and used on all their cars up to 1939.

Peugeot 16 HP Type 116
Peugeot Bébé

Peugeot's origins can be traced back to 1810 when Jean Pierre Peugeot set up a foundry and rolling mill. The enterprise was continued by his sons, Jules and Emile who increased their range of products to include tools, pendulum clocks, springs for wrist and pocket watches, coffee grinders, ribs for umbrellas and crinolines. By 1885 Armand, the grandson of Jean Pierre and the son of Emile, had persuaded his relatives to produce bicycles but he had failed to interest them in cars.

In 1889 Armand bought the manufacturing rights to the Daimler engine and he started to construct quadricycles after having requested the collaboration of Bollée and Serpollet. Armand Peugeot's first quadricycle appeared in 1890. Others followed which became known through the races of the period. His most successful machine was the 1902 Bébé. This was a small car without reverse gear and which weighed just 600 pounds (270 kg). Whilst Armand concentrated entirely on cars the other branch of the Peugeot company continued with its traditional business until Eugene's sons, Pierre, Robert and Jules, expanded into cars. In 1905 they went into competition with Armand and they quickly gained numerous racing successes. To distinguish their machines from Armand's they called them Lion-Peugeot. In 1910 the Peugeots came together again, forming Société Anonyme des Automobiles et Cycles Peugeot which replaced Armand's Société Anonyme des Automobiles Peugeot and Les Fils des Peugeots Frères founded by Eugene, Pierre, Robert and Jules.

The 16 HP made in 1908 was a

conventional car with a side valve engine, high tension magneto ignition and shaft drive. The relatively small engine capacity seemed inadequate for the car's needs. In reality it was quite the opposite and the Type 116 was a very reliable car.

In 1913 the second Peugeot to be called Bébé, appeared. The design was entrusted to Ettore Bugatti. It had the smallest 4-cylinder engine on the market. The 856 cc engine had a T cylinder head and was of an antiquated design but it turned out to be perfectly suited to a car that weighed less than 730 pounds (330 kg). Its maximum speed was a little above 34 mph, there was a 2-litre gearbox and there was a special control lever for reverse. The car's principal defects were the short life of the tires, which, it is said, had to be replaced after less

Car: **Peugeot Bébé**
Year: **1913**
Engine: **4 cylinders in line**
Bore and stroke: **55 × 90 mm**
Cylinder capacity: **856 cc**
Gears: **2 forward**
Brake horse power: **10**
Maximum speed: **34 mph**
Wheelbase: **6 ft 0 ins (1.82 m)**
Suspension: **front: semi-elliptic leaf-springs; rear: upside down ¼ elliptic leaf-springs**

Car: **Peugeot 16 HP Type 116**
Year: **1908**
Engine: **4 cylinders in line**
Bore and stroke: **80 × 110 mm**
Cylinder capacity: **2212 cc**
Gears: **4 forward**
Brake horse power: **—**
Maximum speed: **—**
Wheelbase: **9 ft 2 ins (2.79 m)**
Suspension: **front and rear: semi-elliptic leaf-springs**

than 6,000 miles and the lack of precision in the steering. The Bébé went out of production in 1916. A total of 3,095 cars were built but a much larger number, about 12,205, of the Quadrilette, its successor, were built.

Renault Taxi Type Taxi de la Marne 8 C 2 CIL
Renault coupé 12 CV
Renault 6 CV NN 4 CIL

Louis Renault will be remembered not only for the great cars he produced but also for his patent on the direct-transmission gearbox. He also opened his factory to the Germans in the Second World War, possibly in an effort to save the plant. This resulted, however, in his imprisonment in 1944 and the confiscation of the factory by the government. These two events proved too great a blow for Louis Renault who died the same year.

Possibly one of the most famous events in Renault history is the use of the Marne Taxi in the First World War. Production of the type started in 1905, and many were used as taxis. The engine had side valves, magneto ignition, a cone clutch and shaft drive. The maximum speed was 37 mph. During the First World War, the German Army invaded France and in order to quickly get French troops through to the front line, thousands of the Marne 8 C 2 CIL Paris taxis were used to transport the soldiers. Historians have stated that the government paid the standard fare for each trip, despite the fact that some of the fares were 130 francs.

The 12 CV coupé, also designated EV, had a lowered chassis and the bodywork was built by Kellner. The hand brake acted on the rear wheels and the brake pedal on the transmission. The version illustrated here had a maximum speed of 50 mph. Renault

Car: **Renault Taxi Type Taxi de la Marne 8 C 2 CIL**
Year: **1906**
Engine: **twin-cylinder**
Bore and stroke: **80 × 120 mm**
Cylinder capacity: **1205 cc**
Gears: **3 forward**
Brake horse power: **—**
Maximum speed: **37 mph**
Wheelbase: **6 ft 5 ins (1.95 m)**
Suspension: **front: semi-elliptic leaf-springs; rear: ¼ elliptic leaf-springs with auxillary springs**

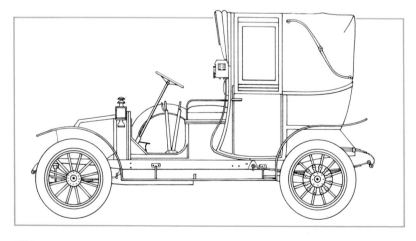

continued to build these vehicles with radiators mounted behind the engine until 1929. From 1922, however, Renault fitted four wheel brakes on large cars (18-40 CV), and, with time, this extended to other models: the 10 CV of 1923 and the 6 CV of 1924.

Again in 1922 a minor stylistic revolution took place: the characteristic alligator (coal scuttle) shaped hood was replaced by a pointed hood whose sharp edges were linked with the lines of the body's waist. Placed centrally in the hood was a circular cast metal badge, in its middle was the word 'Renault' and this was edged by two bars. Two years later the badge took its final, diamond shape.

The 6 CV started as a 3-seater torpedo in 1922 and was intended to compete with the Citroën 5 CV. It was an economical model and it featured

Car: **Renault coupé 12 CV**
Year: **1921**
Engine: **4 cylinders in line**
Bore and stroke: **80 × 140 mm**
Cylinder capacity: **2814 cc**
Gears: **4 forward**
Brake horse power: —
Maximum speed: **50 mph**
Wheelbase: **8 ft 8 ins (2.64 m)**
Suspension: **front and rear: semi-elliptic leaf-springs**

an important technical innovation. It had the first removable cylinder head which made repair work a much easier task.

As a clever publicity stunt, it was arranged for it to travel, apparently driverless, through the streets of Paris to catch the public's attention. In 1924 a 4-seater torpedo entered production, which had four wheel brakes.

The advertising launch of the torpedo dwelt upon the car's qualities of endurance. In 1926, between

March 29, and April 6, this car covered 10,000 miles (16,000 km) on the Miramas circuit in 203 hours, at an average speed of 49 mph, stopping only to refuel. In 1927 it made the first solo crossing of the Sahara. The car was now firmly categorised as being hard-wearing and enduring. The 6 CV NN weighed 2,380 pounds (1,080 kg) and had a maximum speed of 47 mph.

The largest Renault of the 1920s was the 45, with a 6-cylinder engine of 9121 cc capacity. It had servo-assisted brakes, weighed 5,730 pounds (2,600 kg) and had a maximum speed of 84 mph. Its physical power earned it the title *'sa Majeste la 40 CV'* and it was more than 16 feet 5 inches (5.0 m) in length. The chassis provided a basis for variety of coachwork and many designers used a great deal of imagination over it as custom built cars were then very fashionable in France. Renault, however, were also keen to demonstrate its basic qualities and on May 11, 1925 a 4-seater torpedo version of the 45 covered 107 miles (172 km) in one hour on the Parisian circuit of Montlhéry. This beat the world record of 97.903 mph for six hours. A few days later it averaged 100.456 mph over 12 hours and 87.700 mph over 24 hours.

Car: **Renault 6 CV NN 4 CIL**
Year: **1925**
Engine: **4 cylinders in line**
Bore and stroke: **58 × 90 mm**
Cylinder capacity: **951 cc**
Gears: **3 forward**
Brake horse power: —
Maximum speed: **47 mph**
Wheelbase: **8 ft 0 ins (2.43 m)**
Suspension: **front: semi-elliptic leaf-springs; rear: transverse leaf-springs**

Rochet-Schneider was one of the few makes at the beginning of the twentieth century that never raced, but this did not affect its success. It was founded in 1894 by Edouard Rochet and Theophile Schneider in Lyons, and they began by building bicycles. In 1910 Schneider left and set up his own company.

A feature of the cars built by the two partners was their resemblance to Panhard and Benz models. Although this indicated a certain lack of originality in the design it was also widely felt that their cars were better built than their immediate rivals.

The 25 CV of 1911 was one of the most successful models. It had high tension magneto ignition and shaft drive. It was followed up by a 5500 cc 6-cylinder vehicle and gradually side valves were abandoned in favour of

Car: **Rochet-Schneider 25 CV**
Year: **1911**
Engine: **4 cylinders in line**
Bore and stroke: **105 × 140 mm**
Cylinder capacity: **4849 cc**
Gears: **4 forward**
Brake horse power: —
Maximum speed: —
Wheelbase: **10 ft 10 ins (3.30 m)**
Suspension: **front: semi-elliptic leaf-springs;
    rear: ¾ elliptic leaf-springs**

overhead types. The precision and quality of the firm's products led to Rochet-Schneiders being built under licence by Moyea and Sampson in the United States; by Nagant and FN in Belgium; by Florentia in Italy and by Martini in Switzerland. By 1932 Rochet-Schneider concentrated entirely on commercial vehicles but before then a 5400 cc 6-cylinder with dual ignition and servo-assisted brakes had been put into production.

The Talbot Company began as Clement-Talbot in London in 1903 as a joint venture by Adolphe Clément, Lord Shrewsbury and Talbot. Its initial purpose was to import the French Clément-Bayard cars, but in 1906 it started independent production, marketing its cars under the name Talbot. In 1919 Clément-Talbot was bought by the French firm Darracq, and in 1920 this absorbed Sunbeam as well, and S.T.D. Motors was formed. Following this transaction matters became more complicated as Darracq was known as Talbot in France and Talbot-Darracq in Britain. In racing the group's cars were known as either Sunbeam, Talbot or Darracq.

The car pictured here is, in fact, an English-built Talbot. It was a development of the 1922 8/18 and it

Car: **Talbot 10/23**
Year: **1923**
Engine: **4 cylinders in line**
Bore and stroke: **60 × 95 mm**
Cylinder capacity: **1075 cc**
Gears: **3 forward**
Brake horse power: **23**
Maximum speed: **50 mph**
Wheelbase: **9 ft 4¼ ins (2.87 m)**
Suspension: **front and rear: semi-elliptic leaf-springs**

was the work of the designer George Roesch. The engine had overhead valves, coil ignition, the differential was on the rear axle and the wheelbase was longer than the 8/18's, enabling it to carry four people. In 1935 the S.T.D. group was dissolved. The British side was acquired by the Rootes brothers, and the French by Major Antony Lago, whose products became known as Lago-Talbots.

Tracta was only in business between 1925 and 1934, but it was one of the first car manufacturers to adopt front wheel drive. The firm was founded in 1925 by the engineer J. A. Grégoire and Pierre Fenaille at Asnières and it was intended to produce high quality cars.

The front wheel drive Tractas made their name at Le Mans in particular, where they were always successful. Grégoire used a SCAP engine and the Cozette supercharger. A feature of front wheel drive cars was the lack of a transmission (propeller) shaft tunnel and this allowed cars with a very low centre of gravity to be designed, which made them very stable. Pierre Fenaille devised a constant velocity joint which overcame the problem of connecting the transmission directly to the

Car: **Tracta**
Year: **1930**
Engine: **4 cylinders in line**
Bore and stroke: **67 × 105 mm**
Cylinder capacity: **1487 cc**
Gears: **4 forward**
Brake horse power: —
Maximum speed: —
Wheelbase: **8 ft 6 ins (2.59 m)**
Suspension: **front and rear: telescopic shock-absorbers and sliding swinging half axles**

steerable wheels. The car illustrated has an unusually long hood, a tiny passenger compartment and minimal ground clearance.

The development of the constant velocity joint absorbed almost all the small factory's resources, and production ceased in 1934. However, Grégoire and Fenaille continued to work on the constant velocity joint for front-wheel drive and this was later adopted by many car producers, and was even used on the Jeep.

Turcat-Méry is one of the French makes most prized by collectors of veteran cars. The company was formed by two cousins, Léon Turcat and Simon Méry. Their first vehicle was produced in Marseilles in 1897, but the company Société Turcat-Méry et Compagnie was not founded until two years later. Their cars were robust and were distinguished by their 5-speed gearboxes (on some models) and their similarity to the cars of De Dietrich, a firm for whom Turcat and Méry worked. Their collaboration with De Dietrich was so extensive and demanding that the pair moved to be near the latter at Luneville and later in Paris. Louis Méry, Simon's brother remained at Marseilles. The two partners later became fully independent again.

Until 1908 Turcat-Méry cars had

Car: **Turcat-Méry 18 CV**
Year: **1911**
Engine: **4 cylinders in line**
Bore and stroke: **90 × 130 mm**
Cylinder capacity: **3307 cc**
Gearbox: **4 forward**
Brake horse power: —
Maximum speed: —
Wheelbase: —
Suspension: **front and rear: semi-elliptic leaf-springs**

chain drive, but shaft drive from 1909 onwards; their 4-cylinder engines had a stroke of 130 mm, the bore being varied according to the cylinder capacity of the model. The final years of activity were dogged by financial problems. The introduction of a sports car, the 4-cylinder RGH, was well received but it was not, on its own sufficient to restore order to the company's finances. New models with 1200 and 1600 cc engines built by SCAP and CIME similarly failed. In 1929 Turcat-Méry closed.

Gabriel Voisin's name is one of the most highly regarded in France because of the advanced designs that he produced. He was initially a builder of airplanes, in fact it was Voisin who built the first French airplanes on a commercial basis. He always associated automobiles both technically and in appearance with aircraft. They were original and futuristic cars, but were also powerful and luxurious, belonging mainly to royalty and aristocracy.

For his first car Voisin had bought the manufacturing rights to an 18 CV sleeve valve engine from André Citroën, which Citroën had obtained from Panhard and then decided that it did not suit their needs. This engine powered Voisin's C1, which was a sports model developing 150 bhp at 4,000 revs. The touring version

Car: **Voisin C5**
Year: **1925**
Engine: **4 cylinders in line**
Bore and stroke: **95 × 140 mm**
Cylinder capacity: **3969 cc**
Gears: **4 forward**
Brake horse power: **80**
Maximum speed: **93 mph**
Wheelbase: **10 ft 11½ ins (3.34 m)** *or*
   11 ft 8½ ins (3.57 m)
Suspension: **front and rear: semi-elliptic**
   leaf-springs

developed 80 bhp at 2,500 revs and had a top speed in fourth gear of 93 mph and 65 mph in third. The C3 followed, and this also had a very good performance. Finally came the C5. This model differed in having magnesium pistons and a higher compression ratio. It developed 100 bhp at 2,700 revs and had servo-assisted brakes.

The last design of Voisin was a mini car powered by a 125 cc engine called the Biscooter. This highly original model was popular in Spain.

Germany

Germany has produced relatively few types of cars. The number has been reduced even further since the Second World War as contact between manufacturers in East Germany and those in the West has gradually diminished. There is one unusual feature of this industry's history and that is the outstanding success of Mercedes or Daimler Benz.

In 1890 Gottlieb Daimler and William Maybach founded the Daimler Motor Gesellschaft in Cannstatt and granted manufacturing licences to Panhard and Levassor and Peugeot in France. Gottlieb Daimler died in 1900 and was succeeded by his son, Paul. It was at this point that Emil Jellinek, the firm's agent in Western Europe and America, commissioned a number of cars from Daimler provided that they bore his daughter's name; Mercedes. From then on all passenger cars produced by the firm bore the name. In 1926 Daimler merged with Benz and the company name became Daimler-Benz; but the name Mercedes continued to be used for the cars.

Throughout its existence Mercedes has always been distinguished by the great variety of its products.

The company that was responsible for the advent of the car in Germany was Opel. Opel has always principally catered to the lower levels of the market. It was founded in 1862 by Adam Opel for the manufacture of sewing machines, then bicycles in 1886 and cars in 1898.

Opel aimed to cover a large part of the market and engaged in some racing, (at that time it was essential to do so to become known), but its small cars were the most important. 1912, the fiftieth anniversary of its birth coincided with the production of its ten thousandth car. The firm alternated mass production of popular small cars with luxury models. It was the former, however, such as the Püppchen and the Laubfrosch that gave it success and esteem. In 1929 Opel sold most of its shares to General Motors.

Ford entered the German market at almost the same time as General Motors (1925), by opening an efficient assembly workshop with only 37 employees. Rather than an assembly shop this initial establishment provided premises for the customs clearance of cars imported to the United States. It was in 1926 that Ford began assembly work and on April 18 of that year that the first

Model T Ford was put on the market. By 1929 Ford began building a new factory in Cologne. By 1937 the factory had 40,000 employees and production was above 600,000 units.

BMW was another illustrious make whose origin was the result of the merger in 1916 of Rapp and Gustav Otto, two firms from Munich. The new firm was initially known as Bayerische Flugzeugwerke and then in 1917 as Bayerische Motoren Werke. It manufactured engines for airplanes at first and then engines for motorcycles. BMW became involved with cars in 1928 when it bought the manufacturing licence to the Dixi. In 1931 it began to produce cars entirely of its own design. The 328 was announced in 1936 and contained many innovations (mass produced light alloy cylinder heads, overhead valves arranged in a V, three up-draft carburetors and a radiator for cooling the oil). Despite this only 462 examples of the car were built. Subsequently, without abandoning motorcycles, BMW concentrated on the growing luxury car market.

Maybach and Horch, both of which have disappeared, were representatives of the quality of German industry. Wilhelm Maybach was a collaborator of Daimler and in 1912 he founded his own company in Friedrichshafen on Lake Constance.

In 1921 Maybach produced a 5800 cc 6-cylinder which caused a sensation at the Berlin Motor Show. The entire production of Maybach (which survived only 20 years) was studded with technical innovations.

These included: a planetary transmission with just two speeds, carburetors with variable choke tubes, mechanical brakes on four wheels, a single piece cylinder block and head, overdrive, 5-speed synchromesh transmission, an engine block with built-in cylinder barrels and a channel frame chassis. In 1966 Maybach became part of the Daimler-Benz group, but they had ceased making cars in 1941.

August Horch founded Horch, another of the élite German manufacturers, in 1899. This company's most admired models were those with relatively small capacity 8-cylinder engines. The Second World War proved fatal for it, however, as it was in the Eastern part of Germany and it has since been used for completely different purposes.

The need to strengthen and assist companies that were in difficulties led to the creation in 1932 of a consortium linking Audi, DKW, Horch and Wanderer. The new firms's emblem (four interlinked rings) was only used by these four firms, however, in the sporting field. DKW had been founded in 1918, Audi in 1909 and Wanderer in 1885.

German cars were much appreciated for their solidity if not for their appearance. The speed with which the cars have recovered markets after the Second World War is further evidence of the German aptitude for mechanics in general.

The Volkswagen phenomenon remains a case apart. Production of this vehicle easily exceeds 19 million, even beating the Model T Ford of which over 15 million units were built.

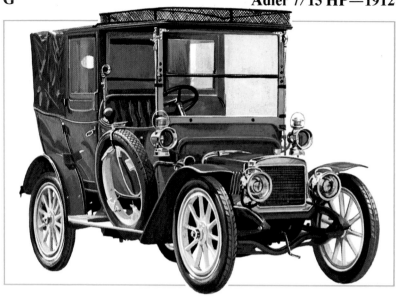

Adler Fahrradwerke was founded in 1886 by Heinrich Kleyer in Frankfurt, initially producing bicycles and then motorcycles and typewriters. Adler turned to cars in 1899 with products that featured single-cylinder De Dion-Bouton engines and shaft drive and continued their involvement for 40 years. The well known engineer Edmund Rumpler had refurbished the cars by 1903, fitting them with independent suspension, and engines and gearboxes in a single unit. In 1912 Adler opened an assembly shop in Vienna. They had also reached an agreement with an English coachbuilder, Morgan. Morgan bought Adler chassis and fitted them with bodywork to suit the tastes of British buyers.

The 7/15 is an example of this collaboration as the body was built by

Car: **Adler 7/15 HP**
Year: **1912**
Engine: **4 cylinders in line**
Bore and stroke: **75 × 100 mm**
Cylinder capacity: **1768 cc**
Gearbox: **3 forward**
Brake horse power: **15**
Maximum speed: **42 mph**
Wheelbase: **7 ft 10 ins (2.38 m)**
Suspension: **front and rear: semi-elliptic leaf-springs**

Morgan. The engine was a derivative of the 1909 6/14 (stroke increased from 88 mm to 100 mm) having side valves, a twin block L cylinder head and magneto and coil dual ignition. An ear trumpet was positioned beside the driver's seat so that the chauffeur could receive the passenger's instructions. Adler stopped producing cars at the outbreak of the Second World War, but it resumed the production of motorcycles in 1957.

Apollo began as Ruppe & Sohn of Apolda in Thuringia but in 1910 it became Apollo Werke. It then started the manufacture of water and air-cooled vehicles (the latter were uncommon at that time) under the management of Karl Slevogt who was both a well respected engineer and a skilled driver. The best known car was the sports version of the 1911 4/12 with a unit construction 1000 cc engine and gearbox that developed 12 bhp at 1,800 revs. There was also a Typ B Spezial (20 bhp at 2,200 revs) illustrated here. A record breaking car was developed from the latter which produced almost twice the power due to the capacity being raised to over 2000 cc. The 4-cylinder engine developed a hefty 28 bhp at 2,000 revs which gave a maximum speed of 56 mph. It weighed less than 1,545 lb

Car: **Apollo 4/12 PS**
Year: **1913**
Engine: **4 cylinders in line**
Bore and stroke: **75 × 116 mm**
Cylinder capacity: **2040 cc**
Gearbox: **4 forward**
Brake horse power: **20**
Maximum speed: **56 mph**
Wheelbase: **7 ft 2½ ins (2.20 m)**
Suspension: **front and rear: semi-elliptic leaf-springs**

(700 kg). Its sporting successes led Apollo to widen its production and it built large capacity engines, also water-cooled and, after the war, a V-8 with four wheel brakes. Apollo went out of business in 1926, leaving behind the memory of a small but well run and highly flexible company. During the period when it was regularly taking part in races it was quite common for its nippy little cars to cause problems for even the most powerful Bugattis on the race track.

Audi was born as the result of a quarrel which in June 1909 forced August Horch to leave the firm that bore his name. A variety of reasons were responsible for his being out-voted, not least of which were Horch's racing failures in 1907. It took him only a month to found Horch Automobil Werke but the court at Leipzig ordered him to change its name (the new company name was very like the old one). August Horch then chose the latinised version of his own name, Audi ('hark' or 'listen'). The 14/50 was also known as the Alpensieger because a string of victories won by Audis in Alpine competitions during 1912, 1913 and 1914 rapidly gave the German firm the reputation of being invincible in this type of event. The 14/50's engine had overhead valves

Car: **Audi K 14/50 PS**
Year: **1923**
Engine: **4 cylinders in line**
Bore and stroke: **90 × 140 mm**
Cylinder capacity: **3563 cc**
Gearbox: **4 forward**
Brake horse power: **50**
Maximum speed: **56 mph**
Wheelbase: **11 ft 6½ ins (3.52 m)**
Suspension: **front and rear: semi-elliptic leaf-springs**

and many of its parts were in light alloy. Rudge spoke wheels were used. It was the first mass produced German car to have the driver's position on the left. There was one brake on the transmission and a pedal brake that acted on the rear wheels. Its maximum speed was 56 mph. The 14/50 PS was replaced by the unsuccessful 18/70 PS Model M. Horch handed the technical direction of Audi to others and in 1928 it was absorbed into DKW.

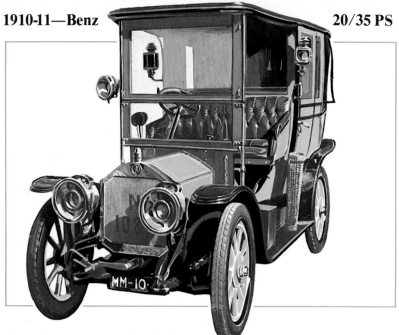

Karl Benz, along with Gottlieb Daimler, was the inventor of the internal combustion engine as a practical means of propulsion. The 20/35 PS, however, still used chain drive. Benz's reputation increased with the arrival of a highly talented engineer, Hans Niebel, although the cars, which were very well built, fast and all powered by 4-cylinder engines (until 1914), remained in essence conservative. Niebel changed over from engines with L cylinder heads to ones with T heads and chain drive was slowly replaced by shaft drive. One of Niebel's masterpieces was the famous Blitzen Benz (200 bhp at 1,600 revs), which, driven by Bob Burman, reached 142 mph in 1911. Its 4-cylinder engine had a capacity of 21500 cc. It was Hans Niebel, who by strengthening the design side of Benz

Car: **Benz 20/35 PS**
Year: **1910-1911**
Engine: **4 cylinders in line**
Bore and stroke: **105 × 140 mm**
Cylinder capacity: **4851 cc**
Gearbox: **4 forward**
Brake horse power: **35**
Maximum speed: **52 mph**
Wheelbase: **10 ft 10 ins (3.30 m)**
Suspension: **front and rear: semi-elliptic leaf-springs**

and enabling it to assert itself in the racing field, was responsible for the German company's return to the ranks of the world's most prestigious manufacturers, in the second decade of this century. The First World War had a very severe effect on it and its recovery was very slow. In 1924 Benz agreed to merge with Daimler and this led to one of the most famous of car manufacturers, also known by the name Mercedes Benz.

DKW is Das Kleine Wunder, which in translation means 'the little wonder'. This name, which later became a make, was given to a 25 cc engine by Jorgen Skafte Rasmussen, a Dane, who had settled in Zschopau, Saxony. DKW's production then moved on from small engines to motorcycles and in 1926, to cars with twin-cylinder two stroke engines of about 600 cc and a self-supporting bodywork of wooden panels covered with imitation leather. In 1931 the front-wheel drive F1 entered production. This had a double member frame with brackets to support the bodywork. It had a unit construction engine and gearbox and independent suspension. The basic 2-seater version of this car weighed a mere 990 pounds (450 kg).

Its production figures give an idea of its success: 4,333 cars in 1931-1932,

Car: **DKW F1 500**
Year: **1931**
Engine: **twin-cylinder in line**
Bore and stroke: **68 × 68 mm**
Cylinder capacity: **490 cc**
Gearbox: **3 forward**
Brake horse power: **15**
Maximum speed: **50 mph**
Wheelbase: **6 ft 10½ ins (2.10 m)**
Suspension: **front and rear: transverse leaf-springs**

13,000 a year in 1934 and 1935, and almost 40,000 cars in 1937. In 1932, DKW, Audi, Horch and Wanderer linked up to form Auto Union which from 1934 until 1937 was especially well known for its powerful racing cars, gaining its victories with rear-engined cars. Auto-Union was absorbed by Mercedes in 1958 and in 1965 it was sold to Volkswagen. DKW suffered the same fate and after having launched a new line of two stroke models the name was dropped in 1966.

Suddeutsche Fabrik of Gaggenau (Gaggenau being the Bavarian town where the factory was situated) started producing cars in 1904. Its origins however go back to 1895 when Bergmanns Industriewerk was founded by Theodore Bergmann. In 1895 he had bought the patent to a car called the Orient Express, designed by Josef Vollmer. The Orient Express was inspired by Karl Benz's vehicles and had a water-cooled, single-cylinder 4-stroke engine, rear mounted and low tension magneto ignition. The Typ 10/18, produced until 1910, had a monobloc engine with dual ignition which developed 20 bhp at 1,600 revs. Its maximum speed was about 50 mph.

Gaggenau also started to produce trucks in 1904 when its products were known interchangeably as Gaggenau

Car: **Gaggenau Typ 10/18 PS**
Year: **1907**
Engine: **4 cylinders in line**
Bore and stroke: **85 × 115 mm**
Cylinder capacity: **2600 cc**
Gearbox: **4 forward**
Brake horse power: **20**
Maximum speed: **50 mph**
Wheelbase: —
Suspension: **front and rear: semi-elliptic leaf-springs**

or SAF (Suddeutsche Automobilfabrik). In 1910 SAF was taken over by Benz, with which it already had common interests. It continued to produce cars for a short time but later it concentrated on truck production. In 1926 Gaggenau was completely absorbed into Benz and it lost its separate identity. Gaggenau is also remembered for its involvement in racing, and was particularly active between 1906 and 1910.

August Horch was just 30 years old and had small financial means when in 1899 he founded the firm that bore his name, setting its factory up in a Cologne stable. Horch concentrated on light vehicles with motorcycle style transmissions and advanced mechanical solutions. In 1902 he moved to Reichenbach in Saxony and in 1903 to Zwickau. The first 4-cylinder was a great success.

However, after internal disagreements August Horch left the company in 1909 to found Audi. Despite Horch's absence the firm continued to make a name for itself through the refinement of its products. After the war Paul Daimler, who had left Daimler became the technical director. Daimler, supported by the advice of Professor Schlesinger, gave Horch an even more distinctive

Car: **Horch 853**
Year: **1938**
Engine: **8 cylinders in line**
Bore and stroke: **87 × 104 mm**
Cylinder capacity: **4944 cc**
Gearbox: **5 forward**
Brake horse power: **105**
Maximum speed: **84 mph**
Wheelbase: **11 ft 6 ins (3.50 m)** *or*
12 ft 3½ ins (3.74 m)
Suspension: **front: independent suspension with transverse leaf-springs and wishbones; rear: axle with semi-elliptic leaf-springs and hydraulic shock-absorbers**

approach by centering its production on multi-cylinders. There were not many variants of the 853 which was built between 1936 and 1939. The engine had an overhead camshaft, pressure lubrication, a 12-volt electrical system, coil ignition and a 5-speed transmission (fourth being direct drive and fifth being overdrive). There was a choice of disc or wire wheels and it had four wheel hydraulic brakes.

Maybach was founded in 1912 in Friedrichshafen on Lake Constance to produce engines for airships and airplanes. It turned to cars as a consequence of the armistice imposed on Germany in 1918. Its first engine was a 6-cylinder and this was adopted by the Dutch firm Spyker. From engines it expanded to complete cars (the body being built elsewhere according to the client's tastes). The designer was Karl Maybach, the son of the founder, Wilhelm. He gave his cars large engines whose flexibility allowed the use of the gearbox to be reduced to a minimum. The W5's transmission only had two speeds (like the Model T Ford's), first gear was for climbing steep slopes and second gear, direct drive, was for starting and normal progress. Naturally there was a reverse gear.

Car: **Maybach W5**
Year: **1927**
Engine: **6 cylinders in line**
Bore and stroke: **94 × 168 mm**
Cylinder capacity: **6996 cc**
Gearbox: **2 forward**
Brake horse power: **120**
Maximum speed: **80 mph**
Wheelbase: **12 ft 0 ins (3.66 m)**
Suspension: **front and rear: semi-elliptic leaf-springs**

The maximum power of the W5's engine was 120 bhp at 2,800 revs (it had side valves operated by rockers and camshafts). The W3, which preceded the W5, was the first German car to have four wheel brakes.

Maybach moved on from 6 cylinders to 12 in an attempt to match its competitors. Maybach, which for years was synonymous with elegance, stopped producing cars in 1945. In 1966 it was absorbed by Daimler-Benz.

Mercedes 28/95 PS
Mercedes-Benz 770
Mercedes-Benz 170 V

The company name has always been and still is Daimler-Benz, but the cars themselves are generally known as Mercedes-Benz. The name Mercedes was imposed by Emil Jellinek who imported the cars into Western Europe and America, as that was the name of his daughter. From 1926 Mercedes was linked to Benz and the three pointed star became the firm's emblem.

The first machine bearing this name was the 35 PS, dating from 1900, which at the turn of the century won numerous races, especially on the Cote d'Azur. Initially the name was only used for the racing cars but with time it came to be used for the entire production. It was followed by the 28/95, which was one of Daimler-Mercedes' most successful racing cars. Although it had a smaller engine, it developed its maximum power of approximately 95 bhp at the same engine speed (1,800 revs). It had an overhead camshaft, side valves, and a maximum speed of about 72 mph. In 1921 a version with a shorter chassis was driven to victory by Sailer in the Coppa Florio and came second in the Targa Florio. These successes however, must be credited to the driver as the car was not ideally suited to the Sicilian circuit. In the post war period modifications were made to the 28/95. These were mainly in the engine which became monobloc instead of twin block. In 1923 front brakes were added to the car.

Car: **Mercedes 28/95 PS**
Year: **1922**
Engine: **6 cylinders in line**
Bore and stroke: **105 × 140 mm**
Cylinder capacity: **7250 cc**
Gearbox: **4 forward**
Brake horse power: **95**
Maximum speed: **72 mph**
Wheelbase: **11 ft 0 ins (3.35 m)**
Suspension: **front and rear: semi-elliptic leaf-springs**

The successes it gained in the sporting field encouraged Mercedes to continue racing. The racing and touring models, however, were kept very separate, the tourers being divided into luxury and medium-small cars. This company policy was continued even after the merger with Benz in 1926.

The 770 of 1930 was one of the company's largest capacity and most prestigious machines. Its claimed maximum power was 150 bhp at 2,800 revs under normal conditions and 200 bhp at the same engine speed with full accelerator power as this cut in a supercharger. The engine had over-head valves, dual magneto and coil ignition, twin bodied carburetors, aluminium pistons, nine main bearings, pressure lubrication with a gear pump and water cooling with a pump and thermostat. The transmission had four synchromesh speeds and third gear was direct drive, fourth being overdrive. The suspension was later changed, the semi-elliptic leaf-springs being replaced by independent wheels with swing axles.

It was inevitable that the car's grandeur, ideal for parades, should lead to the production of both a special closed and open version for use by Hitler. In this form the car's weight increased from 5,960 pounds (2,700 kg), to 8,160 pounds (3,700

Car: **Mercedes 170 V**
Year: **1936**
Engine: **4 cylinders in line**
Bore and stroke: **73.5 × 100 mm**
Cylinder capacity: **1697 cc**
Gearbox: **4 forward**
Brake horse power: **32**
Maximum speed: **69 mph**
Wheelbase: **8 ft 6½ ins (2.60 m)**
Suspension: **front: independent suspension with transverse leaf-springs; rear: independent suspension with coil springs**

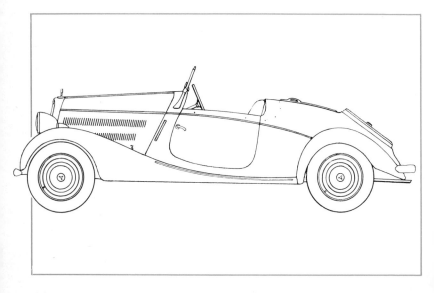

kg). Even the windows were one inch (2.25 cm) thick.

The 170 V of 1936 was typical of the medium class. It had a tubular chassis, independent suspension and the engine had side valves. It was with this car that Mercedes restarted its business after the war even though the bombing had destroyed its factories. The 170 V gave rise to the 170 D which used a diesel engine. This replaced the 260 D of the 1930s which was the first diesel-engined car in the world. As the 170 V was rather heavy it needed a long straight in order to reach its maximum speed of 69 mph.

70,000 170 Vs were produced before the war, 17,000 were supplied to the German Army during the war and 49,000 were produced when activity resumed. A further 94,000 were built in the 170 D and the 170 S

Car: **Mercedes 770**
Year: **1930**
Engine: **8 cylinders in line**
Bore and stroke: **95 × 135 mm**
Cylinder capacity: **7655 cc**
Gearbox: **4 forward**
Brake horse power: **150**
Maximum speed: **107 mph**
Wheelbase: **12 ft 4 ins (3.76 m)**
Suspension: **front and rear: semi-elliptic leaf-springs**

versions. The latter differed in its bodywork and in its engine. This was an enlarged 1767 cc engine, the maximum power increasing to 52 bhp and the maximum speed to 76 mph. There were two other versions, the cabriolet which remained in production until 1957 and the 170 DS which had the same enlarged 1767 cc engine, a maximum power of 40 bhp and a maximum speed of 66 mph. In 1955 a 170 with a monocoque body was named the 180.

Opel 6/16 PS
Opel P4

Opel started by manufacturing sewing machines in 1862. The first factory was at Russelsheim near Frankfurt and it remained there when Adam Opel considered changing it over first in 1866 to the production of bicycles, (because of the passion that his five sons had for two wheeled vehicles), and then to cars.

Car production started in 1898 following an agreement between Opel's heirs and Freidrich Lutzmann, who had designed a motorised carriage. The Opels were far from satisfied with their first vehicle and it was not a commercial success. At this point an agreement was drawn up with Darracq by which Opel bought the manufacturing rights to the Darracq models. The first of these appeared in 1902. Then the Opels broke away from Darracq and produced a car which was entirely their

own and which brought them much acclaim on the race circuit. The 6/16 was one of their most popular cars and it remained in production until 1914. The engine had a monobloc L cylinder head and developed 16 bhp at 1,750 revs. It was one of Opel's first products to have a 4-speed gearbox, it had magneto ignition, a cone clutch and a maximum speed of 41 mph. In 1908 Opel achieved a record that excited much envy at the time: it had produced 10,000 cars. In 1912 the firm, which was already known for producing particularly sturdy cars, brought out the Püppchen (doll) which had four cylinders and four speeds.

The P4 dates from 1935 and its production was based on American methods. Opels had been sold to General Motors in 1929. The particularly attractive price of DM 1,450 made the P4 highly successful but it only remained in production for two years. The reason was probably because it overshadowed the Hitler

régime's 'people's car' or Volkswagen. Technically there was nothing outstanding about the P4, indeed it was rather behind its time. However, Opel and its new owners had an entirely practical objective; this was a sturdy car which lacked frills and was cheap. In this they were imitating the approach of Ford in England. The P4 derived from cars that were already in production by 1929 and 1932; it differed only in having a shorter piston stroke than its stable mates. It developed 23 bhp at 3,600 revs. It had pumped water cooling, a 6 volt electrical system, mechanical brakes, a 3-speed gearbox (a 4-speed gearbox was an extra) and a 2- or 4-door body. Aside from these features, which admittedly do not place the P4 in the forefront of progress, the P4 occupies a place of great importance in the

Car: **Opel P4**
Year: **1935**
Engine: **4 cylinders in line**
Bore and stroke: **67.5 × 75 mm**
Cylinder capacity: **1074 cc**
Gearbox: **3 forward**
Brake horse power: **23**
Maximum speed: **57 mph**
Wheelbase: **7 ft 6 ins (2.3 m)**
Suspension: **front and rear: semi-elliptic leaf-springs**

Car: **Opel 6/16 PS**
Year: **1911**
Engine: **4 cylinders in line**
Bore and stroke: **70 × 100 mm**
Cylinder capacity: **1540 cc**
Gearbox: **4 forward**
Brake horse power: **16**
Maximum speed: **41 mph**
Wheelbase: **8 ft 8 ins (2.6 m)**
Suspension: **front and rear: semi-elliptic leaf-springs**

history of Opel. The P4 was the inspiration for the Kadett manufactured by General Motors which has sold around the world.

Stoewer began to produce motorized vehicles in 1899 which makes it one of the earliest German car firms. From tricycles with single cylinder De Dion engines, the Stoewer brothers, Emil and Bernhard, moved on to cars with 4 and 6-cylinder engines (they were amongst the first in Germany to use the latter layout). The 4 cylinders of the 1912 machine illustrated here had a L cylinder head, side valves and a multi-plate clutch. The brake pedal acted on the transmission and the hand brake on rear wheel drum brakes.

After concentrating on airplane engine production during the First World War, Stoewer resumed car construction with a range of new models. However, they now had to produce smaller machines, though the company continued to sound out the

Car: **Stoewer**
Year: **1912**
Engine: **4 cylinders in line**
Bore and stroke: **78 × 118 mm**
Cylinder capacity: **2247 cc**
Gearbox: **4 forward**
Brake horse power: **22**
Maximum speed: **50 mph**
Wheelbase: **9 ft 8 ins (2.9 m)**
Suspension: **front: semi-elliptic leaf-springs; rear: ¾ elliptic leaf-springs**

luxury car market with 8-cylinder models. In 1930 Bernard Stoewer designed the highly successful V 5. This was the first cheap German car with front-wheel drive and independent suspension. In 1931 and 1932 more than 2,000 were produced. From then on Stoewer restricted itself almost entirely to front-wheel drive cars. It ceased car production at the outbreak of the Second World War and concentrated on supplying components to other manufacturers.

Wanderer began by manufacturing bicycles near Chemnitz in Saxony, under the name of Wanderer Werke of Schonau. In 1911 it started car production after having tried to produce motorcycles. The firm's first car was the 5/12. It had a unit construction engine and 3-speed transmission. The engine had overhead inlet valves and side exhaust valves, and developed 12 bhp at 1,800 revs. The tandem arrangement of the seats explains the vehicle's narrowness of 3 feet 6½ inches (1.08 m) and its wheelbase of 7 feet 2½ inches (2.20 m). It also had a low overall weight of 1,545 pounds (700 kg) but its maximum speed of 44 mph was quite fast for its time. Wanderer called this original mini car Püppchen the name which Opel also gave to one of its models. In its early years Wanderer confined

Car: **Wanderer 5/12 PS**
Year: **1914**
Engine: **4 cylinders in line**
Bore and stroke: **62 × 95 mm**
Cylinder capacity: **1145 cc**
Gearbox: **3 forward**
Brake horse power: **12**
Maximum speed: **44 mph**
Wheelbase: **7 ft 2½ ins (2.2 m)**
Suspension: **front: semi-elliptic leaf-springs; rear: ¾ elliptic leaf-springs**

itself almost exclusively to small-engined cars, but in 1929 it put a 2600 cc 6-cylinder model into production and in 1931 it commissioned 6- and 8-cylinder engines from Ferdinand Porsche. In 1932 Wanderer merged with Audi, DKW and Horch to form Auto-Union. The new models with Porsche-designed engines were in the 1933 Berlin Motor Show.

Wanderer concentrated on producing military vehicles for the army during the war, and car production was never resumed when it was over.

Italy

The first Italian contribution to steam powered locomotion can be attributed to Virginio Bordino. In 1854 he designed and built a Landau which was powered by a vertical shaft steam engine that worked on coke. The twin-cylinder engine was mounted at the rear; the transmission was by driving rods and the steering was a trapezium linkage Ackerman system. The vehicle, which was first seen in Turin, had a maximum speed of 5 mph.

Luigi De Cristoforis of Milan designed a simpler igneous-pneumatic powered vehicle which foreshadowed the use of combustible oil (naptha). Eugenio Barsanti and Matteucci claimed to be the first to invent the atmospheric engine; Spinelli and Schiavi patented a pyronitric gas engine that harnessed the explosions of a gaseous mixture, and Emilio Berio produced various improved versions of Barsanti and Matteucci's engine. In 1879 Murnigotti obtained a patent for the use of a gas engine with electrical ignition and two cylinders with alternated power phases to propel a velocipede and a 3-wheeled car. Five years previously, in 1874 Professor Enrico Bernardi of Padua University had already begun his research on atmospheric engines. His numerous investigations on various aspects of motor vehicle design including the steering, the transmission and engine cooling, led in 1896 to the limited partnership of Bernardi-Miari & Giusti & Compagnia for the manufacture of Bernardi engines and 3- and 4-wheel motor vehicles. A Miari & Giusti 3-wheeler with a Bernardi engine won a motor race from Turin to Alessandria via Asti on July 17, 1898. It covered 120 miles at an average speed of 12 mph and used 12 pounds (5 kg) of fuel. It had a 620 cc single-cylinder engine which developed 2 bhp and engine speeds between 420 and 820 revs.

Bernardi-Miari & Giusti, who between 1896 and 1901 built and sold 100 cars (in 1899 the company took the name of Motori Bernardi-G. Miari, Giusti & Compagnia) represented the start of the Italian motor car industry.

As in the United States, Great Britain and France, the advent of the car in Italy was accompanied by numerous ventures and dozens of models appeared and disappeared within a few years. The major figures in this initial phase were the Ceirano brothers. They were responsible for the founding of a number of companies including Welleyes, Spa, Rapid, Itala and Scat.

In 1899, Fiat, which was to become the principal Italian car manufacturer, was founded in Turin. Fiat started with a vehicle bought from Welleyes, which had been a design of Aristide Faccioli and patented by Matteo Ceirano. The man who worked hardest at launching the Welleyes cars was Cesare Goria-Gatti who, in 1898, had entered the partnership founded by Giovanni Battista Ceirano.

One of the Turin Automobile publications, *Marche Italiane Scomparse* (defunct Italian manufacturers), lists about 300 manufacturers who survived from the early twentieth century through to the outbreak of the First World War. Apart from Fiat, Lancia in 1906 and later Alfa Romeo, also established themselves as strong and successful companies.

The public's interest in motor cars was aroused from racing. Only later did they move into production of light, economical and cheap vehicles. The first popular car manufactured by Fiat was the 509, introduced in 1925 and sold for L18,500. Ninety thousand of these were built before 1929. The first true 4-seater, however, was the 508, or Balilla, which appeared in 1932, followed in 1936 by the 500 or Topolino.

Lancia, whilst not producing great numbers, was renowned for its refinement of some of its cars' advanced mechanics. For instance the monocoque body was used on the Lambda in 1923 with a narrow V engine.

The golden era of the car in Italy was the 1930s. The car was represented by such manufacturers as Isotta-Fraschini whose cars were considered to be the equals of Rolls-Royce, Hispano-Suiza and Duesenberg. Production ceased at the beginning of the Second World War.

The first reliable figures on the progress of car production in Italy date from 1925, when 45,800 cars and 4,600 industrial vehicles were produced. Production then fell again and it was not until 1950 that production exceeded 100,000 units. Manufacture has risen continuously since this period and this has enabled Italian industry to meet the competition from other major European car manufacturers.

A.L.F.A. 12 HP
Alfa Romeo P2
Alfa Romeo RL Super Sport
Alfa Romeo 6C 1750 GS
Alfa Romeo 6C 2300 Pescara
Alfa Romeo 6C 2500 Turismo

Car: **A.L.F.A. 12 HP**
Year: **1911**
Engine: **4 cylinders in line**
Bore and stroke: **80 × 120 mm**
Cylinder capacity: **2413 cc**
Gears: **3 forward**
Brake horse power: **22**
Maximum speed: **56 mph**
Wheelbase: **9 ft 7 ins (2.92 m)**
Suspension: **front: semi-elliptic leaf-springs; rear: semi-elliptic leaf-springs and ½ cantilever springs**

Alfa Romeo arose indirectly from the French firm Darracq. Darracq had set up a factory in Italy to assemble their products, especially a kind of car that would be suitable as a taxi. The car was not a success and a group of Italian financiers stepped in to take over these interests. In 1910 the firm took on a new name: Anomina Lombarda Fabbrica Automobile (A.L.F.A.). The now wholly Italian design of the cars was carried out by Giuseppe Merosi who had been previously employed by Orio Marchand, Fiat and Bianchi.

The 24 HP was the first car in the new line. It appeared in 1911 and had a 4084 cc monobloc engine and enclosed shaft drive. The 12 HP, though less complex, was inspired by the 24 HP and it was with the 12 HP that A.L.F.A. began its racing career at the end of 1911. A car was entered in the first road race at Modena which was restricted to touring cars travelling 940 miles in five stages. The 12 HP was classed among the six equal, unpenalized entrants. The 12 HP's engine developed 22 bhp at 2,100 revs and this was later raised to 25 bhp at 2,400 revs (series B), and to 28 bhp at 2,400 revs (series C). The maximum speed of the first series was 56 mph rising to 63 mph for series C. It was available in two versions: a torpedo and a limousine (the torpedo's dry weight being 2,030 pounds (920 kg)). The 12 HP remained in production from 1910 to 1915 and 330 were built.

In 1915 A.L.F.A. underwent an important change when the majority shareholder, the Banca di Sconto appointed an engineer, Nicola Romeo to run the firm. In 1918 Romeo's various companies were merged under a single name and in 1920 Romeo's name was added to Alfa.

The RL was considered to be Giuseppe Merosi's masterpiece. Displayed for the first time at Alfa Romeo's showroom in the via Dante, Milan in 1921, it immediately entered production in both standard and sports versions. Its manufacture continued until 1927. The RL was raced between 1923 and 1927 and it won 90 victories in the touring class. It competed mainly in hill-climbs and endurance races. Neither the first nor the second series had front brakes, but by September 1923, the third series had front and rear drum brakes.

Vittorio Jano, who succeeded Merosi, began with the P2 then designed the 1500, which later became

Car: **Alfa Romeo P2**
Year: **1924**
Engine: **8 cylinders in line**
Bore and stroke: **62 × 85 mm**
Cylinder capacity: **1987 cc**
Gears: **4 forward**
Brake horse power: **135**
Maximum speed: —
Wheelbase: **8 ft 8 ins (2.64 m)**
Suspension: **front and rear: semi-elliptic leaf-springs**

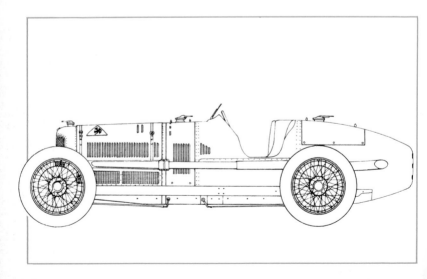

the 1750. Various versions of the 1500 were produced; these differed in their engines particularly as to whether or not there was a supercharger, with power ranging from 64 bhp at 4,500 revs without a supercharger, to 102 bhp at 5,000 revs with. The 1500 was produced from 1929 until 1933 in five series. The difference between the third, fourth and fifth series lay mainly in the adjustable mechanism for heating the mixture in the inlet manifold by means of the exhaust gases. A total of 2,579 were built. The 1750 was designed both for use on motorways and minor roads by using a formula based on a combination of a low weight of 2,000 pounds (900 kg) and high performance at speeds between 80-105 mph.

Another of Jano's designs was the 8C 2300 which was also built between 1931 and 1934, again in several versions. A special feature of the 8-cylinder engine was that it retained the same bore and stroke as the 6-cylinder 1750. The two extra cylinders raised its capacity to 2336 cc and the power developed ranged from 142 bhp at 5,000 revs to 180 bhp at 5,400 revs. This engine also powered a Grand Prix twin-seater, the 8C Monza. The sports versions of the 2300 are amongst the most successful Alfa Romeos. Although it had an unhappy beginning in the 1931 Mille Miglia, Nuvolari then drove on to victory in the 22nd Targa Florio.

Car: **Alfa Romeo RL Super Sport**
Year: **1925**
Engine: **6 cylinders in line**
Bore and stroke: **76 × 110 mm**
Cylinder capacity: **2916 cc**
Gears: **4 forward**
Brake horse power: **83**
Maximum speed: **85 mph**
Wheelbase: **10 ft 3½ ins (3.13 m)**
Suspension: **front and rear: semi-elliptic leaf-springs**

Birkin won the Irish G.P. driving a 2300, while a 4-seater 8C won the Le Mans 24-Hour race with an all British team (Birkin-Howe). In 1932 the 2300 took first and second places in both the Mille Miglia (the teams being Borzacchini-Bignami and Trossi-Brivio) and the Targa Florio (Nuvolari and Borzacchini). In 1933 it took the first eight places in the Mille Miglia (won by Nuvolari) and the first three positions in the Le Mans 24-Hour (won by Sommer-Nuvolari). The success gained in the Pescara 24-Hour gave birth to the little sedan that bore the name Pescara, the maximum power being 95 bhp at 4,500 revs.

The 6C 2500 was less important from a technical point of view but was a link between pre- and post-war production. The 2500, production of which resumed at the end of the war, represented a new policy on the part of Alfa Romeo. Whilst not abandoning racing, Alfa were faced with the ever growing need to increase manufacturing. From the beginning the 6C 2500 was produced in three models (Turismo, Sport and Super Sport) and a total of 1,885 cars were produced, Alfa itself building the body of the Turismo.

Car: **Alfa Romeo 6C 1750 Grand Sport**
Year: **1930**
Engine: **6 cylinders in line**
Bore and stroke: **65 × 88 mm**
Cylinder capacity: **1752 cc**
Gears: **4 forward**
Brake horse power: **85**
Maximum speed: **95 mph**
Wheelbase: **9 ft 0 ins (2.74 m)**
Suspension: **front and rear: semi-elliptic leaf-springs and friction shock absorber**

Car: **Alfa Romeo 6C 2300 Pescara**
Year: **1934**
Engine: **6 cylinders in line**
Bore and stroke: **70 × 100 mm**
Cylinder capacity: **2309 cc**
Gears: **4 forward**
Brake horse power: **95**
Maximum speed: —
Wheelbase: **9 ft 10 ins (3.3 m)**
Suspension: **front and rear: semi-elliptic leaf-springs**

▼

Car: **Alfa Romeo 6C 2500 Turismo**   ▲
Year: **1939**
Engine: **6 cylinders in line**
Bore and stroke: **72 × 100 mm**
Cylinder capacity: **2443 cc**
Gears: **4 forward**
Brake horse power: **105**
Maximum speed: —
Wheelbase: **10 ft 8 ins (2.64 m)**
Suspension: **front: cylinder encased coil springs; rear: longitudinal torsion bar**

The 4C was the third model to appear on the market in the brief history of Ansaldo. Its overhead camshaft engine made the 4C a very advanced machine for its time. However the new firm's hopes of opposing Fiat's dominance was not successful as it could not withstand the political and economic crisis at the end of the First World War.

This company was founded in 1853 by the engineer, Giovanni Ansaldo and was known chiefly for the building of ships and the manufacture of artillery. Ansaldo partially changed over to the production of automobiles at the end of the war when he attempted to find a use for the Transaerea factories at Turin.

The 4C was designed by Guido Soria, an ex-employee of Fiat. The engine had a removable cylinder

Car: **Ansaldo 4C**
Year: **1920**
Engine: **4 cylinders in line**
Bore and stroke: **70 × 120 mm**
Cylinder capacity: **1804 cc**
Gears: **3 forward**
Brake horse power: **36**
Maximum speed: **50 mph**
Wheelbase: **9 ft 0 ins (2.74 m)**
Suspension: **front and rear: semi-elliptic leaf-springs**

head, magneto ignition, pumped water-cooling, fan and radiator and single plate clutch. The hand brake acted on the transmission. Its maximum speed was about 50 mph. In 1923 an engine of about 2000 cc entered production.

In 1924 there came a 6-cylinder engine with the same capacity and in 1929 a 3500 cc 8-cylinder engine. In 1928 the 4-cylinder models or types were given a 4-speed gearbox. The Ansaldo gained a strong reputation in hill-climbs.

Bianchi had a long life as a car manufacturer. It ceased to exist as such in
1955 as the result of an agreement
between Fiat and Pirelli. Prior to cars
it had been actively involved with
bicycles and motorcycles. The company first became associated with cars
in 1899 (though this is not historically
definite), when its founder, Edoardo
Bianchi, built a 4-wheeler powered by
a single-cylinder De Dion-Bouton
engine. One of Bianchi's designers
was Giuseppe Merosi, who moved on
to A.L.F.A. and hence to Alfa
Romeo.

Bianchi built simple, solid machines
powered by 4-cylinder engines with
side valves in T-shaped cylinder
heads, with low tension magneto ignition, a steel chassis, a honeycomb
radiator and double chain drive.
From 1909 onwards, engines with

Car: **Bianchi 20/30**
Year: **1910**
Engine: **4 cylinders in line**
Bore and stroke: **110 × 130 mm**
Cylinder capacity: **4939 cc**
Gears: **4 forward**
Brake horse power: **30**
Maximum speed: **40 mph**
Wheelbase: **10 ft 6 ins (3.2 m)**
Suspension: **front and rear: semi-elliptic
    leaf-springs**

L-shaped cylinder heads, high tension
magneto ignition and shaft drive were
adopted and all these features are
found on the 20/30. When the 20/30
appeared it had chain drive and an
engine with a twin block L-shaped
cylinder head but it was later modern-
ized and fitted with a monobloc
engine and shaft drive. The increase
in the bore brought the capacity up to
5700 cc and its maximum speed rose
to about 50 mph.

Ceirano Tipo CS
Ceirano Tipo N 150

The Ceirano Brothers, Giovanni Battista, Giovanni and Matteo, provide one of the best examples of the initiative and vitality of the early car manufacturers. On October 23, 1898, the limited partnership of Ceirano Giovanni Battista & Company was founded in Turin. One of the most significant names in Italian automobile engineering, Aristide Faccioli, was its technical director. Its first vehicle was produced the following year and was powered by a 663 cc twin-cylinder engine.

Known as Welleyes this car was almost immediately rechristened Fiat as it was sold together with equipments and patents for a total of L30,000 to a group of Turinese manufacturers who had just founded Fiat (Fabbrica Italiana Automobili Torino). Giovanni Battista himself joined Fiat but in 1901 he went into business for himself again and founded Fratelli Ceirano with his brother Matteo.

In 1905 Giovanni Ceirano founded the firm Scat (Società Ceirano Automobili Torino). Giovanni left Scat in 1916 when the shares were sold to a Frenchman called Brasier. However, in the postwar period Scat's production declined to such an extent that Giovanni was able to reunite it with another company, Giovanni Ceirano Fabbrica Automobile S.A., and the two merged in 1923.

Scat had racing successes and in 1914, Ernesto Ceirano, Giovanni's son, drove a Scat to victory in the Tour of Sicily. Ernesto also won the 1914 Parma-Piaggio di Berceto hill race driving a Scat.

Giovanni Battista had founded a company with his brother in 1903. It was called G.G. Fratelli but it was a short-lived venture and the two brothers split up. Giovanni Battista went on to found Ceirano & Compagnia. He was also responsible for the company called Star (Società Torinese Automobili Rapid).

Matteo's career was no less complicated. In 1904 he founded Itala which built huge Edwardian cars with overtones of Mercedes. He then moved on to smaller and more conventionally designed cars. In 1906 he founded Spa (Società Piemontese Automobili).

The two vehicles illustrated here were Giovanni Ceirano's products.

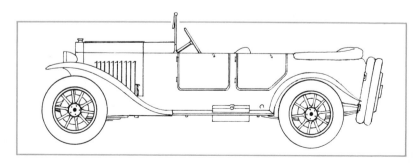

The CS, from 1921, had a side valve engine and developed 22 bhp at 2,200 revs. This car gave rise to two sporting versions, the Tipo CS 22 and the Tipo SC 4, the latter having a capacity of 2843 cc and a bore and stroke of 85 × 130 mm. The CS 2 developed 35 bhp at 3,000 revs.

The second car illustrated was nick-named the Ceiranina because of its engine capacity. The engine also had side valves, but a sports version, the 150 CS, had overhead valves.

The erratic company of Scat and of Ceirano in general came to an end when Fiat, who had become the principal shareholder of Scat, decided in 1932, that it should be absorbed by Spa of which they had taken control in 1926.

Ceirano was therefore placed in liquidation, its trademark was sold to

Car: **Ceirano Tipo CS**
Year: **1921**
Engine: **4 cylinders in line**
Bore and stroke: **75 × 130 mm**
Cylinder capacity: **2166 cc**
Gears: **4 forward**
Brake horse power: **22**
Maximum speed: —
Wheelbase: —
Suspension: **front and rear: semi-elliptic leaf-springs**

Car: **Ceirano Tipo N 150**
Year: **1925**
Engine: **4 cylinders in line**
Bore and stroke: **65 × 110 mm**
Cylinder capacity: **1460 cc**
Gears: **4 forward**
Brake horse power: **40**
Maximum speed: **60 mph**
Wheelbase: **8 ft 9 ins (2.97 m)**
Suspension: **front and rear: semi-elliptic leaf-springs**

Scat and all car production was entrusted to Scat. In 1931 Giovanni Battista Ceirano left Scat permanently and in 1933 he founded Fata with his son Ernesto but it did not manufacture cars.

Antonio Chiribiri, the founder of this make, started in the aircraft industry (Fabbrica Torinese Velivoli Chiribiri & Compagnia). In 1910 the shortage of orders for aircraft forced him to transfer to the car industry. Chiribiri set up a small, efficient team, one of the administrative people being Vittorio Valletta who was later to become the leading figure in Fiat. The car which brought Chiribiri most fame was a 1600 which had the gearbox mounted in with the differential gear on the rear axle.

In 1922 a twin cam shaft model was put into production and this won numerous races with the famous Tazio Nuvolari as driver. The illustration here is of the standard version. The twin cam shaft engine developed 45 bhp at 3,500 revs (65 bhp at 5,000 revs in the racing version). The maxi-

Car: **Chiribiri Tipo Milano**
Year: **1925**
Engine: **4 cylinders in line**
Bore and stroke: **65 × 112 mm**
Capacity: **1485 cc**
Gears: **4 forward**
Brake horse power: **45**
Maximum speed: **75 mph**
Wheelbase: **—**
Suspension: **front and rear: semi-elliptic leaf-springs**

mum speed of the former model was 75 mph and of the latter 94 mph. A Grand Prix racer called the Monza was also produced. Another version had a supercharger and the maximum power rose to 93 bhp at 5,700 revs. With a light body, this last car could reach over 110 mph. The economic crisis caused a large drop in sales and Chiribiri went out of existence in September 1928. Its factories were taken over by Lancia.

Diatto began in 1835 as Turin coach builders. In 1905 Vittorio and Pietro Diatto made an agreement with the French firm of Clement-Bayard to create an automobile business. A 1884 cc twin-cylinder car and a 3770 cc 4-cylinder car already being produced by Clement-Bayard were chosen. In 1909 Adolphe Clement, who had been chairman of the firm Diatto-A. Clement Vetture Marca Torino, withdrew, leaving the two brothers in full control of Diatto. The company changed its name to Officine Fonderie Frejus Diatto and in 1909 put the first 4-cylinder monobloc into production. In 1915 a body building shop was added to the factory.

The Diatto 20 dates from 1922. It did not originate in the firm but was the work of Veltro of Turin who handed the design over to Diatto. The

Car: **Diatto 20 A**
Year: **1927**
Engine: **4 cylinders in line**
Bore and stroke: **80 × 100 mm**
Cylinder capacity: **1996 cc**
Gears: **4 forward**
Brake horse power: **40**
Maximum speed: **—**
Wheelbase: **10 ft 2 ins (3.09 m)**
Suspension: **front and rear: semi-elliptic leaf-springs**

overhead valves and camshaft classed the 20 as a modern car. The engine of the 20 S developed 75 bhp as opposed to the 40 bhp of the 20 A. In 1923 the company was placed in liquidation and it changed its name once again to Autocostruzioni Diatto S.A. A Grand Prix car also featured again in its program. This was commissioned from Alfieri Maserati and he produced a 2000 cc 8-cylinder vehicle which made its first appearance at the 1925 Italian Grand Prix. Nothing came of this project.

Fiat 12-15 HP Zero
Fiat 501
Fiat 520 Superfiat
Fiat 519 S
Fiat 508 Balilla 3 Marce

The type Zero was the name Fiat gave to one of its most famous cars. The Zero appeared after the Model I and was slightly shorter in length; 12 feet (3.66 m) to the Model I's 12 feet 5 inches (3.78 m) whilst being powered by an engine of the same capacity. As the car was smaller than the Model I, it was given the name Zero. The Zero was Fiat's first mass produced car to have a relatively small capacity and had only one style of body which was the torpedo. Over

two thousand were produced between 1912 and 1915 and the Zero was also furnished with an electrical system. The Zero had a maximum speed of 39 mph, did an average of 24 miles per gallon and had a dry weight of 1,990 pounds (900 kg). Its engine developed 19 bhp at 2,000 revs and had a compression ratio of 4.2:1. The spider and landaulet versions were entirely the work of coach builders who, as with preceding models, were supplied with the bare chassis.

The 501 appeared in 1919 and

Car: **Fiat 12-15 HP Zero**
Year: **1912**
Engine: **4 cylinders in line**
Bore and stroke: **70 × 120 mm**
Cylinder capacity: **1846 cc**
Gearbox: **4 forward**
Brake horse power: **19**
Maximum speed: **39 mph**
Wheelbase: **8 ft 8 ins (2.64 m)**
Suspension: front: **semi-elliptic leaf-springs;**
 rear: **¾ leaf-springs**

remained in production until 1926. 69,478 of these were built of which 2,614 were the Model S. The 501 was another milestone in Fiat's career, not only because of the high level of production but also because it became such a popular car with the Italians. The car was similar to the Model T Ford as its mechanics were simplified so that no specialist skills would be required for repair work.

The 501 was Fiat's first post World War I car and was designed by a lawyer, Carlo Cavelli. The standard version's maximum speed was 44 mph, whilst for the S version it was 59-62 mph.

The Super was Fiat's only car to have a 12-cylinder engine. The angle of the V was 60 degrees and it developed 80 bhp at 2,000 revs with a maximum speed of 75 mph. It is not

Car: **Fiat 501**
Year: **1919**
Engine: **4 cylinders in line**
Bore and stroke: **65 × 110 mm**
Cylinder capacity: **1460 cc**
Gearbox: **4 forward**
Brake horse power: **23**
Maximum speed: **44 mph**
Wheelbase: **8 ft 9 ins (2.66 m)**
Suspension: **front and rear: semi-elliptic leaf-springs**

certain how many of the Superfiats were built, though it is maintained that there were only five. The Turin firm intended this car for the export market, as a rival to the highly esteemed Rolls-Royces and Hispano-Suizas, but the large capacity Fiat was not very successful abroad. Fiat, both then and later, was particularly connected with small capacity cars and it excelled in the design and manufacture of these cars. The financial crisis in 1922 also played a part in the

Car: **Fiat 520 Superfiat**   ▲
Year: **1921**
Engine: **V-12**
Bore and stroke: **85 × 110 mm**
Cylinder capacity: **6805 cc**
Gearbox: **3 forward**
Brake horse power: **80**
Maximum speed: **75 mph**
Wheelbase: **12 ft 8 ins (3.86 m)**
Suspension: **front: semi-elliptic leaf-springs;
   rear: semi-elliptic leaf-springs and
   mechanical shock-absorbers**

Car: **Fiat 519 S**
Year: **1922**
Engine: **6 cylinders in line**
Bore and stroke: **85 × 140 mm**
Cylinder capacity: **4766 cc**
Gearbox: **4 forward**
Brake horse power: **77**
Maximum speed: **79 mph**
Wheelbase: **10 ft 9½ ins (3.28 m)**
Suspension: **front and rear: semi-elliptic
   leaf-springs and mechanical
   shock-absorbers**   ▼

failure of the ambitious Superfiat venture.

The 519 S assumed the role of leading lady amongst Fiat's products and it was also their only car to have a V radiator similar to the early style Mercedes. The 519 was a fast car, having a maximum speed of 79 mph despite its considerable weight of 4,400 pounds (2,000 kg). Together with the standard models, the 519 and 519 B, a total of 2,411 cars were produced.

The 508 or Balilla, which was presented to the public at the 1932 Milan Motor Show, revealed Fiat's true policy. Its length of 11 feet 3 inches (3.44 m), its ability to carry a driver and three passengers, its low weight of 1,510 pounds (685 kg) and its fuel consumption of 36 miles per gallon made it their first popular car.

Car: **Fiat 508 Balilla**
Year: **1932**
Engine: **4 cylinders in line**
Bore and stroke: **65 × 75 mm**
Cylinder capacity: **995 cc**
Gearbox: **3 forward**
Brake horse power: **20**
Maximum speed: —
Wheelbase: **7 ft 5 ins (2.26 m)**
Suspension: **front and rear: semi-elliptic leaf-springs and hydraulic shock-absorbers**

Initially the Balilla had a 3-speed transmission; by 1934 41,396 had been built. In 1934 the sedan, the roadster and the coupé were provided with a fourth gear. The weight of the sedan rose to about 1,565-1,640 pounds (710-745 kg) although its maximum speed remained unchanged. 71,700 cars with the fourth gear were produced.

Isotta-Fraschini OC 5
Isotta-Fraschini Tipo 8

Two of Isotta-Fraschini's most admired products were the Tipo 8, launched in 1920 and its larger sister the Tipo 8A, launched in 1924. Both these cars were comparable with the most celebrated cars of their period such as Rolls-Royce, Hispano-Suiza and Duesenberg. Isotta-Fraschini was founded in 1900 under the name of Società Milanese d'Automobili Isotta Fraschini & Compagnia by Cesare Isotta and Vincente, Oreste and Antonio Fraschini. Riccardo Bencetti, Paolo Meda and Ludovico Prinetti were also involved.

Isotta-Fraschini began by representing, in Italy, the Renault with the single-cylinder De Dion-Bouton engine. Then it cautiously began to build its own cars using French single-cylinder Aster engines. Isotta-Fraschini's designer was Giuseppe Stefanini who produced a large number of models. In 1905 Stefanini was succeeded by Giustano Cattaneo who was already known for working

with Brixia-Zust. Cattaneo was to make Isotta-Fraschini one of the most advanced types of car and gave it a world class stature.

The OC 5 and the Tipo 8 are held to be the most typical of Isotta-Fraschini's vast range of products. In 1907, Isotta-Fraschini approached the Société Lorraine des Anciens Etablissements De Dietrich & Compagnie for help and it bought half their shares. The OC 5's engine developed 36 bhp and it had a maximum speed of 47 mph. Apart from the single-cylinder with which it began production in 1902, Isotta-Fraschini used an unbroken series of 4-cylinder engines from 1904 until the appearance of the highly celebrated Tipo 8. The engine had overhead valves, developed 80 bhp, magneto ignition and a multi-plate clutch. As the Tipo 8 had a variety of bodywork an exact figure for its overall length cannot be given, but it was about 16 feet 6 inches (5 m). The Tipo itself was fast, with a maximum speed of 87 mph and the 8 A SS and the 8 B could reach speeds of 100 mph.

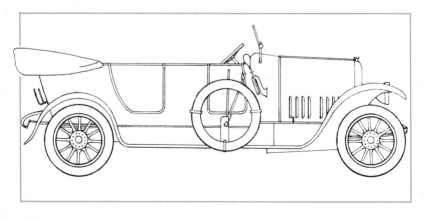

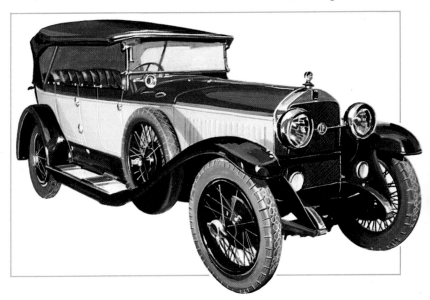

Isotta-Fraschini made a name for itself in the field of military equipment with engines for airplanes and naval vessels. When much later it was forced to abandon car production because of poor management it turned to trucks, using German M.A.N. engines. Cattaneo left and design was entrusted to Giuseppe Merosi, who was already known for the work he had done at Bianchi, A.L.F.A. and Alfa Romeo. Shortly after the Second World War it again took an interest in cars with a model that had a rear-mounted 8-cylinder engine. It was called the Monterosa after the name of the street where Isotta had had its factory since 1906. As well as being rear-mounted the engine's V-8 layout was another feature of this car. Prototypes of the Monterosa were built and Caproni,

Car: **Isotta-Fraschini Tipo 8**
Year: **1920**
Engine: **8 cylinders in line**
Bore and stroke: **85 × 130 mm**
Cylinder capacity: **5898 cc**
Gearbox: **3 forward**
Brake horse power: **80**
Maximum speed: **87 mph**
Wheelbase: **11 ft 2½ ins (3.41 m)** *or*
   12 ft 1 in (3.68 m)
Suspension: **front: semi-elliptic leaf-springs;**
   rear: semi-elliptic leaf-springs and
   hydraulic shock-absorbers

Car: **Isotta-Fraschini OC 5**
Year: **1914**
Engine: **4 cylinders in line**
Bore and stroke: **100 × 140 mm**
Cylinder capacity: **4398 cc**
Gearbox: **4 forward**
Brake horse power: **36**
Maximum speed: **47 mph**
Wheelbase: **10 ft 4½ ins (3.16 m)** *or*
   10 ft 8½ ins (3.26 m)
Suspension: **front: semi-elliptic leaf-springs;**
   rear: ¾ elliptic leaf-springs

which from 1935 was the majority shareholder in Isotta-Fraschini, proposed to manufacture them but nothing developed from the proposal.

Itala 35/45 HP
Itala 61

This manufacturer will always be linked with two great sporting events: Alessandro Cagno's victory in the first Targa Florio (1906) and the victory of Scipione Borghese, Luigi Barzini and Ettore Guizzardi in the Peking-Paris race of 1907.

In 1903 Matteo Ceirano founded Ceirano Matteo & Compagnia. In 1904 there was a change in both its name (Ceirano Matteo & C. Vetture Marca Itala) and in its premises (from Via Guastalla to Via Petrarca, Turin). The first automobile to be produced was a 4562 cc 4-cylinder 24 HP. Matteo himself immediately gave the company a sporting association by carrying the 24 HP to victory in the Susa-Moncenisio hill-climb of that year. In 1905 Ceirano Matteo & C. Vetture Itala again changed its name, this time to Itala Fabbrica Automobili

S.A. With the vital flow of new capital, its founder left and with Michele Ansaldi set up Spa. Matteo was succeeded as designer by Alberto Belloco.

The 35/45 HP was the machine in which Borghese, Barzini and Guizzardi undertook their extraordinary adventure in the Peking-Paris race of 1907. For length and difficulty this race ranks as the greatest race in the entire history of the car. They left Peking on June 10, 1907, and arrived in Paris on August 10. The actual length of the race was 10,000 miles and this was covered in 44 days. They reached the French capital 20 days ahead of the car that came second. Apart from modifications to the body, the addition of extra fuel tanks and removable fenders, the 35/45 was a normal production machine and it was obviously the most famous of Itala's cars. There were, however, quite a number of models in the course of this

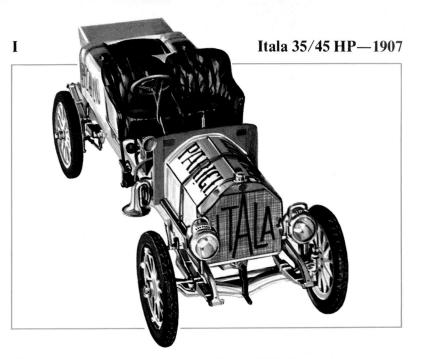

firm's rather troubled career before it disappeared from the motoring scene in 1934.

Another famous model was the 61 which was a tourer and the work of Giulio Cesare Cappa, one of the most productive minds in Italian engineering. The 61 had 6 cylinders with overhead valves and a camshaft in the crankcase, developing 60 bhp at 3,500 revs. Another of Cappa's designs was for a front-wheel drive racing car with a wooden chassis and independent suspension, powered by a 1100 or 1500 cc 12-cylinder engine. Unfortunately this advanced car never ran under its own power. In 1929, in an attempt to save Itala, a merger was made with Officine Meccaniche & Metallurgiche di Tortona and the new company took on the title of Itala S.A. In 1931 it was

Car: **Itala 35/45 HP**
Year: **1907**
Engine: **4 cylinders in line**
Bore and stroke: **130 × 140 mm**
Cylinder capacity: **7433 cc**
Gearbox: **4 forward**
Brake horse power: —
Maximum speed: —
Wheelbase: —
Suspension: **front and rear: semi-elliptic leaf-springs**

Car: **Itala 61**
Year: **1927**
Engine: **6 cylinders in line**
Bore and stroke: **65 × 100 mm**
Cylinder capacity: **1995 cc**
Gearbox: **4 forward**
Brake horse power: **60**
Maximum speed: **70 mph**
Wheelbase: **9 ft 10 ins (2.99 m)**
Suspension: **front and rear: semi-elliptic leaf-springs**

altered to Itala-Saca (Società Anonima Costruzioni Automobilistiche). The survival of the new company depended upon the 75 (which was a modified Tipo 61) but in 1934 Itala-Saca was forced to close.

Lancia Alpha Tipo 51
Lancia Theta Tipo 61
Lancia Lambda Tipo 67
Lancia Aprilia Tipo 97

The Alpha was the first car built by Vincenzo Lancia and it was also the first car to be given a Greek name, a fashion that this firm was to continue to follow to this day. The Alpha was offered for sale in five versions: double phaeton, coupé de luxe, limousine, partly openable landaulette and fully openable landaulette. Although orthodox in its general conception, like all the succeeding Lancia models it was a revolutionary machine. The maximum engine speed was very high for its time (1,800 revs) and its almost square bore and stroke was highly original. This feature was to be adopted again more than half a century later because of the need to achieve high engine speeds. When the prototype of the Alpha had been finished, it was discovered that it

could not get through the door of the small workshop that Vincenzo Lancia had chosen for his research laboratory. Various solutions to the problem were proposed, such as tipping the chassis on its side. Vincenzo Lancia objected and instead chose a more drastic but fundamentally more rational solution of knocking down the door!

A version of the Alpha, the Dialpha (the prefixes 'di' and 'tri' were to be frequently used to denote sports or other nonstandard versions of a model), showed Vincenzo Lancia's passion for racing (he had been a team driver for Fiat). The Dialpha had a maximum speed of 68 mph and a 6-cylinder in line engine, which is the only example of this number and

Car: **Lancia Alpha Tipo 51**
Year: **1908**
Engine: **4 cylinders in line**
Bore and stroke: **90 × 100 mm**
Cylinder capacity: **2543 cc**
Gears: **4 forward**
Brake horse power: **28**
Maximum speed: **50 mph**
Wheelbase: **9 ft 3 ins (3.04 m)**
Suspension: **front and rear: semi-elliptic leaf-springs**

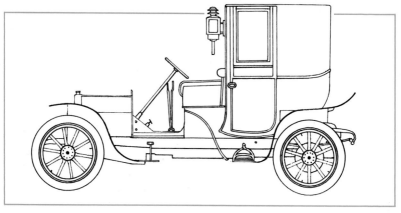

arrangement of cylinders in Lancia's history. Only 23 Dialphas, which had an engine capacity of 3815 cc, were built, as opposed to 108 Alphas.

Another important step was the Theta, which was derived from a truck. The Theta had a 4940 cc 4-cylinder in line engine which was originally intended for a light truck called the Zeta. This vehicle was light and easy to handle and won Lancia a large order for the Italian Army who used it in the war in Libya. In the Theta the 4-cylinder in line engine developed considerable power: 70 bhp at 2,200 revs. With the Theta, Lancia offered for the first time in Europe, along with Hispano-Suiza, an electric starter motor. The ignition, the starting lights, the horn, the dashboard lights and the controls placed on the adjustable steering

Car: **Lancia Theta Tipo 61**
Year: **1913**
Engine: **4 cylinders in line**
Bore and stroke: **110 × 130 mm**
Cylinder capacity: **4940 cc**
Gears: **4 forward**
Brake horse power: **70**
Maximum speed: **55 mph**
Wheelbase: **10 ft 10 ins (3.30 m)**
Suspension: **front and rear: semi-elliptic leaf-springs**

column were further new features on this car. Some 1,696 Thetas were sold, a very high proportion of which were destined for export. The Theta had a maximum speed of 55 mph and was the car with which Lancia began to gain a reputation abroad.

The Kappa and the Dikappa were the last Lancia cars to have engines with cylinders in line. The Trikappa marked the change to V-8 engines. A peculiar feature of these engines was the narrow angle, only 14°, of the V.

227

The 8-cylinder derived from a 12-cylinder with the same angle, designed as an aircraft engine.

The Lambda was a model with several innovations and entirely new design features. It had a narrow angle V-4 engine of 14° capable of turning over rapidly at 3,250 revs. Another of the Lambda's innovations was that it was the first car to have a monocoque hull. The idea for the new suspension system apparently came to Vincenzo Lancia following the breakage of a rear leaf-spring whilst he and his mother were travelling in a Kappa.

The Lambda was a great commercial success. A total of 12,999 were built in nine different series. It was first shown to the public at the 1922 Paris Motor Show and it gained an enthusiastic reception. The angular body was also one reason for

Car: **Lancia Lambda Tipo 67**
Year: **1923**
Engine: **V-4**
Bore and stroke: **75 × 120 mm**
Cylinder capacity: **2120 cc**
Gears: **3 forward**
Brake horse power: **49**
Maximum speed: **70 mph**
Wheelbase: **10 ft 2 ins (3.09 m)**
Suspension: **front and rear: telescopic independent suspension; front: hydraulic damping device**

its popularity. The absence of a chassis made it remarkably low and yet another innovation was the integration of the trunk into the body, rather than jutting out. This was also a technical solution to the problem posed by the lengthened body which needed to be closed at the rear end to give it greater rigidity. The engine capacity rose in the seventh series from 2120 to 2370 cc, the bore being increased from 75 to 79.37 mm and consequently the maximum power

increased from 49 to 59 bhp at the same engine speed. The eighth series featured another increase in capacity (2570 cc, bore 82.55 mm, power 69 bhp), some modifications of detail and an increase in accessories, one such being a rev counter.

The Aprilia, which appeared in 1937, was a very popular product of this Turin company. Vincenzo Lancia gave his collaborators strict specifications regarding the volume, spaciousness, wind resistance and weight of this car. The car may not have been very attractive but the line of the body fulfilled strict scientifically obtained requirements. Amongst production cars it still has one of the best coefficients of penetration (Cx = 0.47). The Aprilia was powered by a narrow angled V-4 (slightly more than 17°) with a single overhead

Car: **Lancia Aprilia Tipo 97**
Year: **1937**
Engine: **V-4**
Bore and stroke: **73 × 83 mm**
Cylinder capacity: **1388 cc**
Gears: **4 forward**
Brake horse power: **46**
Maximum speed: **80 mph**
Wheelbase: **9 ft 0 ins (2.74 m)**
Suspension: **front: telescopic; rear: transverse leaf-spring and torsion bars**

camshaft and valves arranged in a V. It had an aluminium engine block and cylinder head. It had telescopic front suspension whilst the rear suspension was by transverse leaf-spring and torsion bars. The Aprilia was built both before and after the war and the total number produced was 27,608. The capacity was increased in the second series to 1486 cc, the bore and stroke rising to 74.61 × 85 mm, although the maximum power remained virtually the same.

The company of OM was started in 1848 when Benedetto Grondona began to build carriages outside the Porta Nuova in Milan. He was succeeded by his son Felice who, together with Giovanni Miani and Paolo Zambelli, broadened its interests to include other sorts of vehicles including railway vehicles. In 1880 Miani founded a new firm, Miani, Venturi & Compagnia, in association with Girolamo Silvestri and Prospero Venturi, with the aim of building a steam engine of the Viennese SIGL design. On the death of Prospero Venturi the company became Miani, Silvestri and Compagnia. The OM factory was in Porta Vicentina, Milan, where the first Italian electric streetcar was built (it would link Florence and Fiesole).

In 1918 the first OM, which was

Car: **OM Tipo 469**
Year: **1922**
Engine: **4 cylinders in line**
Bore and stroke: **69 × 100 mm**
Cylinder capacity: **1496 cc**
Gears: **4 forward**
Brake horse power: —
Maximum speed: —
Wheelbase: **9 ft 2 ins (3.25 m)**
Suspension: **front and rear: semi-elliptic leaf-springs**

very similar to the Brixia-Zust, was produced. The next to appear was the 465; this number had a definite significance, the 4 standing for the number of cylinders, and the 65 standing for the bore. The 465 was followed by the 467 and the 469, the latter being regarded as this car manufacturer's war horse. The 469's engine had a detachable cylinder head and the cooling system's fan had wooden blades. Magneto ignition was added later. In 1930 the engine capacity was increased to 1680 cc.

The Ceirano brothers were responsible for the formation of Spa. It was founded in 1906 by Michele Ansaldi (who came from Fiat) and Matteo Ceirano (who had previously worked for Itala). Spa enjoyed a long period of prosperity because of the quality of their products and the foresight of Ansaldi and Ceirano. They saw the inevitable slump in the market before the war and turned also to manufacturing aircraft engines. Once the war had begun, many of these were sold to the Italian Air-Force.

The car illustrated here is a sports version. The engine developed 30 bhp at 1,300 revs; was fed by a single body carburetor; had high tension magneto ignition, side valves, and a camshaft in the crankcase; pumped water cooling with a fan; and had a honeycomb radiator. There was a multi-

Car: **Spa 25/30**
Year: **1913**
Engine: **4 cylinders in line**
Bore and stroke: **100 × 140 mm**
Cylinder capacity: **4398 cc**
Gears: **4 forward**
Brake horse power: **30**
Maximum speed: **65 mph**
Wheelbase: **9 ft 2 ins (3.25 m)**
Suspension: **front: semi-elliptic leaf-springs;**
   rear: ¾ elliptic leaf-springs

plate clutch, a chassis with two channel side members, acetylene headlights and oil burning side lamps. The seats were slightly staggered, mainly to make the driving position more comfortable. The failure of the Banca Nazionale di Sconto placed Spa in difficulties and in 1926 Fiat took control and turned Spa over exclusively to truck production. The Spa name was dropped in 1947, but the factory is still used by Fiat for production of its heavy trucks.

The company of Züst goes back to 1871, when the Swiss engineer Robert Züst became a partner of Guller and Groff of Intra on Lake Maggiore. This had been founded in 1854 and specialised in mechanical engineering. In 1893 Züst took over completely and the company took the name of its new owner. In 1905 it moved to Milan and concentrated on car production. Amongst its first designers was Giustino Cattaneo who was to become one of the most admired car engineers in Italy. Züst's cars had 4-cylinders in line, twin block, high capacity engines with low tension magneto ignition, 4-speed gears and chain drive. Production of relatively low engine capacity cars, such as the 14/18 HP (3770 cc), was delegated to Brixia-Züst, a small firm formed in 1905 in Brescia in which Züst retained

Car: **Züst 25/35 HP**
Year: **1913**
Engine: **4 cylinders in line**
Bore and stroke: **100 × 150 mm**
Capacity: **4714 cc**
Gears: **4 forward**
Brake horse power: **50**
Maximum speed: **60 mph**
Wheelbase: **9 ft 7½ ins (2.93 m)**
Suspension: **front and rear: semi-elliptic leaf-springs**

a majority shareholding. Züst was dissolved in 1917 with the transfer of its plant to Officine Meccaniche già di Miani, Silvestri & Compagnia, which resulted in the birth of OM.

In common with certain large engined models the 25/35 HP had a pear shaped radiator. In practice Züst's tendency to produce exclusive cars left the buyer free to choose between several shapes of radiator.

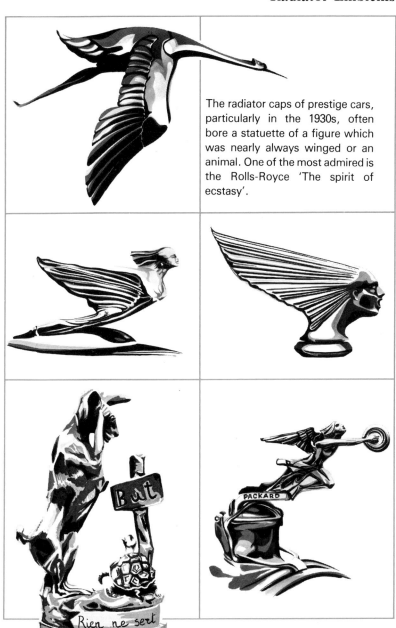

The radiator caps of prestige cars, particularly in the 1930s, often bore a statuette of a figure which was nearly always winged or an animal. One of the most admired is the Rolls-Royce 'The spirit of ecstasy'.

Other Countries

A variety of other countries, apart from the United States, Great Britain, France, Germany and Italy, possessed a car industry. These, both large and small, were completely wiped out or drastically reduced in size either by the crisis at the end of the 1930s or an inability to change from quality to mass production.

Austria had two large car manufacturers, Austro-Daimler and Steyr. Steyr was founded near Graz in 1864 by Josef Werndl and the highly original work of its first designer, Ledwinka, influenced the firm's production for many years.

Gottlieb Daimler created three enterprises, one of which was Austro-Daimler in Austria (the other two being in England and Germany). Ferdinand Porsche's presence at Austro-Daimler ensured that it produced highly prestigious models.

From the beginning of the century until the outbreak of the Second World War the Belgian car industry was one of the most active in Europe. In 1900 300 cars were in use in Brussels alone. There were many successful companies such as Germain, F.N. (or *Fabrique Nationale d'Armes de Guerre*), Nagant, Pieper, Delin, V. Antoine, Lefert, Linon, Mans and Vincke, as well as a large number of coach building workshops. The leading company, at least in terms of quality, was Minerva which had been founded in 1903. Between 1905 and 1908 a number of other makes appeared, such as Imperia and Springuel, and Métallurgique reorganised its entire production. In 1912 there were 16 car factories in Belgium, employing 5,000 workers.

The First World War dealt an initial, severe blow to the strength of the Belgian car industry. There were many attempted mergers, agreements and groupings, with the result that the number of car manufacturing groups in the country was reduced to two. Both Minerva and F.N. were forced to give up independent manufacturing. The assembly of foreign firms' models, which has been developed since the Second World War, has been the salvation of the industry.

In Czechoslovakia the car has always been considered a luxury despite the attempts of many front ranking engineers to popularise it. One particularly popular make was the Tatra. Designed by Hans Ledwinka, it had a large tubular backbone frame chassis and air cooling. The same chassis was used by Skoda, Praga and Jawa.

Skoda has always specialised in small capacity cars but its production cycle also included two large 4-cylinders, three 6-cylinders and even a 3880 cc 8 inline. The production of Praga has been along roughly the same lines as Skoda.

Walter, which specialised in airplane engines, offered, in 1930, seven different models, five of them built under licence from Fiat. Another Czechoslovak make known in the sporting field was Wikov, who constructed under licence from Ansaldo.

Aero began in 1929 with a 500 cc single-cylinder car which was rather austere both in appearance and in substance. It was later replaced by a 662 cc twin-cylinder. Between 1934 and 1939 Aero changed to front-wheel drive, initially with a 1000 cc twin-cylinder engine and then with a 2000 cc 4-cylinder engine.

Jawa specialised in motorcycle production, turning to four wheels in 1934, first with the 'Meisterklasse' built under licence from DKW, and then with a model of its own, the 'Minor', though this was still related to the DKW (chassis, 615 cc engine and 3-speed transmission). The last of the Czech firms was Z (the letter stood for Zbrojovka, an arms factory) and this also concentrated on sports cars.

The Swiss industry, like the Austrian one, existed for a relatively short time only and specialised in sturdy vehicles. Fischer, founded in Zurich in 1909, had only a fleeting existence, but Fischer himself was an important designer. He developed an innovative gearbox which had internally toothed pinions and a sleeve-valve engine. He granted the manufacturing rights to this to a German firm which never produced it.

Martini had a much more fortunate career, remaining active from 1902 until 1934. They also made a name for themselves with their racing cars. Friedrich von Martini had started in 1860 as a manufacturer of sheet pressing machinery and, later, of guns.

Turicum (the old Latin name for Zurich) is another important name in the history of the Swiss car industry. This factory was founded in 1904 and closed in 1914. Its guiding force, particularly from the point of view of design, was Martin Fischer.

Though there was only one well-known Dutch make of car, the Spyker, the innovative solutions adopted on its vehicles give Holland an important place in the history of automobile engineering. Its innovations included dust and water proof hood, the production of the first 6-cylinder engine, 4-wheel drive and overhead camshafts.

For many years the Spanish car industry was identified with the luxurious Hispano-Suiza cars designed by Marc Birkigt. After the war Spain gradually became more industrialised and car manufacturing became increasingly important. The first companies to be founded were SEAT (Fiat) and Pegaso. Recently Ford have also opened a factory in Spain. Citroën, Renault and Chrysler all assemble their own products in Spain.

In Sweden Scania had been making cars since 1901 and Vabis since 1897. In 1911 the two companies merged (Scania-Vabis) and produced the only important Swedish make until 1929.

The Austrian division of Daimler of Cannstatt originated in 1899 and subsequently became associated with the Bierenz Fischer company (which had specialised in machine tools since 1848. Austro Daimler was managed from 1902 by Paul Daimler and in that year it became the independent Osterreichische Daimler Motoren Gesellschaft. After 1905 the management passed to Ferdinand Porsche.

The AD 617 was the first 6-cylinder car built by the Austrian firm; it was designed by Porsche himself and was fitted with an engine clearly derived from that of an aircraft, having a single aluminium engine block, steel liners screwed into the engine block and an overhead camshaft. It developed a power of 60 bhp at 2,300 revs and had a maximum speed, according to the manufacturers, of about 72

Car: **Austro Daimler AD 617**
Year: **1921**
Engine: **6 cylinder in line**
Bore and stroke: **85 × 130 mm**
Cylinder capacity: **4426 cc**
Gears: **4 forward**
Brake horse power: **60**
Maximum speed: **72 mph**
Wheelbase: **11 ft 4 ins (3.45 m)**
Suspension: **front: semi-elliptic leaf-springs; rear: cantilever springs**

mph. From 1923 to 1926 the AD became the ADV (the V indicating front brakes). As the large capacity of its engine indicates, the ADV was essentially a luxury car. All the products of this factory were based on highly original principles. It began to make a name for itself in races before the First World War, especially those sponsored by Prince Heinrich of Prussia which, for a while, were the culmination of the racing activities of many car manufacturers of the period.

Like Austro Daimler, Graf und Stift consistently produced luxury cars which bore comparison with Rolls-Royce, Hispano-Suiza and Isotta-Fraschini. The firm was founded by the Graf brothers who began, shortly before the end of the last century, with a small front wheel drive car powered by a single-cylinder De Dion-Bouton engine. The company made a fresh start with an agreement between the Graf brothers and Willy Stift, the owner of Celeritas. The latter did not build cars independently but assembled ones imported from France. Graf und Stift was born in 1902 and in the beginning constructed cars on behalf of, and under the name of, Arnold Spitz. Spitz was one of the principal car dealers in Austria. The failure of Spitz in 1907 freed Graf und Stift and it took the company name of

Car: Graf und Stift SP 8
Year: **1933**
Engine: **8 cylinders in line**
Bore and stroke: **85 × 132 mm**
Cylinder capacity: **5992 cc**
Gears: **4 forward**
Brake horse power: **125**
Maximum speed: **88 mph**
Wheelbase: **12 ft 4 ins (3.76 m)**
Suspension: **front and rear: semi-elliptic leaf-springs**

Wiener Automobilfabrik A.G. This specialised in the production of large 4-cylinder cars. It was whilst he was in a Graf und Stift that Archduke Franz Ferdinand was assassinated at Sarajevo. The SP 8 had an 8-cylinder engine which developed 125 bhp; it had an overhead camshaft, aluminium engine block, 9 main bearings and a synchromesh transmission. It had a maximum speed of 88 mph. It was this model in particular that earned Graf und Stift the title of the 'Austrian Rolls-Royce'.

Excelsior was active from 1903 until 1932, quite a long period for a company that never aimed at mass production of their cars. It began by using French Aster engines, but from 1911 onwards it built its own 6-cylinder 4500 cc engine with which it equipped a range of prestige cars. After the war it restarted production, still with a 6-cylinder engine which powered a model that has gained a place in history through one of its features. This was a system of diagonal braking in which the front right and rear left wheels and the front left and rear right wheels were linked; for safety reasons this system has been readopted on cars in the 1970s. The Albert I went into production in 1922. Initially it had a 4768 cc engine, but subsequently, the bore having been increased, a larger

Car: **Excelsior Albert I**
Year: **1926**
Engine: **6 cylinders in line**
Bore and stroke: **90 × 140 mm**
Cylinder capacity: **5343 cc**
Gears: **3 forward**
Brake horse power: **130**
Maximum speed: **100 mph**
Wheelbase: **10ft 10 ins (3.30m)**
Suspension: front: **semi-elliptic leaf-springs**; rear: **cantilever springs**

capacity (5350 cc) engine. It is the sports version of the Albert I that is pictured here. With the help of 3 carburetors it developed over 130 bhp and had a maximum speed of 100 mph. This car had servo brakes and these, again, were diagonally linked. This machine gained two racing successes. It came second in the Belgian Grand Prix of 1926 and in the following year it won the same race. In 1932 Excelsior was taken over by Minerva.

Founded in 1897, in Monceau-sur-Sambre, Germain began by assembling Daimler cars. Only in 1903 did it start independent production with the 15/18 HP which had an engine with an L-shaped cylinder head and dual ignition. The 35 HP had a rounded radiator and this became a characteristic of the make. In 1905 the 14/22 was put into production. This had a T-shaped cylinder head and a 3-speed transmission and was very fast for its capacity (3000 cc). It was thus able to make a name for itself in the racing world. The 18/22 is a derivation of it, the increase in capacity being achieved by increasing the bore (from 92 to 102 mm). This model remained in production until 1914.

Germain was involved in some sporting activity, taking part in the French Grand Prix of 1908. Sub-

Car: **Germain 18/22 HP**
Year: **1908**
Engine: **4 cylinders in line**
Bore and stroke: **102 × 110 mm**
Cylinder capacity: **3595 cc**
Gears: **3 forward**
Brake horse power: **22**
Maximum speed: **42 mph**
Wheelbase: **9 ft 3 ins (2.82 m)**
Suspension: **front: semi-elliptic leaf-springs;
    rear: ¾ elliptic leaf-springs**

sequently the company took up a manufacturing licence for the sleeve-valve engine and its history is strewn with numerous attempts to keep pace with the other Belgian and International makes. The 1914 war put an end to its business. Historically this make will be remembered for the mechanism introduced on the 1906 range of models for lifting the valves. A centrifugal speed governor was fitted which limited the engine speed to 1,000 revs to protect the engine from damaging over-use.

In the history of the Belgian car industry, so rich in makes once well known but which have all now disappeared, Métallurgique occupies a place in the front rank, in particular because of its intense activity in the sporting field. Founded in 1898, in Marchienne-au-Pont under the name of SA L'Auto Métallurgique, it began by producing cars with twin-cylinder engines. The company's destiny took a decisive turn when the famous engineer from Daimler, Ernst Lehmann, was engaged. Lehmann completely changed the products, experimenting with large capacity cars inspired by Mercedes. Metal chassis, honeycomb radiators and 4-cylinder engines with T-shaped cylinder heads (monobloc from 1908 and from 1911 with a 4-speed gearbox) were immediately adopted.

Car: **Métallurgique 12 CV**
Year: **1910**
Engine: **4 cylinders in line**
Bore and stroke: **80 × 130 mm**
Cylinder capacity: **2614 cc**
Gears: **4 speed**
Brake horse power: **32**
Maximum speed: **52 mph**
Wheelbase: **10 ft 1¾ ins (3.09 m)**
Suspension: **front: semi-elliptic leaf-springs; rear: cantilever springs**

The car illustrated here was the smallest built in the pre-war years and was made until 1914. The pointed radiator became a characteristic of the Métallurgique range which used, almost exclusively, Van den Plas bodies. The valve arrangement, a single overhead inlet valve and two side exhaust valves, was distinctive of the sports engines. The Adex brake system with diagonal linkage was noteworthy. Métallurgique merged with Minerva in 1927 and production ceased.

Minerva, perhaps the most famous of the Belgian makes of car, was the creation of a Dutchman, Sylvain de Jong, who had settled at Antwerp and begun by building bicycles and motorcycles. Automobile production started with small capacity cars and expanded into the production of the Minervette, a small car with a 636 cc single-cylinder engine. De Jong then made a major shift in production, concentrating on large cars. The 30 CV was the first of these with a 6-cylinder engine. It had a monobloc Knight engine with seven main bearings. Initially it had a cone clutch, but on subsequent models this was replaced by a multi-plate clutch. It could reach a speed of 75 mph. Servo brakes were fitted in 1923 and in 1927 the capacity was increased to 6000 cc. With the loss of de Jong in 1928,

Car: **Minerva 30 CV**
Year: **1921**
Engine: **6 cylinders in line**
Bore and stroke: **90 × 140 mm**
Cylinder capacity: **5344 cc**
Gears: **4 forward**
Brake horse-power: **110**
Maximum speed: **75 mph**
Wheelbase: **11 ft 11 ins (3.63 m)**
Suspension: **front: semi-elliptic leaf-springs;**
    rear: cantilever springs

Minerva stressed the design and construction of luxury cars which, though they earned widespread praise, did not sell well. In 1938 Minerva ceased building their own cars and in 1951 they concentrated on assembling Rovers and Armstrong-Siddeleys. The unveiling of a prototype derived from the CEMSA Caproni F II at the Brussels Motor Show of 1953 was the final attempt to re-start independent production. However, there was no follow-up.

The origins of this firm go as far back as 1850, but actual car production did not begin until 1897. This was synonymous with the arrival of Hans Ledwinka, an exceptionally gifted engineer who has left an indelible mark on the history of the car. The 77, which is considered his masterpiece, appeared at the 1934 Berlin Motor Show, where it excited great interest because of its advanced features, including independent suspension to all four wheels, an air cooled rear mounted V8 engine, hydraulic brakes, a gearbox with 4 synchromesh gears and a centralised lubrication system. The body shape was also highly original, its aerodynamic design being of particular importance. Other ingenious details were the central driver's seat, the space for luggage

Car: **Tatra 77**
Year: **1935**
Engine: **V-8**
Bore and stroke: **80 × 84 mm**
Cylinder capacity: **3380 cc**
Gears: **4 forward**
Brake horse power: **60**
Maximum speed: **100 mph**
Wheelbase: **10 ft 4 ins (3.15 m)**
Suspension: **front: independent with transverse leaf-springs; rear: independent with coil springs**

under the back seat and the two spare wheels kept in the front trunk. The maximum speed of this highly original car was about 100 mph. The 77 was followed by the 77A which had a reduced capacity of 2900 cc and a maximum speed of about 95 mph. The distinctive body shape of these cars suggested a stylistically similar design to Ferdinand Porsche for his now legendary Volkswagen Beetle. Hans Ledwinka has passed into motoring history as one of the most innovative automobile engineers.

The Netherlands today, apart from DAF, lacks a car industry but at the beginning of the century it had a very active one. Spyker, in particular, was a leading car manufacturer, producing the first 6-cylinder engine and the first car with 4-wheel drive. The firm started in 1880 by building carriages, but changed over to cars because one of the Spijker brothers (Spijker was their real name) became the Dutch agent for Benz. There was nothing exciting about Jacobus and Hendrik Spijker's first car. In 1903 they produced the first 6-cylinder engine, shortly before the English Napier, and one of the Dutch firm's 6-cylinders is known to have appeared in London in 1903. This car also had 4-wheel drive and brakes on each wheel. It was intended for racing, but so far as is known it never competed,

Car: **Spyker**
Year: **1905**
Engine: **4 cylinders in line**
Bore and stroke: **90 × 100 mm**
Cylinder capacity: **2546 cc**
Gears: **3 forward**
Brake horse power: —
Maximum speed: —
Wheelbase: **7 ft 9 ins**
Suspension: **front and rear: semi-elliptic leaf-springs**

and only one was made. Cars made by Spyker were characterised by a rounded radiator.

Spyker's decline started to become apparent in 1920, as its innovative streak faded, though its last car was a 6-cylinder of high quality. It used a 5700 cc Maybach engine with dual ignition. S. F. Edge set some endurance records (24 hour) at Brooklands circuit in one of these cars. Spyker terminated production in 1925.

Hispano-Suiza Alfonso XIII
Hispano-Suiza H6 B
Hispano-Suiza Type 68 and 68 Bis

Hispano-Suiza, one of the world's most famous car manufacturers, was founded in Barcelona by Damian Mateu (a Spaniard) and Mark Birkigt (who was Swiss). With two business associates (Fonctuberta and Seix), Mateu had taken over a small manufacturer of cars called La Cuadra, whose technical director was Marc Birkigt. The latter had been invited to Spain by a fellow student who, with others, was hoping to build electric buses. One of these was in fact built but it failed to live up to expectations. The unsuccessful enterprise and the firm for which Birkigt worked was taken over by Mateu who retained him as its technical director. From 1904 onwards the company was known as Hispano-Suiza.

Marc Birkigt and Henry Royce had much in common. Both began as specialists in the electrical field, both marketed their first car in 1904, and both took part in some races as part of their complete dedication to the design of high class cars. Both Rolls-Royce and Hispano-Suiza reached the peak of their fame with models powered by 12-cylinder engines. Finally, both firms built powerful airplane engines which were very successful and even used for record attempts.

The first sports car produced by Hispano-Suiza was named the Alfonso XIII in respectful homage to the Spanish King, who as well as being an enthusiastic racegoer was an expert driver. The cars bearing his name did not do well in the first Catalonia Cup but they performed much better against their competitors in the second of these races. The Alfonso

Car: **Hispano-Suiza Alfonso XIII**
Year: **1911**
Engine: **4 cylinders in line**
Bore and stroke: **80 × 180 mm**
Cylinder capacity: **3617 cc**
Gears: **3 or 4 forward**
Brake horse power: **64**
Maximum speed: **72**
Wheelbase: **9 ft 10 ins (2.30 m)**
Suspension: **front: semi-elliptic leaf-springs; rear: semi-elliptic or ¾ leaf-springs**

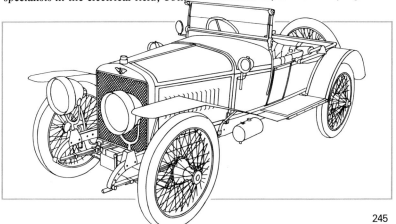

XIII, improved and perfected by racing, became one of the Spanish company's best cars and indeed, one of the best cars built anywhere before the Great War. The engine developed 64 bhp and it had a maximum speed of over 70 mph.

The success that Hispano-Suiza cars were enjoying led to an important step in the company's history. Both Birkigt and Mateu were convinced that the construction of a second factory in France (at Bois-Colombes near Paris) would increase the sales of the company's products. In time, the French Hispano-Suiza became much more important than its parent company.

The H6, the first car developed and produced in France and until 1930 the only model built there, is considered to be one of Hispano-Suiza's most successful cars. At the same time it was also built in Spain, though in small numbers intended mainly for the domestic market and fitted with a 3700 cc engine. Its technical details (the engine developed 135 bhp at 2,750 rpm), its performance (a maximum speed of around 95 mph) and the ease with which it could be driven made the H6 a much admired and sought after model. The engine was a derivative of one built for airplanes; it had a single camshaft, overhead

Car: **Hispano-Suiza Type 68 and 68 Bis**
Year: **1931**
Engine: **V-12**
Bore and stroke: **100 × 100 mm**
Cylinder capacity: **9420 cc**
Gears: **3 forward**
Brake horse power: **220**
Maximum speed: **100 mph**
Wheelbase: **12 ft 5½ ins (3.80 m)**
Suspension: **front and rear: semi-elliptic leaf-springs**

valves, two spark plugs per cylinder, alloy pistons and pressure lubrication was used for the crankshaft, which had seven bearings. The exceptional rigidity of the crankshaft explains why only a 3-speed transmission was required. It had 4 servo-operated drum brakes.

The Type 68 and the 68 Bis were launched in 1931 with the specific intent of competing with Rolls-Royce's cars. The magnificent 12-cylinder engine was, at the time, regarded as a marvel and it is still considered to be one of the most refined units ever to have been put into production. The first version (9424 cc) developed 220 bhp at 3,000 revs and the second versions (11310 cc, the stroke being increased from 100 to 120 mm) developed 250 bhp. The chassis, like all those built by this

Car: **Hispano-Suiza H6 B**
Year: **1922**
Engine: **6 cylinders in line**
Bore and stroke: **100 × 140 mm**
Cylinder capacity: **6597 cc**
Gears: **3 forward**
Brake horse power: **135**
Maximum speed: **95 mph**
Wheelbase: **12 ft 1¼ ins (3.70 m)**
Suspension: **front: semi-elliptic leaf-springs; rear: cantilever springs**

company, was especially rigid and was available in light, normal and long versions, thus allowing a wide choice of body. With this car Hispano-Suiza regained its position alongside Rolls-Royce and Duesenberg. However the outbreak of the Second World War placed the company in serious difficulties. The Spanish company was absorbed by ENASA and the French company attempted, without success, to re-enter the car market with a V-8 front wheel drive car.

247

The history of the merger between Scania and Vabis for the production of cars is a rather unusual tale. Scania (Maskin A.B. Scania of Malmo) began by producing Humber bicycles and later, cars powered by front-mounted Kamper twin-cylinder engines. AB Vabis of Sodertalje was founded in 1891 and specialised in the manufacture of railway coaches, starting to build cars in 1897 whilst still carrying on with the former activity. In 1911 Scania and Vabis decided to merge, the former concentrating on truck production and the latter on cars. In 1911, the year of their agreement, they offered two sorts of car: both had 4-cylinder engines and bore each company's trade mark, differing in size and in degree of finish. In 1914 the two companies amalgamated almost en-

Car: **Scania-Vabis 18/20 HP**
Year: **1911**
Engine: **4 cylinders in line**
Bore and stroke: **85 × 100 mm**
Cylinder capacity: **2270 cc**
Gears: **4 speed**
Brake horse power: **22**
Maximum speed: **40 mph**
Wheelbase: —
Suspension: **front and rear: semi-elliptic leaf-springs**

tirely and they used a single trade mark. The 18/20 had a short life, appearing in 1911 and remaining in production for just a year. Until 1924 there was nothing new of importance. The numbers produced by Scania-Vabis were never large and they were subject to the needs of the market. Car production was abandoned in 1929, but Scania-Vabis continued to be a major producer of commercial vehicles and today still trades under the name Scania.

This make also had a short life (from 1909 to 1914). It was founded in Zurich by Martin Fischer who had gained his design experience at Turicum and who was considered one of his country's most versatile and eclectic designers. Amongst other things he invented a gearbox with internally toothed pinions and a sleeve valve engine.

The 10/33 was a successful model. It incorporated the two technical features already mentioned and its wheels could be fitted quickly because there was only a single, central bolt. The front-mounted engine was water cooled and developed 33 bhp at 1,200 revs. The 10/33 had shaft drive, Bosch magneto ignition and a multiplate clutch. The brake pedal acted on the transmission and the hand brake controlled drum brakes.

Car: **Fischer 10/33 CV**
Year: **1913**
Engine: **4 cylinders in line**
Bore and stroke: **85 × 120 mm**
Cylinder capacity: **2723.5 cc**
Gears: **4 forward**
Brake horse power: **33**
Maximum speed: **46 mph**
Wheelbase: —
Suspension: **front: semi-elliptic leaf-springs; rear: elliptic leaf-springs**

Before the outbreak of the First World War Fischer had designed a 6-cylinder car but he was only able to produce three examples. After the war he began again as an independent designer putting forward, in 1919, an idea for a small car with seats in tandem, and in 1921 a new engine with sleeve valves which he handed over to a German firm.

Fischer's most valuable invention was perhaps the gearbox with internally toothed gear-wheels.

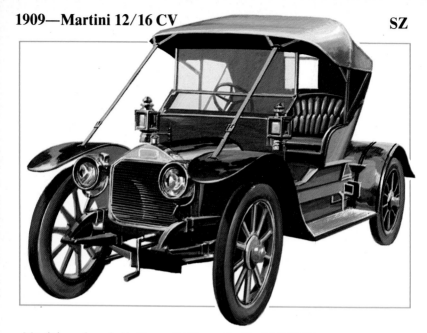

Martini was founded in Frauenfeld by Friedrich von Martini and it specialised in sheet pressing and the manufacture of rifles. In 1902 it began to construct cars, specifically the French Rochet-Schneider (though having previously made an attempt at independent manufacture in 1897 with a car powered by a rear mounted twin-cylinder engine and again in 1908 with a *vis-à-vis* with a front mounted engine). The early years were troubled; Martini moved in 1903 to St Blaise in the canton of Neuchâtel. In 1906 the factory was sold to an Englishman, Deasy, and he in turn handed it over to a group of Swiss bankers in 1908, in which year it was renamed the Société Nouvelle des Automobiles Martini.

The 12/16 had a monobloc engine with overhead inlet valves and shaft

Car: **Martini 12/16 CV**
Year: **1909**
Engine: **4 cylinders in line**
Bore and stroke: **80 × 110 mm**
Cylinder capacity: **2212 cc**
Gears: **4 forward**
Brake horse power: **16**
Maximum speed: **40 mph**
Wheelbase: —
Suspension: **front and rear: semi-elliptic leaf-springs**

drive, features that placed it amongst the most up to date cars of the time. The company again ran into difficult times which it attempted to overcome first by handing over half the shares to the German firm Steiger, then by buying the manufacturing rights to the Wanderer and finally by producing a luxury car entirely designed by Martini. However, nothing succeeded in saving the company and it went into liquidation in 1934.

This firm's strange name is made up of the first three letters of the surnames of its two founders (Piccard and Pictet). Initially it only manufactured car parts. In 1904 it was taken over by SAG (Société d'Automobiles à Genève) whose designer was Marc Birkigt, later to gain fame with Hispano-Suiza. Piccard and Pictet broke away from SAG, becoming fully independent and producing sturdy and efficient cars. The 1919 one pictured here had Argyll's patented sleeve-valve engine, developing 50 bhp at 1,800 revs, a Zenith carburetor and Scintilla magneto ignition. The dashboard, which had a mileage counter, a clock, an ammeter and a voltmeter, gives an idea of how refined this car was. There was also an instrument which showed the lubricating oil level.

Car: **Pic-Pic**
Year: **1919**
Engine: **4 cylinders in line**
Bore and stroke: **85 × 130 mm**
Cylinder capacity: **2950.5 cc**
Gears: **4 forward**
Brake horse power: **50**
Maximum speed: **60 mph**
Wheelbase: **10 ft 3 ins (3.12 m)**
Suspension: **front and rear: semi-elliptic leaf-springs supplemented by Houdaille hydraulic shock absorbers**

The First World War brought the company many orders due to the sturdiness of its vehicles but in 1920 it began to run into serious difficulties because of competition from imported cars. Pic-Pic finally disappeared in 1924, although in 1922, two years after it had ceased activity for the first time, it was taken over by a new financial group which gave the Swiss firm the go ahead to produce a 4-cylinder 3-litre. However, only 300 of these were sold.

Radiators

Since the first cars, makes have been distinguished by the shapes of their radiators. A good example is the radiator of the Morris Oxford which resembled the nose of a bull, so much so that the car passed into history under the name of the 'bullnose'. Many makes of car, such as Rolls-Royce, have never changed the shape of their radiators. Mercedes is another traditionalist, though the radiators on its models have become progressively smaller and have lost their original function.

Alfa Romeo

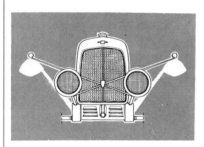

Aston Martin

Bentley

Bugatti

Bugatti

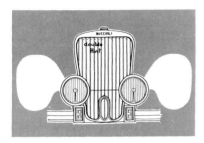

Bucciali

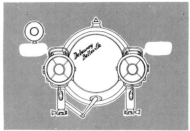

Delaunay Belleville

Duesenberg

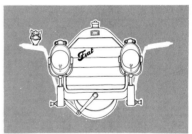

Fiat

Hispano-Suiza

Isotta-Fraschini

Radiators

Isotta Fraschini

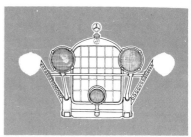

Mercedes

Rolls-Royce

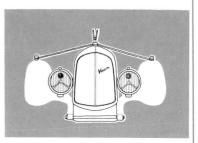

Voisin

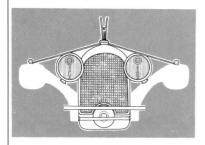

Voisin

Zeppelin

Evolution of the Car Body

The car developed from the horse-drawn carriage and for years its origins were obvious. In the early days motorised carriages were exclusively open. The 'torpedo' was the first to offer some protection. This was followed by the 'limousine' which introduced the class division between the driver and the passengers. Gradually the body became more and more closely suited to the design requirements of a motor vehicle.

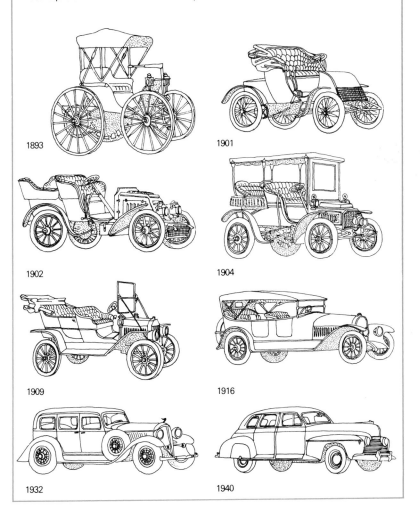

1893

1901

1902

1904

1909

1916

1932

1940

Cars That Sold a Million

In that period after the Second World War the car ceased to be the status-symbol that it had been in the 1930's and became a functional object. The American car industry had produced its first million units by 1912; by 1952 it had reached 100,000,000 and in 1971 237,000,000. The annual production is now around 10 million cars. The Italian car industry built 45,800 cars and 3,600 trucks in 1925 (the first year for which there are reliable statistics) and by 1939 it had reached just under 55,000 cars and 13,000 trucks. The first million units were only achieved in 1963, but by 1973, its best year, it produced well over 1,800,000 cars, and including trucks it reached 2,000,000 vehicles.

West Germany, France and the United Kingdom all went through the same process of expansion in car numbers in the post-war period until the energy crisis of 1973. However the greatest phenomenon, the most dramatic expansion in the world's car industries, has been that of Japan. Starting from nothing in the post-war period, Japan has firmly established itself in second place behind the United States.

It is estimated that at the end of 1975 there were 323,833,000 cars in the world. Of these more than 112,000,000 were in Europe (about 79,000,000 in the EEC countries), over 36,000,000 in Asia, more than 160,000,000 in the Americas (with about 122,000,000 of these in the United States alone) and just over 6,500,000 in Africa.

The fact that in recent years (from 1969 to 1976) 271,000,000 vehicles have been produced in the world gives an idea of the enormous expansion of the car industry. This development has taken place in the industrially more advanced countries, which have reached densities of one car for every three or four inhabitants, with ever increasing numbers of families that possess two or more cars.

This chapter is concerned with the spread of motor cars throughout the world and it will consider all the models of which more than a million have been built.

It is well known that the first car to exceed this level of production was the Model T Ford. The career of this car has been fully discussed earlier in the book, so here it is sufficient to record that it took two years to design and reach production. It was not for another 70 years that Henry Ford's record was beaten, when Volkswagen put the Rabbit into production from scratch in eighteen months.

When Ford introduced the T the public were told that it had undergone the most severe tests in all weather conditions (snow in winter, in the mountains during summer, and on sand and on mud). With this sort of presentation Henry Ford was ahead of his time in publicity. Today's manufacturers still emphasise that the prototypes of a particular model have undergone the same harsh treatments before moving on to the production line. Ford also told the public that it had spent $150,000 (a large sum in 1908) on new machines and tools. He also added a passage that, in view of the incredible success later enjoyed by the Model T, seems highly unlikely. A brochure of 1908 states, 'we do not know how many units of this model will be built in the next 12 months. However, the car's price has been fixed assuming a production of 25,000'. In fact 15,007,033 Model T's were produced and nobody would have then believed that this record would one day be broken. Whilst it is true that the car industry has become stronger and capable of producing more and more cars every year, the habit of remodelling and embellishing the body and adjusting the mechanics or, even scrapping a model shortly after putting it into production in order to stimulate the market has become the norm. However, the car industry's pundits had failed to take account of an ugly and uncomfortable car which Hitler's régime intended to be known as the 'people's car'—the Volkswagen. As the figures show, nearly twenty million have been produced in the course of about thirty years. The Volkswagen was the brainchild of Adolf Hitler, who wanted a sturdy car that could seat four people and which, above all, could be sold at a low price in order to motorise his country. The task of producing it was given to Ferdinand Porsche who was very famous as a designer, particularly of racing cars, in both Germany and Europe (although he was Austrian Hitler pretended that Porsche had requested German citizenship).

For the first time, after having worked for various car manufacturers, Porsche was able to give full vent to his talents, without any limits to the cost, in producing the prototype. In May 1937 the Nazi party founded a firm the 'Volkswagen Development Company' ('Gesellschaft zur Vorbereitung des Volkswagen') with a capital of 480,000 Marks with Ferdinand Porsche as its head. In 1939 the capital was increased to 150 million Marks. Initially thirty prototype cars were built in a small factory that Porsche had at Zuffenhausen near Stuttgart. Another thirty were built at Unterturkheim, also in the Stuttgart suburbs, in the Mercedes factories. His purpose in placing sixty cars on the road was to get as much information on the reliability of the car in as short a time as possible. At the end of the trials the first thirty prototype Volkswagens had covered a total of about 12.5 million miles. It was the first time that the tests on a new model had been carried out on so many cars. The consequence was that the costs rose astronomically (30 million Marks according to reliable sources). In the meantime Porsche and his close collaborators made two tours of the United States, paying special attention to Ford, to familiarise themselves with the production methods there. Some American engineers were recruited.

When ready, the car fully satisfied

Cars That Sold a Million

British Leyland	
Morris Minor	1,600,000*
Mini	4,200,000
Land-Rover	1,025,000

Citroën	
2 CV A2	3,000,000
Dyane	over 1,000,000
Ami 8	1,800,000
GS	1,209,000
DS	1,456,000*

Fiat	
1100	2,025,000*
600	2,612,000*
500	3,678,000*
850	2,203,000*
124	1,920,000*
128	2,545,000
127	2.419,000

Ford (Europe)	
Anglia	1,083,955*
Taunus	5,900,000
Cortina	3,600,000
Escort	3,200,000
Capri	1,300,000
Transit	1,500,000

Mercedes	
200-280	1,752,008

Nissan	
Skyline (180K/240K)	1,485,293
Bluebird (160B/180B)	3,544,757
Sunny (120 Y)	3,704,070

Opel	
Rekord	6,011,760
Kadett	4,398,713
Ascona	1,228,760

Peugeot	
403	1,300,000*
404	2,450,000**
204	1,600,000*
504	1,800,000
304	1,000,000

Renault	
4 (1945-61)	1,105,543*
Dauphine	2,120,220*
8	1,329,372*
4 (from 1962)	5,020,721
5	1,732,331
6	1,480,071
12	2,519,459
16	1,743,259

Simca	
1000	1,660,309
1100	1,718,847

Toyota	
Crown	1,489,742
Cressida	1,492,543
Corona	3,243,595
Celica	1,080,456
Corolla	4,655,668

Vauxhall	
Viva	1,529,579

Volkswagen	
Beetle	19,137,131
Rabbit	1,450,538
Dasher	1,135,131

NOTE

In addition to the above figures: 291,705 Crown vans have been built (total inc. cars: 1,781,447); 219,920 Cressida vans (total inc. cars;. 1,712,463); 731,773 Corona vans (total inc. cars: 3,975,368); 1,167,627 Corolla vans (total inc. cars: 5,823,295). By June 30, 1977, 712,324 Toyota Publica cars and 579,970 vans had been built making a total of 1,292,294 units. By the same date 147,308 Simca 1100 'utilitaires' and 261,576 'petites collections' (cars shipped in pieces and assembled abroad) had been built as well as 257,013 Simca '1000' petites collections.

  * production of this model has ceased
** this model is still being produced in Nigeria

Adolf Hitler but it was obvious that the price he had set (900 Marks) could not be met. The lowest that it could be kept down to was 990 Marks, this included the cost of two years' guarantee and maintenance. In actual fact the price finally rose to 1,240 Marks of which 990 were production costs, 200 were two years guarantee and 50 were delivery charges. The car could only be bought for 1,240 Marks by members of the Labour Front. The cost to non-members was in proportion to their income as assessed by the same Labour Front. The delivery or transport charge could be avoided by collecting it directly from the factory. To facilitate this bus services were set up between the country's major centres and Wolfsburg.

It was also decided that the capital would be put up by the workers themselves through a weekly levy of 5 Marks (or 10 or 15 according to their means). By this method of finance the 336,668 workers raised, through their contributions, no less than 280 million Marks.

On May 26, 1938 Adolf Hitler laid the foundation stone of the factory. Then the war broke out and the entire production of the Wolfsburg factory (designed to be 150,000 units per year) went to the Wehrmacht. In fact, Volkswagen did not even produce 60,000 cars and derivatives during the whole war and American military sources place the total at little more than 48,000.

At the end of the war the problem arose of what to do with the factory. In March 1948 a meeting took place at Cologne which was attended by Henry Ford II, the chairman of Ford England and of Ford Germany, Colonel C. R. Radclyffe who represented the British military government, and Heinz Nordhoff, who had been put in charge of Volkswagen (the last mentioned had spent some time with Opel before the outbreak of the war). Rejected by the British, Volkswagen was now offered to Ford. Henry Ford II, asked the advice of Ernest Breech, one of his closest associates. Breech replied with the famous remark that what was offered was not worth a damn. Given these circumstances, Volkswagen was returned to the Germans and Heinz Nordhoff remained in charge. Contrary to the predictions of the British and American experts in this field the 'Beetle' went on to become one of the

Volkswagen Beetle

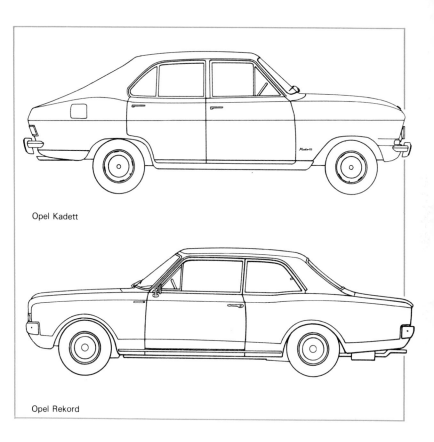

Opel Kadett

Opel Rekord

Citroën 2 CV

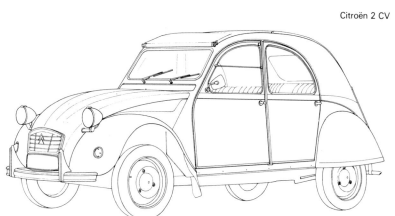

greatest successes in the history of cars not only in Europe but on the American market.

It was inevitable that at some point the Beetle would begin its decline and that it was foolhardy industrial policy to rely on a single model. Recently the Beetle has been replaced by the Rabbit, which is well past the million mark and the Dasher which also sold a million in a brief space of time.

After the Beetle the model which has been built in the largest numbers is the Opel Rekord, a sturdy, medium sized machine which has enabled the German subsidiary of General Motors to penetrate several markets. Already more than six million Rekords have been sold and at the 1977 Frankfurt Motor Show it was unveiled, at least as far as the body was concerned, in a completely new form. The Rekord is followed by the Kadett which passed the 4,500,000 mark on June 30, 1977. Opel's astute policy was confirmed by the success of the Ascona which entered production in 1975 and which has sold in its turn, more than a million.

The Rekord was born in 1953 as a replacement for the Olympia and it retained some of its predecessor's features. In appearance it resembled the Chevrolet of that year (the sides, in a continuous sweep covered the wheels, a technique known in America as the pontoon side; the windshield being curved and in a single piece). The main differences between it and the Olympia were in the suspension, the Rekord having ball joints and telescopic shock absorbers. Though it was roomier inside

than the Olympia the Rekord weighed less than its stable-mate and this feature was much appreciated. The new car received a favourable reception from its first appearance because of the space inside it and the feeling of strength that it conveyed simply by its appearance. The best reward for its designers was the fact that it was the first car built by Opel that General Motors imported into the United States (October 1957). In 1959 the range was extended by the addition of a 4-door version with a 1680 cc engine and in 1960 the body was restyled. The recent restructuring of this car on top of the earlier changes made in its appearance and mechanical modifications suggest that this car will remain in production for quite a few years. A version with a 2100 cc diesel engine came out in September 1972 and this important step has added to growth in the Rekord's production.

The Kadett has a singular history. When Opel decided to re-enter the small car market it was thought best to build a new factory which would be capable of producing at least 1,000 cars per day (one a minute in two 8-hour shifts). After various studies the choice fell on Bechum, an area in the Ruhr where the exhaustion of the coal mines had created unemployment and had left large expanses of vacant land. Construction of the new factory began in September 1960 and 25 months later it was ready for production. The Kadett, like the preceding model bearing the same name, was produced from scratch and engineers from Chevrolet were involved in its design.

Renault 4

The Kadett has also been remodelled several times though the mechanical parts have been left basically unchanged. It has occupied an important position in General Motors' industrial strategy, as it has provided the basis for the creation of a universal car. It was felt that the market was turning towards small cars and General Motors have built the Kadett, under different names and with different engines, in Brazil, Japan, Argentina and in the United States. The common feature of all these models, in their various configurations and under their assorted titles, is a wheelbase of 7 ft 10 ins (2.39 m).

The next best seller after the Volkswagen Beetle and the Opel Rekord is the Renault 4, with sales of over 5 million. The French firm can boast of several 'millionaire' models; these are, after the 4, the 12, the Dauphine, the 5, the 6, the 16, the 1945-61 4CV and the 8. This list clearly shows the success of all these models.

The first Renault 'millionaire' was the post-war 4CV, this, it is said, had an outstanding supervisor, none other than Ferdinand Porsche whilst he was still a prisoner of the French. Though ugly in appearance the first 4CV had two features that were very attractive to the public of its day; these were a small engine capacity and four doors. It marked the renaissance of the French firm, under the new title of 'Regie Nationale des Usines Renault', after the war. Accused of collaborating with the Germans, Louis Renault was imprisoned and died in jail. The 4CV was followed by the roomier and more comfortable Dauphine which, though its road holding was suspect, immediately gained the favour of the public for the same reasons as the 4CV. As the market leader, Renault deceived themselves into thinking that they could concentrate all their production on a single model, as Volkswagen were doing. The decline of the Dauphine, which was possibly more rapid than had been foreseen, put the French firm in a very critical position. The danger that had been run led the new chairman, Dreyfus, to change the policy completely and to progressively put a large number of models into production. The end of the Dauphine was also the end, as far as Renault were concerned of the rear mounted engine (the first 4 had also

263

used this arrangement) and, today, all this firm's cars have front-wheel drive. Another great success is the 5 which was launched in January 1972 and of which nearly two million have been sold.

The first British car to pass the million mark was the Morris Minor which was designed by Alec Issigonis, one of the brightest designers in automobile engineering since the war and the only true innovator in this field. He deserves this recognition for having got the Mini, the first modern car with a front mounted transverse engine, onto the road in a very short space of time. The Mini passed the four million mark on June 30, 1977. Alec Issigonis was not a designer in the strict sense of the word but a 'creator' of cars (he received a mechanical engineering degree *honoris causa* after the enormous success of the Mini). When, because of the Suez crisis, the British Motor Corporation decided to market a small car with low fuel consumption, Issigonis held that this could only be achieved by mounting the engine transversely so as to take up as little room as possible. As this was the first attempt at producing a transverse engine in a block with the gearbox and the differential gear, there were some mechanical problems for users and to BMC itself (in the production costs). However, it is still today the best example of a small car; with an overall length of 10 ft ½ in (3.05 m) it is capable of carrying 4-5 people. When the Mini appeared on the British market in 1959, Issigonis accurately predicted that its layout would have many imitators.

The Land-Rover has also had a unique career in the history of cars. Intended for mainly cross-country use, in imitation of the wartime Jeep, the Land-Rover has passed the million mark and far exceeded the hopes of its creators and builders.

The Citroën 2 CV and its close relative the Dyane (together, more than four million units had been built by June 30, 1977) are milestones in the history of the car. They were designed before the outbreak of the last war as spartan vehicles, as a basic method of transport (the then chairman of Citroën asked his designers for 'an umbrella on four wheels'), and the 2 CV and the Dyane have fulfilled the roles assigned to them by the French company. At the opposite end of the range, the numbers of the DS that were built are impressive as are the numbers of the Ami 8 and the GS (the former went into production in 1961 and the latter in 1970). All the Citroën 'millionaire' models have front-wheel drive.

The first Peugeot model to pass the million was the 403, a sturdy medium sized car and many regret its passing (especially the Parisian taxi drivers). The 404, also out of production, holds Peugeot's production record, followed by the 504 which is approaching two million. The 204 (which went out of production with sales of 1,600,000), the 304 and the 104 which was launched in 1972 show Peugeot's belief in front-wheel drive. However, Peugeot has not completely changed over to front-wheel drive as rear-wheel drive has been retained on the 504 and the luxurious 604.

Peugeot 104

Morris Mini Minor

Fiat 500

265

The Simca 1000 owes its success (it is one of the few remaining cars with a rear mounted engine) mainly to the fact that it was conceived as an economical, family car. The four doors helped greatly in classifying it as such. It is significant that the 1000 was designed by Dr Oscar Montabone of Fiat at a time when a majority of Simca's shares were held by the Italian company. On the other hand the 1100 has front-wheel drive and its success is based on its versatility (it was one of the first to have a rear door).

Like Renault, Fiat has many models that have passed the million mark. The first of these was the 1100, which was put on the market before the war (1939) and was completely redesigned as the 103 at the end of the war. The 600 (1955-70), which was their first family car produced on a large scale, was another of Fiat's warhorses. It should have had front-wheel drive and a transverse engine but because of the cost exactly the opposite arrangement was used. The 500 (1957-75) was also rear-engined and in its turn a great success. However, it was introduced on to the market at a bad moment for business (August 1957) and it received a cold reception. For a time its poor sales led to ill feeling between the designers and the marketing division, the former were accused of having thrown together a car, whilst the latter were held to have promoted it badly. The 850, a derivation of the 600 (1964-72), was intended to counter the expansion of the American manufacturers in Europe, which at that time was a

real threat. The public's reception of this car was vital to Fiat's future, so fortunately it was another success. The 124 was the Turin company's first medium sized car to be produced on a large scale. Solid and spacious, with its 4-5 seats, it was intended for the family. It has migrated to the Soviet Union and it will presumably continue to be produced there for years though its production on the Mirafiori assembly lines stopped some years ago. Fiat's other 'millionaires', both transverse front mounted engines, are still in production; they are are the 128 and the 127. The 127 is destined to carry on for some time, as it is now produced in Brazil as well. It is recognised as the precursor of the medium-small front-wheel drive cars such as the Renault 5, the Volkswagen Rabbit and the Ford Fiesta.

The German and English subsidiaries of Ford have also produced highly successful models. It could hardly be otherwise considering the role played by the Model T in the spread of the car. As a group, Ford Europe is well endowed with car 'millionaires'; the Taunus, of which nearly six million had been sold by June 30, 1977, is followed by the Cortina with three-and-a-half million, the Escort with more than three million and the Capri with more than a million. The Transit van had sold 1,500,000 units by June 30, 1977.

Vauxhall's only 'millionaire' model is the Viva. No Mercedes model has ever sold a million and it is unlikely that one ever will. However, if the 200 series, which includes the 200 D, the 220 D, the 240 D, the 240 D 3.0, the

Fiat 1100

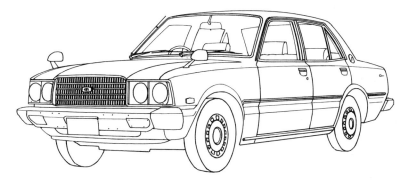

Toyota Corona

200, the 220, the 230/4, the 230/6, the 250, the 280 and the 280 E and which were produced from October 1967 up till the end of 1976, is totalled then its sales reached 1,752,008.

If any industry deserves special recognition for the speed with which it has raised itself to the level of the world's major manufacturers, it is the Japanese industry. Toyota has six models that are well past the million mark, these are the Crown, the Cres-

sida, the Corona, the Celica, the Carina and the Corolla.

Nissan has three: the Skyline, the Bluebird and the Sunny. Bearing in mind that at the end of the Second World War the Japanese car industry was practically non-existent, the results that it has achieved are remarkable. It is because of such successes that it today ranks second behind the United States amongst the car producing countries of the world.

Car Body Designers

Whether looking at the cars of the pioneering period or the sumptuous limousines of the 1930s with their enormous engines, one should not overlook the important role of the car body designer. In the early stages the body was adapted to the shape and size dictated by the needs of production. However, as time went on new needs arose from a desire to make vehicles more personal and individual. Thus, since the post war period the car body designers have contributed much to not only making the motor car more elegant but faster and more economical as well.

The custom built cars of the past were merely beautiful, luxurious or imposing, but those of the 1970s are first and foremost designed to reduce wind resistance and therefore be more economical in fuel consumption, an aim that is much in harmony with the times in which we live. However, even though today most car design is seen in terms of safety, followed by versatility and reliability, there are still a surprising number of very expensive specialist cars being produced. The Mercedes 300 SL was first produced in the early 1950s, at which time it was a revolutionary design. Similarly, despite its huge cost the Ford GT series was developed in the 1960s as the direct result of Henry Ford's desire to compete in Grand Prix racing.

It was during the 1960s that the idea that a car was judged solely on its external design died out, but conversely it is also true that a low cost machine need not be mediocre from the point of view of styling. Today, the majority of cars are seen as a whole: firstly in terms of safety, followed by versatility and reliability.

When Giovan Battista Farina, later to become Pininfarina, set up on his own he did not consider the question of aerodynamics. That was yet to come. Pininfarina, who was self taught, believed that a custom built body should firstly please the eye, and be more functional than a mass produced car. At the time this aim was comparatively easy to achieve as the mass produced bodies of the post war period were neither elegant nor comfortable.

Within the space of a few years, Pininfarina's sense of proportion and his innate good taste brought him acclaim. The designs of his son Sergio and brother-in-law Renzo Carli have been more futuristic, and perhaps more interesting to the engineer than

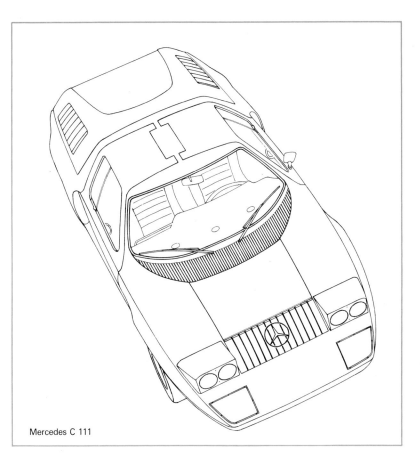

Mercedes C 111

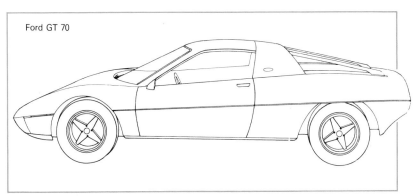

Ford GT 70

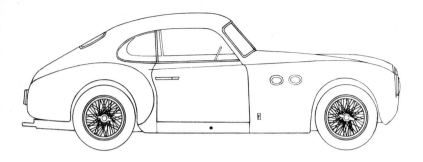

Cisitalia 202— Pininfarina

to the man in the street. The wind tunnel built by Pininfarina some years ago has enabled this celebrated workshop to achieve unforeseeable, streamlined shapes. Thus David Bache's prediction that the bodywork of cars of tomorrow will be designed more by a computer than the pencil of a stylist, whatever his flair, seems to be coming true. On the other hand, Sergio Pininfarina is convinced that in the future the public will still choose the more beautiful of two equally safe and functional cars that are offered at the same price. Though it is becoming more an instrument of work and less a status symbol with

every day, the motor car continues to be shaped to please the eye so it seems likely that there will continue to be a place for the car body designer for some time to come.

The Cisitalia, produced by Pininfarina in collaboration with the engineer Giovanni Savonuzzi and on display at the Museum of Modern Art in New York can be regarded as the originator of the stylistic trend whose most prominent feature is known as the 'pontoon side' in America. This consists of having the fenders flush with the sides of the car. This stylistic approach has had a great impact and has been adopted by

Alfa Romeo Carabo— Bertone

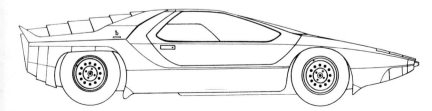

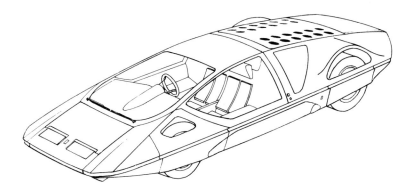

Modulo—Pininfarina

almost every car builder. If there is a single car that expresses the future of Pininfarina's style in a tangible form then it is definitely the Modulo, which is considered a true masterpiece. Similarly, the talent and imagination of Bertone are merged in an exemplary fashion in the Carabo, another shell that is assured of its place in the history of the car. It is interesting to see that one of these exhibition machines, the Stratos, has, most unusually, gone into mass production after some adjustments and modifications. The Stratos, with Lancia-Ferrari mechanics, completely dominates the major international

rallies. This shows that futuristic, dream cars produced initially for exhibition are not always ends in themselves.

Today, the stylist who combines taste, style and a sense of the future is Giorgio Guigiaro who, though young, already has several famous pieces to his credit. At the age of 21 he joined Carrozzeria Bertone (Bertone Car Body Design) but quickly left to set up Ital-Design. The Testudo, with Chevrolet Corvair Monza mechanics is regarded as one of his most significant creations, and has ensured him of a permanent place amongst the great men of styling.

Lancia Stratos—Bertone

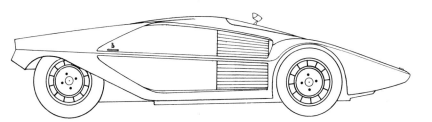

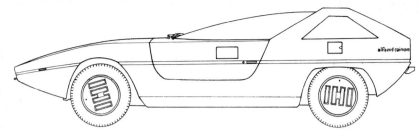

Alfasud Cainano—Ital-Design

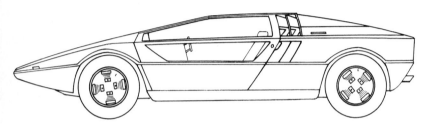

Maserati Boomerang—Ital-Design

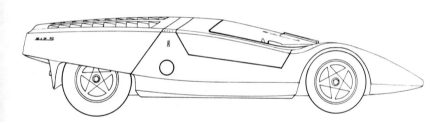

Ferrari 512/S—Pininfarina

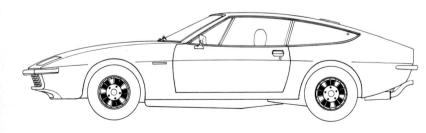

Opel Diplomat

Engines

The descriptions of the models included in this book provide irrefutable evidence of the outstanding imagination of the designers of the past. The conditions prevailing during the period of their inventiveness often proved an insurmountable obstacle to the actual realisation of their technical solutions which recently put forward again have enjoyed more success and have been, improperly, represented as new.

The most popular engines at the beginning of the century were single-cylinder ones. These were quickly supplanted by twin-cylinder engines, either in line or V, water or air cooled, and mounted in a large number of different positions (on the front axle, in the middle of the vehicle, beneath the floor, on the rear axle) both longitudinally and transversely. The twin-cylinder which has never totally disappeared (eg, the Fiat 500 and later the 126) gave way to the 4-, the 6- and later the 8-cylinder engine, especially in American products.

The valveless or sleeve-valve engine enjoyed considerable success. Its main feature was that it was free from valve floating at high engine speeds, noise, the breakage of springs and the burning of the valve seats. The best known sleeve-valve engine was the one designed by Charles Y. Knight. In this the combustion chamber was alternately open to the inlet and to the exhaust ducts. The gas flowed during those periods of the reciprocating and rotary oscillation of the sleeve when the ports cut in it aligned with the combustion chamber ports. It seemed

that 8 cylinders marked the upper limit to the number of cylinders but in the 1930s more than one manufacturer adopted 12-cylinder (Auburn, Franklin, Lincoln, Packard, Lagonda, Rolls-Royce, Hispano-Suiza, Napier, and Lancia, the latter two only using it on airplane engines) and 16-cylinder engines. These were the upper limits of the number of cylinders other than in aircraft engines where 24-cylinder examples existed.

The advent, though modest, of the 12- and 16-cylinder engines was due to the desire of certain manufacturers to offer the maximum of comfort in their luxury models. The 4- and 6-cylinder engines of the period had rather poor performances because of the low engine speeds and they were noisy and inflexible. The multi-cylinders eliminated many of these drawbacks but they were very expensive. The publicity which surrounded their appearance described them as being silent and free of the vibrations and coarseness that characterised the fours and sixes.

In 1930 Cadillac put both a 16- and a 12-cylinder engine into production. The 16 had a 45° V and was designed without regard for production costs. It had a capacity of 7413 cc and a maximum power of 165 bhp and engine speed of 3,400 revs in the initial version. In 1934 its maximum power rose to 175 bhp (185 bhp in 1936).

The Marmon 16-cylinder was regarded as a mechanical jewel. Several highly experienced engineers (Howard Marmon, George Freers, Thomas Little) worked on this engine. Besides

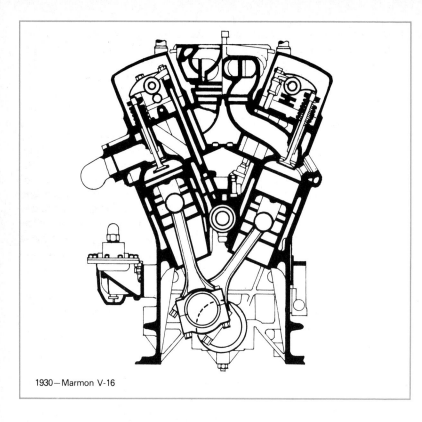

1930—Marmon V-16

being admired for its technical merits this engine was one of the largest fitted in a touring car (8044 cc). Like the Cadillac it had a 45° V, developed 200 bhp at 3,400 revs and its compression ratio was 6:1. Due to the widespread use of light alloys the weight-power ratio was amongst the best, approx 4.65 pounds (2.11 kg) per bhp. Another important feature of the Marmon 16 was the ventilation of the crankcase which reduced the flow of gas to the exhaust.

The Peerless 16, of which only one was built, also had a 45° V. It had a capacity of 7604 cc and it developed 173 bhp at 3,300 revs. In 1937 Cadillac produced another 16-cylinder (514 units until 1941). This had much in common with its predecessor, but differed in having side valves, fewer components, a reduced weight 247 pounds (112 kg) and a greater compactness. As regards costs and maintenance it was a big step forward.

Another 16, of which only one was made, was the Bucciali. This make was founded by Angelo and Paul Albert Bucciali in 1923 in Paris. It began in racing and it lasted ten years. The car in which it was mounted was displayed at the Paris Motor Show of

1931. The 16-cylinder engine used Continental components and had the same capacity as the Peerless (7604 cc). It had a maximum power of 155 bhp and a 22.5° V, exactly half that of the Cadillac, Marmon and Peerless 16s. Engines with 16 and more cylinders were built for purely sporting purposes or for powering fighting aircraft.

The first racing 16 was produced by the Duesenberg brothers in 1919 for the record breaking car in which Tommy Milton reached a speed of 156 mph over a flying mile. The capacity of this engine was 9730 cc. It in fact consisted of two 8-cylinder in line engines with separate drive shafts and no differential gear. Another racing 16 was designed by Frank Lockart on behalf of Stutz who mounted it in the 'Black Hawk'. This was a record breaking car and Lockart was killed in it on a record attempt after having exceeded 220 mph. This 16 was also composed of two sets of 8 cylinders (Miller) and two crankshafts, though there was a single crankcase. Each engine had a capacity of 1491 cc (the overall maximum power was 350-375 bhp). In 1930 this engine was brought back by Sampson who mounted it in the car which he drove in the Indianapolis 500 Mile Race. The next year Sampson again took part at Indianapolis but this time his car had a U 16-cylinder engine. This consisted of four superimposed 4-cylinder engines. It was a two stroke with a capacity of 3818 cc and was a total failure.

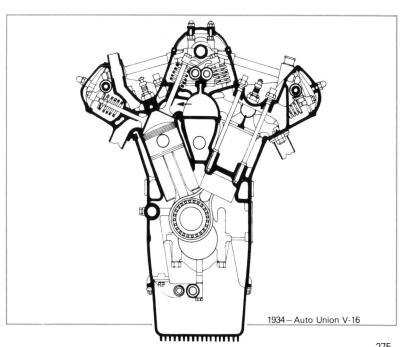

1934 — Auto Union V-16

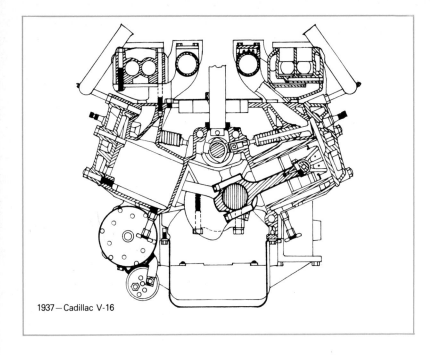

1937—Cadillac V-16

There have been two 16-cylinder cars built in Italy, one by Alfa Romeo and the other by Maserati (two versions). The Bimotore, which was prepared in the Ferrari Stable, was an attempt by Alfa Romeo in 1935 to challenge the domination of Mercedes and Auto-Union. The originality of this single-cylinder lay in the arrangement of its two 8-cylinder in line engines, each having a capacity of 3165 cc (total capacity 6330 cc and a maximum power of 530 bhp), one of which was mounted at the front and the other at the rear. The rotation of the rear engine was transmitted to the front one's clutch via a shaft. The rear drive wheels were connected to the gearbox-differential gear unit by two angled shafts and two pairs of bevel gears. The driver's seat was between the two engines. The Bimotore has won a place in history through a series of successful record attempts made by Tazio Nuvolari on the Firenze-Mare autostrada.

The Maserati 16-cylinder had a capacity of 3961 cc and developed 305 bhp at 5,200 revs. A car powered by this engine and driven by Mario Umberto Borzacchini entered the 1929 Indianapolis but retired on the seventh lap. The Maserati 16 was subsequently restructured and in 1933 it was designated the V5. Its capacity was increased to 4905 cc and it developed 360 bhp at 5,200 revs.

A very successful rear mounted 16-cylinder (the first rear-engined car of the modern era) was the one de-

276

signed by Ferdinand Porsche for Auto-Union in 1933 just before the start of full scale Formula 750, so called because of its maximum weight 1,650 pounds (750 kg). It had a 45° V. In 1936 the capacity rose from 4368 cc (295 bhp at 4,500 revs) to 5998 cc (520 bhp at 5,000 revs). It had a single stage Roots supercharger. One of the basic features of the Auto-Union 16-cylinder was that it weighed a mere 450 pounds (204 kg).

From a 16-cylinder engine built initially for the French air-force and perfected, again for military uses, in the United States by Duesenberg Ettore Bugatti developed an engine for a racing car and for a sports car intended for long distance races. It had two 8-cylinder in line engines arranged in a U. The racing car, the Type 45, had a capacity of 3798 cc, and three of these were built. The other, the Type 47, had a capacity of 2951 cc and a maximum power of 300 bhp.

The most recent 16-cylinders, both post war, are the English BRMs. Both were restricted to racing use. The first was built with a view to the Formula 1500 (cc) with supercharger which contained the races of the driver's world championship of 1950 and 1951. A team of engineers made up of Eric Richter, Frank Will May, Harry Mundy and led by Peter Berthon took part in the project from 1947 onwards. In 1949 it was ready and this engine was fitted in two single-seater cars which made their debut at Silverstone. In the event one of the cars was withdrawn after its trials and the other remained on the starting line because of a broken transmission.

This first unhappy appearance was the forerunner of a series of mishaps which raised a question mark over the ability of the combined forces of the British industry to field a car that could defend its prestige in the world. On paper this 16-cylinder, with a claimed maximum power of 525 bhp at 10,500 revs (390 bhp/litre), was a magnificent engine. Its weak points (the ignition system and the cylinder liners/sleeves) were ironed out but by then the first Formula 1 of the post war period had finished.

Considering the bad experience that BRM had had with this engine, it was surprising that they should turn, in 1966, to a 16-cylinder again for their entrance into the new Formula 1 (3000 cc), which still applies today. The new 16 had an H configuration like the Rolls-Royce Eagle aircraft engine. Though powerful (418 bhp at 10,750 revs), this engine was extremely complicated and it was rapidly abandoned. It does, however, have Jim Clark's victory in the 1966 United States G.P. with a Lotus to its credit, as BRM allowed other teams to use this engine.

A 'boxer' 16-cylinder (i.e. horizontally opposed cylinders or a flat 16), was announced in 1965 by the British Coventry-Climax firm for the Formula 1500 (cc) (not to be confused with the Formula 1500-4500 from the period after the Second World War). It had a predicted maximum power of 220 bhp at 11,000 revs. Coventry-Climax became part of Jaguar and later, with Jaguar, part of British Leyland. It then sadly ceased all involvement in racing.

Index

(Numbers in black refer to illustrations)

279

282

Bibliography

Books

Angelo Tito Anselmi, *Bolaffi Book on Fiat,* Giulio Bolaffi Editore, Turin, 1970.

Automobile Quarterly, *World of Cars,* Automobile Quarterly, New York, 1971.

J. Barron & D. B. Tubbs, *Vintage Cars,* B. T. Batsford Ltd., London, 1960.

Anthony Bird & Ian Hallows, *The Rolls-Royce Motor Car,* B. T. Batsford Ltd., London, 1964.

Anthony Bird, *Veteran Cars,* B. T. Batsford Ltd., London, 1960.

J. R. Buckley, *Cars of the Connoisseur,* B. T. Batsford Ltd., London, 1960.

Piero Casucci & Tommaso Tommasi, *The Story of Ferrari, Alfa Romeo World Champions,* Arnoldo Mondadori Editore, Milan, 1975.

Adriano Ceci & Vittorio Venino, *Great Sporting Makes,* Editoriale Domus/Quattroruote, Milan, 1976.

Floyd Clymer, *Historical Catalogue of 1912 Cars,* Floyd Clymer, Los Angeles, 1955.

Floyd Clymer, *Henry's Wonderful Model T 1908-1927,* McGraw-Hill Book Co. Inc., 1955.

Floyd Clymer, *Historical Catalogue of 1914 Cars,* Floyd Clymer, Los Angeles, 1955.

Floyd Clymer, *Historical Catalogue of 1918 Cars,* Floyd Clymer, Los Angeles, 1957.

Floyd Clymer, *Historical Catalogue of 1921 Cars,* Floyd Clymer, Los Angeles, 1958.

Floyd Clymer, *Historical Catalogue of 1924 Cars,* Floyd Clymer, Los Angeles, 1958.

C. Clutton, P. Bird & A. Harding, *The Vintage Motor Car Pocketbook,* B. T. Batsford, London, 1959.

H. G. Conway, *Bugatti—le pur-sang des Automobiles,* G. T. Foulis & Co. Ltd., London, 1963.

George H. Dammann, *Illustrated History of Ford 1903-1970,* Crestline Publishing Co., Illinois, 1970.

Pierre Dumont, *The Age of Motoring,* Edita, Lausanne, 1965.

J. L. Elbert, *Duesenberg The Mightiest American Motor Car,* The Motor Car Classic Bookhouse, Arcadia, Calif., 1951.

Luigi Fusi, *Alfa Romeo Cars from 1910,* Editrice Adiemme, Milan, 1965.

Paul Kestler, *Bugatti, Evolution of a Style,* Edita Denoël, Lausanne, 1975.

Mileruote Encyclopedia of the Automobile, Vols. 1, 2, 3, 4, 5, 6, 7, 8, 9, 10, Editoriale Domus/Quattoruote, & Istituto Geografico De Agostini S.p.A. Novara, 1973.

David Scott-Moncrieff, *Veteran and Edwardian Motor-Cars,* B. T. Batsford Ltd., London, 1955.

David Scott-Moncrieff, *The Thoroughbred Motor-Car 1930-40,* B. T. Batsford, Ltd., London, 1963.

Elizabeth Nagle, *Veterans of the Road,* ARCO Publications Ltd., London, 1959.

T. R. Nicholson, *Cars of the World in Colour, Passenger Cars 1905-12,* Blandford Press Ltd., London.

T. R. Nicholson, *Cars of the World in Colour, Sports Cars 1907-27,* Blandford Press Ltd., London.

T. R. Nicholson, *Cars of the World in Colour, Passenger Cars 1913-23,* Blandford Press Ltd., London.

Yves Richard, *Renault 1898-1965,* Editions Pierre Tisne, 1963.

Gianni Rogliatti, *The Most Beautiful Period Cars,* L'Editrice dell'Automobile, 1970.

Jacques Rousseau, *Delahaye,* L'Anthologie Automobile, S.E.D.E.C., Paris.

Jacques Rousseau, *World History of the Automobile,* Librairie Hachette, Paris, 1958.

Michael Sedgwick, *Cars of the World in Colour, Passenger Cars 1924-42,* Blandford Press Ltd., London, 1975.

All the Fiats, Editoriale Domus, Milan, 1970.

Joseph H. Wherry, *Automobiles of the World,* Chilton Book Co., Philadelphia, 1958.

Edward Young, *40 Years of Motoring, 1919-1959,* Stanley Paul, London, 1959.

Periodicals

Quattroruote, Editoriale Domus, Milan.